Hiding from the Internet

Eliminating Personal Online Information

Second Edition

2015 Revision

Michael Bazzell

Hiding From the Internet:
Eliminating Personal Online Information
Second Edition (2015 Revision)

Project Editor: D. Sapp

First Published: July 2014

Library of Congress Cataloging-in-Publication Data
Application submitted

ISBN-13: 978-1500397814

ISBN-10: 1500397814

Contents

About the Author

Michael Bazzell

Michael Bazzell spent 18 years as a government computer crime investigator. During the majority of that time, he was assigned to the FBI's Cyber Crimes Task Force where he focused on Open Source Intelligence (OSINT) analysis. As an active investigator for multiple organizations, he has been involved in numerous high-tech criminal investigations including online child solicitation, child abduction, kidnapping, cold-case homicide, terrorist threats, and high level computer intrusions. He has trained thousands of individuals employed by state and federal agencies, as well as the private sector, in the use of his investigative techniques. He has also taught several college courses including Ethical Hacking, Computer Forensics, and Computer Crime Investigation.

The previous editions of "Open Source Intelligence Techniques" and "Hiding from the Internet" have been top sellers in both the United States and Europe. They are used by several government agencies as training manuals for intelligence gathering and securing personal information.

Introduction

Hiding from the Internet

In *Open Source Intelligence Techniques*, I demonstrated how anyone can use the internet to locate personal information about oneself or others. From social networks to people search engines, it is simply too easy to find private information about each of us online. The internet will usually identify your residence, family members, telephone numbers, shopping habits, vehicles, employers, date of birth, education history, and many other details that should not be public. This book will help you maintain your privacy from the general public searching the internet.

Almost every online repository of personal information will allow you to remove your personal information. Since these companies make money from selling your private data, they do not make this removal process obvious. You will not see a website such as People Finders list a huge graphic on the top of their home page that says "remove your data here". Instead, they bury these links to keep the majority of viewers away from online removal submissions and written removal request instructions. This book identifies the best effective ways to remove your personal information from public databases.

Second Edition

The first printing of *Hiding from the Internet* was released in August of 2012. Since then, a lot has changed. Many of the techniques for information removal were slightly different than the requirements today. Some of the companies simply stopped responding to removal requests. More importantly, numerous new online companies indiscreetly announce to the world all of your private information. This edition attempts to tackle these issues and provide new thoughts about how to effectively protect your personal details. Additionally, several new chapters have been added to discuss complete online protection, anonymous purchases, disinformation, and ways to keep up with the changes that will take place after this book is printed. The entire book has been re-structured to provide an orderly solution to protecting your privacy.

Why do you care?

The process of removing your personal information from the internet is not quick. It may take quite some time and may never be 100% complete. For some, it may not be worth the time. For many people though, it is worth every minute. The most common reasons for removing personal information from the internet usually fall into three categories.

Identity Theft Victims

Some sources estimate that one in every three Americans will be impacted by identity theft at some point in their lives. When I speak to groups, I usually poll the audience and discover that at least 25% of the room has been a victim of this type of crime. Most people make it extremely easy for a criminal to obtain enough information from the internet about them to obtain identification and start a line of credit in the victim's name. Following the procedures in this book will make this process more difficult, causing the criminal to move on to someone else.

Targeted Subjects

As a police officer that conducts investigations against "hackers", I have a strong desire to keep my information private. There are many professions that are often targeted for personal information such as members of law enforcement, judges, lawyers, executives, celebrities, and wealthy people. These subjects should put extra effort into protecting their details from the general public. More importantly, the victims of violent crimes, such as domestic battery and those with orders of protection, should clean up their information to make it more difficult to be located.

General Privacy Concerns

Many of you have not been a victim of a crime and are not in a profession that is commonly targeted by criminals. That does not mean that you should not harden your identity. You still have valuable information to protect as well as a family and assets. The earlier you start on this path, the more effective it will be for your future. The methods identified here can be conducted by anyone. Parents may want to start their children on this path early. Teaching teenagers how to not provide information to marketers may save both them and you headaches in the future.

Will this help you disappear?

Yes and no. Eliminating your personal information from the internet will make it much more difficult for someone to locate you, but not impossible. As long as you have a house in your name, property taxes in your name, utilities in your name, or personal vehicles registered at your address, you can be found with legal action. Nothing in this book will hide you from the government. It will, however, stop the general public from obtaining your personal information. For those reading this that hope to use the techniques to hide from the IRS, pending litigation, active warrants, or paying child support, please move along. This book will do nothing for you. If you want to prevent nosey co-workers and sleazy criminals from finding out where you live, this book has you covered.

What will you need?

This book will provide all of the instruction that you will need to remove the personal information stored about you on the internet. A special page has been created on my website to help with the process. Navigate to **www.computercrimeinfo.com** and highlight the "links" section. Along with other helpful categories, there is a page titled "Hiding from the Internet". This page will have every link that is presented in this book, without the instruction. As links change, I will update this page to reflect the changes. As new services arrive, I will include new links to eliminate your data. The page is divided into sections for each chapter. You will also find related posts on my blog at this same location.

Ready?

Whatever led you to this book, your interest in the topic indicates that you are ready to begin a journey into online personal information removal. Let's get started.

Chapter One

Pre-Assessment

Before you embark on the adventure of removing your personal information from the internet, you should take a moment to identify the types of personal information present. Everyone will have different types of content visible about them. Each situation will require a unique strategy for removal. A person that owns a home and has a property tax record will find much more personal details online than a person that rents a home with included utilities. Also, a person with several social networks will see many more details than a person that has none. This chapter will help you quickly discover the amount of work that you will have ahead of you.

Search Engines

The first basic step is to identify the standard information available about you within search engines. In order to properly search your information, you will need to do much more than a standard Google search. Search engines will help you tremendously, but you will need to provide specific instruction when conducting your queries. For the first group of searches, assume that the following information describes you.

John Williams
1212 Main Street
Houston, TX 77089
713-555-1212

Searching "John Williams" will likely not be productive. Even if it were a unique name, the results would include spam and websites that provided no valuable information. Instead, conduct the following searches including the quotation marks.

"John Williams" "77089"

This query instructs the search engine to locate web pages that have exactly John Williams and 77089 on the same page. This will eliminate many unwanted pages that do not contain relevant information. If your name is generic, such as John Williams, you may still be bombarded with unwanted results. Try the following search.

"John Williams" "1212 Main"

This query instructs the search engine to locate web pages that have exactly John Williams and 1212 Main on the same page. This will likely display pages that announce your home address to the world. These will be the pages that you will target for information removal. You should also search the following example to locate pages that display your home telephone number.

"John Williams" "555" "1212"

This query instructs the search engine to locate web pages that have exactly John Williams and 555 and 1212 on the same page. The two sets of numbers were searched separately in case the target websites did not use a hyphen (-) when separating the numbers.

If you live alone, these searches will likely suffice. However, your listing may be displayed in the name of your spouse, a parent, or roommate. Alter the searches to include any appropriate names. If you have a unique last name, such as mine, you could try the following searches to catch all family members.

"Bazzell" "1212 Main"
"Bazzell" "555" "1212"

These queries will locate online content that references you and your home. Additional searches should be conducted based on your name and associations such as your employer, interests, or organizations. Create your own custom queries based on the following example searches.

"Michael Bazzell" "Accountant"
"Michael Bazzell" "software programming"
"Michael Bazzell" "International Police Association"

The quotation marks in the above searches are vital to the queries. They inform the search engine to only look for exactly what is presented. This will prevent Google and others from adjusting your search in order to "help" you. Each search engine that you use will likely give different results. You may want to try variations of your name. In my case, I would want to search "Mike" and "Michael". If you do not receive any results, you may want to repeat the search without the quotation marks.

Every engine has its own algorithm for search and also its own sneaky ways of collecting information during your search. Chapter Four will explain many ways to protect you while searching. For the purposes of this chapter, you only need to apply two policies.

First, never conduct these searches while you are logged into an email or social network account. If you are conducting queries on Google while logged into your Gmail account, Google stores this information about you. If you are searching on Bing while logged into your Facebook page, Bing now associates your queries with your profile. Overall, you do not want any companies to store your searches and associate them with you.

Second, you should not conduct these searches while using a web browser that knows a lot about you. All browsers store "cookies" that record the sites that you visit and the activity that you perform on the sites. Ideally, you should eliminate all of your cookies within a web browser before you conduct any searches. Chapter Four will explain further details. For now, this step is not vital for these basic searches.

Alternative Search Engines

There is no lack of search engines that could be used. While Google and Bing are the two main players, there are many other specialty engines that display results that the others miss. The following is a list of recommended engines for your pre-assessment.

Google	Google.com
Bing	Bing.com
Yandex	Yandex.com
Exalead	Exalead.com
Google Groups	Groups.google.com
Google Blogs	Google.com/blogsearch
Google News	News.google.com
Google Images	Google.com/images
Bing Images	Bing.com/images

Duck Duck Go (duckduckgo.com)

There are many people that do not trust Google due to their policies on data collection and advertisements. If you would like to conduct a query within a search engine that does not track you or record your actions, consider Duck Duck Go. This engine combines several sources to give you a collection of search results. None of your actions are recorded and the search engines that supply the content do not see your information. This can be a great search engine for daily queries. However, I believe that you will be missing many results if you do not use engines such as Google directly for the searches in this chapter. Chapter Four will outline additional steps that you can take in order to protect your privacy while on the internet.

Start Page (startpage.com)

If you want to take advantage of Google's search abilities but insist on hiding yourself from their intrusive monitoring techniques, you can use Start Page. Start Page searches Google for you. When you submit a search, Start Page submits the query to Google and returns the results to you. All Google sees is a large amount of searches coming from Start Page's servers. They cannot associate any traffic to you or track your searches. Start Page discards all personally identifiable information and does not use cookies. It immediately discards IP addresses and does not keep a record of any searches performed.

All-In-One (inteltechniques.com/osint/user.html)

I maintain a page on my website that will allow you to conduct a single query across multiple websites in one click. This is my preferred method when conducting a pre-assessment on someone. The website listed above will present many search fields that will allow you to execute a query on various services. The last search field at the bottom will allow you to execute any query on all of the listed services.

Figure 1.01 displays this page with one of the previous examples within this last search field. Clicking the "Submit All" button will open a new tab for each service. This currently requires Firefox or Safari web browsers. Chrome and Internet Explorer block the required code to perform this action. However, any browser can conduct individual queries through the listed services. This utility will search the following services with associated descriptions.

Google	Standard Google Results
Bing	Standard Bing Results
Yahoo	Standard Yahoo Results
Yandex	Russian Search Results
Exalead	Business Results
Google Groups	Current and Archived Newsgroups
Google Blogs	Current and Archived Blog Entries
Google Discussions	Discussions and Responses on Forums
Google Scholar	Case Law and Educational Documents
Google Patents	Every Patent in the United States
Google News	Current and Historical Online News
Baidu	Chinese Search Result

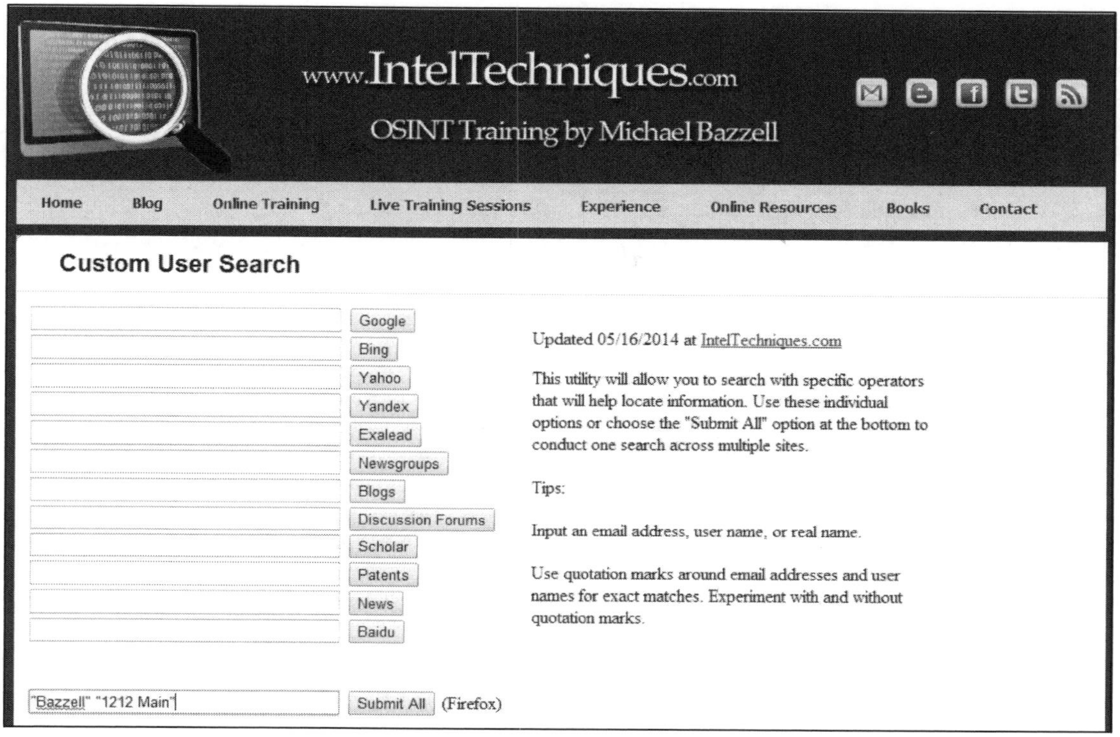

Figure 1.01: A custom search page on IntelTechniques.com.

Email Addresses

After you have identified the various websites that display your residence and telephone information, you should identify services that are connected to your email address. In years past, providing an email address to a company or service did not seem too alarming. Today, this unique identifier can be used to create a detailed record about you and your interests. To obtain accurate results of your email search, quotation marks must be used before and after your email address.

Figure 1.02 displays a Google search result for one of my email addresses. The listed websites are present because my email address is associated with my website. Notice the blue "Sign in" button in the upper right corner. That is an indication that I am not logged into any Google account which provides a small layer of privacy. Chapter Four will discuss the three main levels of online privacy and how to apply the level that works best for you.

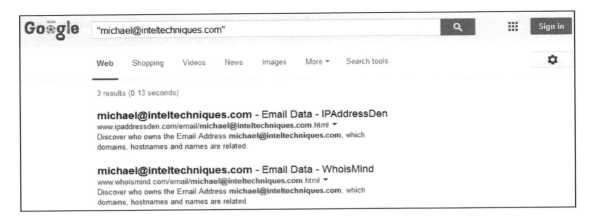

Figure 1.02: A Google search result from an email address within quotation marks.

It is important to know what information is associated with your email address. Many people will conduct a quick search on your address when you contact them. If you locate embarrassing or inappropriate content, you may want to use a different email account when corresponding about business or other important matters. The information found during this search will be very difficult to remove. You may consider switching to a new email address.

User Names

You may wish to search for any social networks that you have visible on the internet. You probably remember your Facebook and Twitter pages, but how many networks did you create and abandon when they lost popularity? We often forget about MySpace, Friendster, and other profiles that we no longer use. Often, those profiles are still visible and may contain personal information. Consider identifying any accounts that you wish to delete.

The easiest way to discover any accounts that may still be lingering is to search by your user name. Since we usually use the same user name for numerous accounts, you may look at known social networks for a hint. You may want to search your Twitter name, Facebook profile name, or the first part of your email account. If your email address is "michaelb911@yahoo.com", you may want to search for only "michaelb911". Locating your old network profiles can be a daunting task. Fortunately, we have services to assist us.

Knowem (knowem.com)

Knowem is one of the most comprehensive search websites for user names. The main page provides a single search field which will immediately check for the presence of the supplied user name on the most popular social network sites. In Figure 1.03, a search for the user name "mikeb5" provides information about the availability of that user name on the top 25 networks.

If the network name is slightly transparent and the word "available" is stricken, that means that there is a subject with a profile on that website using the supplied user name. When the website is not transparent and the word "available" is orange and underlined, there is not a user profile on that site with the supplied user name. For your purposes, these "unavailable" indications suggest a visit to the site to locate your profile. The results in Figure 1.03 indicate that the target user name is being used on MySpace and Twitter, but not Flickr or Tumblr.

The link in the lower left corner of Figure 1.03 will open a new page that will search over 500 social networks for the presence of the supplied user name. These searches are completed by category, and the "blogging" category is searched automatically. Scrolling down this page will present 14 additional categories with a button next to each category title stating "check this category". This search can take some time. If you had a unique user name that you liked to use, the search is well worth the time.

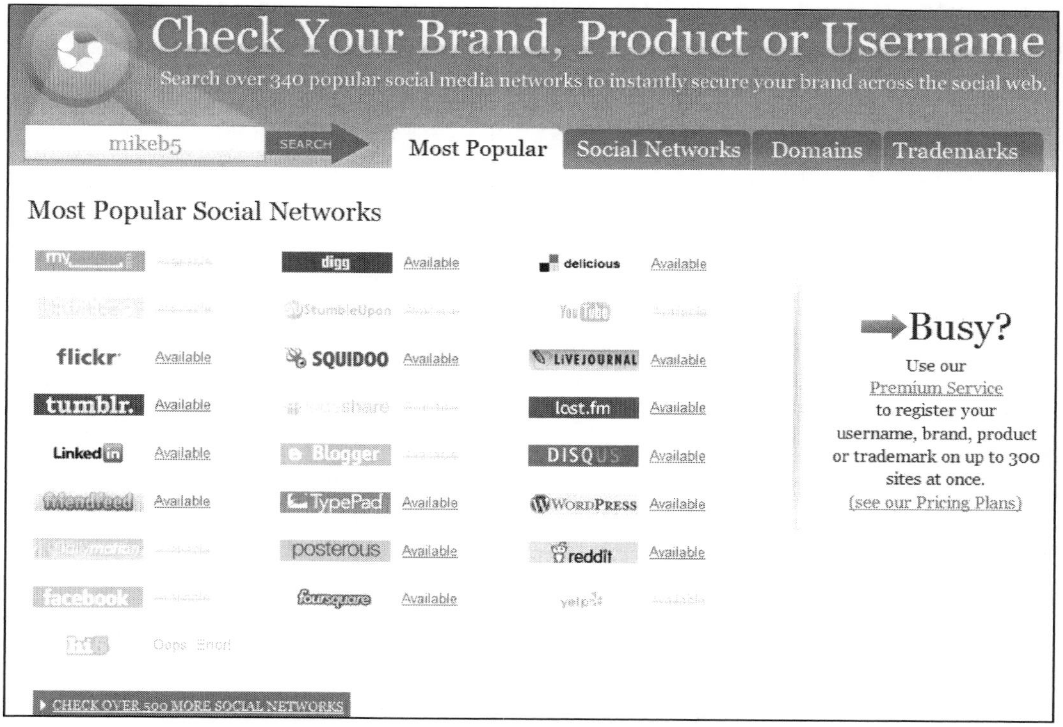

Figure 1.03: A Knowem search result identifying target profiles.

Location Based Searches

You have now likely located the publicly available content that we will attempt to remove from the internet. This will often be easy to find because it is searchable by your name, address, or telephone number. However, there is often social network information that is defined by the location from where it was posted. Many services such as Twitter and Instagram embed the GPS coordinates of the user along with the posted content. This can quickly identify where a person lives or works. It is likely that you are not uploading this type of detail. However, your children, friends, and family may not think about this type of technology and unintentionally compromise your privacy. You should consider conducting searches based on location as well as text. The easiest way to do this is through Echosec.

Echosec (app.echosec.net)

This simple website allows you to zoom to any location and query social network posts that were submitted from that location. Conduct the following steps to search your targeted area.

- ✓ Connect to app.echosec.net in your web browser.

- ✓ Either navigate through the interactive map or type your address directly into the search box in the lower left.

- ✓ Click the "Select Area" button in the center bottom portion of the page. Draw a box around the target area and release the mouse.

- ✓ Navigate through any results displayed below the map.

Figure 1.04 displays search result from an address. The square icons within the map identify Instagram posts by the location they were uploaded. Figure 1.05 displays two of the results from the three posts. The first post identifies the person's date of birth. The second post displays a business card with a name, workplace, email address, and telephone number. All of this information could be used against the people that posted it publicly.

After searching your home, consider a query for your workplace, relatives, or child's friends' houses. You will likely locate personal information that would have been difficult to find based on keyword searches alone. This can be a useful technique to find a child's account when they are unwilling to share it with you.

Now that you have identified the basic types of information that is publicly visible about you through search engines, consider the content that you would like removed. Most privacy seekers want to eliminate any reference to their home address and telephone number. Some people just want to remove those embarrassing photos posted in college. Regardless of your situation, the later chapters in this book will assist with erasing this data. This assessment was only a first step in establishing the scale of information available about you. It is recommended that you conduct the following self-background check to identify more details.

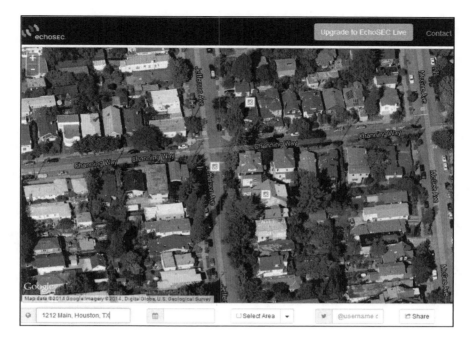

Figure 1.04: A map view of Instagram posts on Echosec.

Lunch treat because I turn 24 tomorrow ▢

chandini ▢

6/17/2014 3:23:04 PM @ Bi-Rite Creamery

▢ via *Instagram*

Yay! We got new business cards. Our organization is a real boy.

jami430

6/17/2014 3:38:18 PM

▢ via *Instagram*

Figure 1.05: Two location based posts identified through Echosec.

Chapter Two

Self-Background Check

At this point, you have completed the basic steps to identify your personal information visible in public view from search engines. You are now ready to conduct a complete self-background check. This will be done in two phases. The first phase will include only public internet websites that anyone could use to find you. The second phase will involve you requesting personal reports that will identify information stored about you in private databases not visible from the internet. The entire check should be completed at least once every five years.

Phase One: Public Websites

Chapters Eight through Fifteen outline the exact removal processes for the majority of the websites that display your personal information. Before attempting removal, you should identify those sites that have a record visible on you. Navigate to each of these websites and conduct a search on your name, address, telephone number, or user name as appropriate. Be sure to take notes of which services possess information that you wish to remove.

People Directories

People directory website removal will be explained in Chapter Eight. Before you can target these websites to remove your information, you should identify which services contain information about you. You should also consider searching for your children's information. If personal information is located, conduct the removal process for that specific website.

Spokeo	spokeo.com
Pipl	pipl.com
Yasni	yasni.com
Zaba Search	zabasearch.com

Intelius	intelius.com
ZoomInfo	zoominfo.com
Infospace	infospace.com
KGB People	kgbpeople.com
PeepDB	peepdb.com
Radaris	radaris.com
WebMii	webmii.com

Telephone and Address

These are the directories mentioned in Chapter Thirteen. Search your name, home address, and telephone number on these websites. Most of them will allow you to reverse search all three.

411	411.com
White Pages	whitepages.com
Yellow Pages	yellowpages.com
Addresses	addresses.com
Infospace	infospace.com
Super Pages	superpages.com
411 Org	411.org
Searchbug	searchbug.com
Reverse Phone Lookup	reversephonelookup.com
Phone Detective	phonedetective.com
Reverse Genie	reversegenie.com
Free Phone Tracer	freephonetracer.com
Privacy Star	privacystar.com

Social Networks

If you use social networks, you should occasionally look through your profiles for any sensitive data that reveals personal information. Even if you no longer use social networks or deleted your account completely, you cannot ignore these sites. Your family and friends are still likely to post sensitive information about you. It could be a photo identifying your home address, vehicle license plate, or the location of your child's favorite hangout. It could also be a family member posting your telephone number to other family members, intending to be helpful. Searching the publicly available information on these sites is easy. The websites listed here will display a search option to find the most common information. Some services require you to be logged into an account in order to search their data. If you do not already have an account on a service, I do not recommend creating one for this purpose.

Facebook Search	facebook.com
Twitter Search	twitter.com/search-advanced
MySpace	myspace.com/discover/people
Google Plus	plus.google.com
LinkedIn	linkedin.com

Facebook (facebook.com)

The Facebook data visible about you may extend beyond the content that is visible on your main profile page. There is often additional personal information leaking into other areas of the network. Use the following techniques to locate further details about your own and your family's profiles. This may help you decide if deleting your entire account is the way to go.

Facebook collects a lot of additional information from everyone's activity on the social network. Every time someone "Likes" something or is tagged in a photo, Facebook stores that information. Until recently, this was very difficult to locate, if not impossible. You will not find it on the target's profile page, but the new Facebook Graph search allows us to dig into this information.

In order to conduct the following detailed searches, you must know the user number of your account. This number is a unique identifier that will allow you to search otherwise hidden information from Facebook. The easiest way to identify the user number of any Facebook user is through the Graph API. While you are on your main profile, look at the address (URL) of the page. It should look something like Figure 2.01.

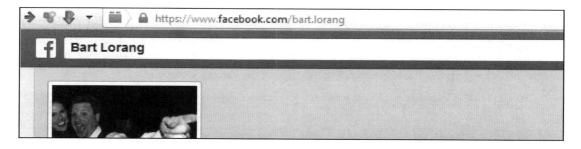

Figure 2.01: A web address (URL) of a Facebook Profile.

The address of the page is https://www.facebook.com/bart.lorang. This identifies "bart.lorang" as the user name of the user. In order to obtain the user number, replace "www" in the address with "graph". Figure 2.02 displays the results when this is conducted on the same profile.

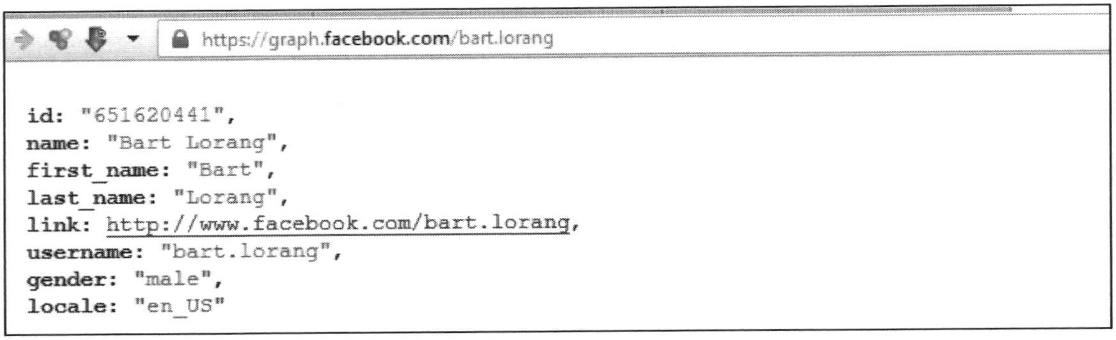

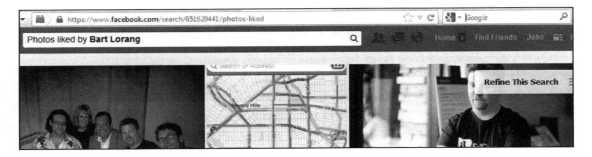

https://graph.facebook.com/bart.lorang
id: "651620441",
name: "Bart Lorang",
first_name: "Bart",
last_name: "Lorang",
link: http://www.facebook.com/bart.lorang,
username: "bart.lorang",
gender: "male",
locale: "en_US"

Figure 2.02: A web address (URL) of a Facebook Graph profile.

The first number that you see in this result is the person's user number on Facebook. This data will allow us to obtain many more details about the account. Repeat this process on your own Facebook page. If we want to see any photos on Facebook that you have "liked", we can type the following address into a web browser. Replace 651620441 with your own Facebook user number.

https://www.facebook.com/search/651620441/photos-liked

This basic structure contains the website (facebook.com), the action (search), the user number (651620441), and the requested information (photos-liked). Figure 2.03 displays the partial results of this address.

https://www.facebook.com/search/651620441/photos-liked
Google
Photos liked by Bart Lorang
Home
Find Friends
John
Refine This Search

Figure 2.03: A web address (URL) of a "liked photo" page of a Facebook user.

Notice the "Refine this search" option in the upper right. Hovering over this expands the options which will allow us to filter the results by the people in the photo, location, time, and the person that posted the photo. This allows me to display only recent photos or focus only on a specific location. Since these are photos that were "liked" by you, the results will include photos on other people's pages that would have been difficult to locate otherwise.

If we had asked Facebook for this information with only your name, we would have been denied. If we asked within the search filter options mentioned earlier, we could only search by general name and could not identify a specific user. If you have a common name, this would not work. The method described here works because we know your user number. There are many other options with this search. We can navigate to the following addresses to see more information about you (user number 651620441). Explanations of each address will be explained after the list.

https://www.facebook.com/search/651620441/places-visited
https://www.facebook.com/search/651620441/places-liked
https://www.facebook.com/search/651620441/pages-liked
https://www.facebook.com/search/651620441/photos-of
https://www.facebook.com/search/651620441/photos-liked
https://www.facebook.com/search/651620441/photos-commented
https://www.facebook.com/search/651620441/friends
https://www.facebook.com/search/651620441/videos
https://www.facebook.com/search/651620441/videos-by
https://www.facebook.com/search/651620441/videos-of
https://www.facebook.com/search/651620441/videos-liked
https://www.facebook.com/search/651620441/videos-commented
https://www.facebook.com/search/651620441/apps-used

The "places-visited" option will identify locations that you have physically visited and allowed Facebook to collect the location information. This is often completed through a smart phone, sometimes unintentionally.

The "places-liked" option will list any physical locations that you have clicked "like". This will often identify vacation spots, favorite bars, and special restaurants. This can be priceless information for an investigator or skip-tracer.

The "pages-liked" option will identify any Facebook pages that you clicked "like". This will often display your interests such as a favorite sports team, musical group, or television show. These results will include a button labeled "liked by".

The "photos-of" option will identify any photos that you have been tagged in. This search became possible in 2014 and has already proved very effective in many investigators. This will immediately locate additional photos of you that may not be visible on your profile.

The "photos-liked" option was explained on the previous pages. This will identify any photos on Facebook that you "like". If the photos of interest are on someone else's profile that is not private, you will be able to see all of them.

The "photos-commented" option will identify any photos on profiles where you left a comment on the photo. This can be important because you may not have "liked" the photo or been tagged in it. The option may produce redundant results, but it should always be checked.

The "friends" option should display a list of all of your friends on Facebook. This will be the same list visible on the main profile page. Occasionally, a person with their friend's list set to "private" can be exploited with this method. Your results may vary.

The "videos" option will identify videos visible on your profile. These may or may not be directly connected to you. They could also be videos linked to the original source with no personal ties to you.

The "videos-by" option identifies videos that were actually uploaded by you. These will be much more personal to you and will usually include more relevant content.

The "videos-of" option is similar to the "photos-of" filter. This will identify videos that supposedly contain images of you within the video itself. It could be compared to "tagging" someone inside a video.

The "videos-liked" option will identify any videos that you clicked "like". This can also be used to establish your personal interests.

The "videos-commented" option will identify any videos on profiles where you left a comment on the video. Again, this can be important because you may not have "liked" the video or been tagged in it. The option may produce redundant results, but it should always be checked.

The "apps-used" option will identify your apps installed through Facebook. These are usually games that can be played with other people. Many of these specify the environment that they work with such as "IOS". This would indicate that you are using an iPhone or iPad instead of an Android device.

Custom Facebook Search Tool

You may now be wondering how you are going to implement all of these searches in an easy format. I had the same thought and developed my own website to handle this task. Navigate to the following website in order to access an all-in-one option.

http://inteltechniques.com/osint/facebook.html

This page will allow you to conduct all of the Facebook Graph searches that were mentioned in this chapter. The current state of this tool is visible in Figure 2.04. The first search will find your profile based on an email address. Copy and paste your user name from the profile address into the second option to identify your user number.

The next group of searches will display the "liked", "tagged", and "by" information that we previously discussed. The third from last option will conduct all of the searches at one time into separate tabs in your browser. Make sure you are logged into a Facebook account for this to function. I also recommend using the Firefox browser which will be discussed later. Chrome tends to block the script required to make this work.

Phase Two: Private Databases Reports

The websites and services in this section can be queried at any time. Most of these businesses do not publicly share your information and do not offer opt-out methods. The data stored is shared with other businesses and can affect your credit score, insurance rates, and ability to obtain a line of credit. While you cannot remove your profile from these databases, you can correct any errors in the reports. These corrections could save you money if you find yourself paying rates that appear to be higher than normal.

Free Credit Report (annualcreditreport.com)

There are several websites that offer a free credit report. Most of these will try to convince you to sign up for premium offers and never offer a free credit report. The only official government supported free credit report website is at **annualcreditreport.com**. This website allows you to view your credit report without any fee once yearly from each of the three credit bureaus. This means that you actually get three free credit reports every year. Instead of viewing all three reports at the same time, create a schedule to spread out the viewings. I recommend the following:

- ✓ In January, connect to **annualcreditreport.com** and request a free report from Equifax.

- ✓ In May, request a free report from Experian.

- ✓ In September, request a free report from TransUnion.

These months can be adjusted. The important element is that you are viewing your credit report throughout the year. The process for viewing your report varies by state. The website will explain every step. When you receive your report, pay close attention to the areas visible in Figures 2.05 through 2.09.

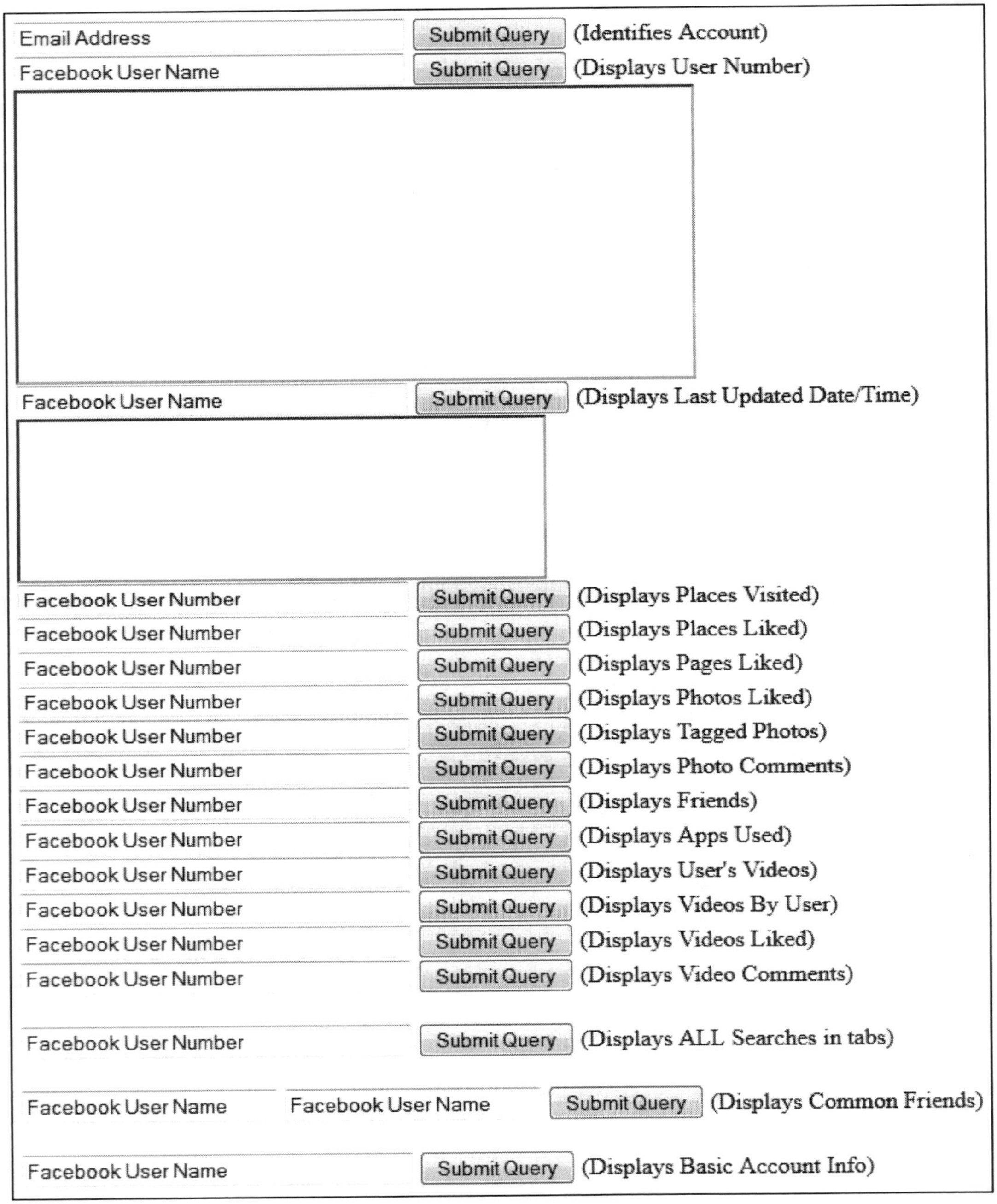

Email Address	Submit Query	(Identifies Account)
Facebook User Name	Submit Query	(Displays User Number)

(large empty box)

Facebook User Name	Submit Query	(Displays Last Updated Date/Time)

(empty box)

Facebook User Number	Submit Query	(Displays Places Visited)
Facebook User Number	Submit Query	(Displays Places Liked)
Facebook User Number	Submit Query	(Displays Pages Liked)
Facebook User Number	Submit Query	(Displays Photos Liked)
Facebook User Number	Submit Query	(Displays Tagged Photos)
Facebook User Number	Submit Query	(Displays Photo Comments)
Facebook User Number	Submit Query	(Displays Friends)
Facebook User Number	Submit Query	(Displays Apps Used)
Facebook User Number	Submit Query	(Displays User's Videos)
Facebook User Number	Submit Query	(Displays Videos By User)
Facebook User Number	Submit Query	(Displays Videos Liked)
Facebook User Number	Submit Query	(Displays Video Comments)
Facebook User Number	Submit Query	(Displays ALL Searches in tabs)
Facebook User Name Facebook User Name	Submit Query	(Displays Common Friends)
Facebook User Name	Submit Query	(Displays Basic Account Info)

Figure 2.04: A website of custom Facebook search tools on inteltechniques.com.

Inquiries - Requests for your Credit History

Numerous inquires on your credit file for new credit may cause you to appear risky to lenders, so it is usually better to only seek new credit when you need it. Typically, lenders distinguish between inquiries for a single loan and many new loans in part by the length of time over which the inquiries occur. So, when rate shopping for a loan it's a good idea to do it within a focused period of time.

| Inquiries in the Last 2 Years | 0 |
| Most Recent Inquiry | N/A |

Figure 2.05: The inquiries section of a credit report. It will identify any companies requesting a copy of your report. This will usually be creditors verifying your details for a loan request.

E*TRADE FINANCIAL	01/23/12
EQUIFAX	08/13/11
EQUIFAX	07/09/12
EQUIFAX INFO SVCS.	08/29/11, 08/17/11, 08/10/11, 08/05/11

Figure 2.06: The non-impact section of a credit report. These inquires include requests from employers, companies making promotional offers, and your own requests to check your credit.

Address Information

Current/Previous	Street Address	Date Reported	Telephone
Current		Last Reported 07/02/2012	
Former Address1		Last Reported 08/29/2011	

Figure 2.07: The address information of a credit report. This will identify any addresses used for current and previous lines of credit. If you see an unfamiliar address, you should report this.

Account Name	Account Number	Date Opened	Balance	Date Reported	Past Due	Status
CHASE BANK USA, NA		03/07/2	$530	03/2012		PAYS AS AGREED

Chase Card Services

P.O.Box 15298
Wilmington , DE-19850
(800) 955-9900

Figure 2.08: The open accounts section of a credit report. It will identify any unused open accounts and a contact number to close the account if desired.

Closed Accounts

Account Name	Account Number	Date Opened	Balance	Date Reported	Past Due	Status
CHASE BANK USA, NA	▮▮▮▮▮▮	11/06/2	$0	06/2012		

Chase Card Services

P.O.Box 15298
Wilmington , DE-19850
(800) 955-9900

Figure 2.09: The closed accounts section that will verify that an account was successfully closed.

LexisNexis (lexisnexis.com)

Chapter Ten will explain how to conduct an advanced removal from LexisNexis. This includes instructions to opt-out of non-public databases. Whether or not you apply these techniques, you should request your personal file from this company. Even if you requested information removal, you will find that the company maintains a file on you. This does not mean that your information is available to the public. The steps below will allow you to review the data LexisNexis stores about you.

- ✓ Navigate to **lexisnexis.com/privacy/for-consumers/CD307_Accurint_Person_ Report_Info_Form.pdf** and complete this form providing your real information. LexisNexis does not use this data to update your current profile. It is only used for verification. Print the form when complete.

- ✓ Print a redacted copy of your driver's license as discussed in Chapter Three. Mail both forms to the following address:

LexisNexis Risk Solutions FL Inc.
Accurint Customer Inquiry Department
PO Box 105610
Atlanta, GA 30348-5610

Westlaw / Clear / Thompson Reuters (clear.thomsonreuters.com)

This is another large company that was discussed earlier. The detailed content of your personal report will probably surprise you. This report can often identify attempted fraud or identity theft conducted in your name. Follow these instructions to obtain your free report:

- ✓ Navigate to the following website:

    static.legalsolutions.thomsonreuters.com/static/pdf/info_request_form.pdf

- ✓ Complete the document with your real information. The information is only used to verify you for the report. New information is not added to any databases.

- ✓ Print a copy of your redacted driver's license (Chapter Three). Mail it and the printed form from step one to the following address:

    Westlaw and CLEAR Public Records
    ATTN: D5-S400 – Personal Information Removal Request
    610 Opperman Drive
    Eagan, MN 55123

Acxiom (acxiom.com)

Acxiom offers two types of personal reports. The first is a fraud detection and prevention report. This report exists if you have returned a large amount of merchandise to retail stores. It is used to identify fraud and probably does not apply to the audience of this book. This report costs $5.00 to obtain and can be found at the following address:

isapps.acxiom.com/rir/rir.aspx

The second option is the background screening report. This is provided to potential employers that request the product. Inaccurate information in this report could explain difficulty in obtaining employment. This report is free.

- ✓ Telephone 800-853-3228 and select option 3. State the following to the customer services representative.

    "I believe that there are errors on my background screening report. Per the rules of the Fair Credit Reporting Act, I would like to request a free copy of my report."

- ✓ You will need to supply your personal information as verification, which is not collected or placed into your profile.

Sterling Infosystems (sterlinginfosystems.com)

This is another service that provides employment related consumer reports to potential employers. An online or mail request can be conducted.

✓ Navigate to **sterlingbackcheck.com/About/Fact-Act-Disclosure.aspx** and complete the online form. Provide a valid email address to receive your digital report.

✓ Alternatively, you can request a report via postal mail at the following address.

SterlingBackcheck
ATTN: Consumer Reports
6111 Oak Tree Blvd
Independence, OH 44131

Innovis (innovis.com)

This is another consumer credit information company that is similar to Equifax, Experian, and TransUnion. One big difference is that you cannot obtain your Innovis credit report through the free website annualcreditreport.com. Innovis encourages mailed requests for a personal credit report, but the automated telephone system is easier and more efficient.

✓ Telephone **800-540-2505** and listen to the recorded message. Choose "1" for the first two menu options. You will then be asked to enter your social security number, date of birth, zip code, and numeric portion of your home address to verify your identity.
✓ You will be informed that you can obtain a free credit report if you are unemployed, on public assistance, or suspect that you may be the victim of identity theft. The first two choices are obvious, but the third is open to interpretation. There are an estimated 20 million victims of identity theft every year. Most of them do not find out about this fraud until they request a credit report. Therefore, if you believe it is POSSIBLE that you are a victim of identity theft and want to verify this through a credit report, select option "4" as instructed. You will receive a copy of this report in a few days.

Approximately one month before I requested credit reports from Equifax, Experian, TransUnion, and Innovis, I contacted my bank and changed my telephone number to an anonymous forwarding number. The only credit report that obtained this new number was Innovis. The number is now associated with my name and will be shared with several companies. This intentional form of disinformation will help mask my real telephone number from the public.

Core Logic (corelogic.com)

Core Logic was discussed in earlier as a consumer information powerhouse. If you completed the opt-out process described there, the company will no longer share your information. However, they still maintain your profile and will allow you access to the report. An email will obtain the best results. You should receive an email response within three business days.

✓ Use your new personal email account and create an email message with the subject of "Opt-Out" to **srumph@corelogic.com**. State the following and include your personal details:

"Per your policy as published at corelogic.com/privacy.aspx, I would like to request my consumer report maintained by Core Logic."

Your Name
Your Home Address
Your Date of Birth

Safe Rent (corelogic.com)

If you currently rent your residence or plan to seek rental housing in the future, you should request a copy of your consumer file maintained by Safe Rent, a Core Logic company. You must complete a form and submit via fax or postal mail.

✓ Print the form at the following address:

http://www.corelogic.com/downloadable-docs/nbd03-104-disclosure-request-web-packet.pdf

✓ Complete the form with your real information and submit via postal mail to the following address:

CoreLogic National Background Data, LLC
Compliance Division
PO Box 772277
Ocala, FL 34477-2277

There is a small fee to access your report. However, there are certain situations that allow for a free report. If you meet ANY of the following conditions, the fee will be waived:

Denial of your housing application
Required to have a deposit not required by others
Required to have a cosigner
Assessed a higher rental rate than others
Denied employment or promotion
Reassigned or terminated
Unemployed or filing for unemployment within 60 days
Public welfare recipient
Have reason to believe your file may contain errors

I believe that practically everyone can qualify through one of these conditions. The last option can apply to anyone that believes "typos" are possible on their report. Follow the instructions on the form and expect your report within two weeks.

Insurance Services Office (iso.com)

Your vehicle and home insurance rates can be influenced by your loss history report. Inaccuracies in this report can cause unnecessary rate increases. The Insurance Services Office will provide a free copy of your report. Included in this copy are any losses reported to your insurance company in the past five years.

- ✓ Place a telephone call to **800-627-3487**. Provide the information requested for verification purposes. Your report will arrive via postal mail in about one week.

- ✓ Verify any losses listed in the report. If you find discrepancies in the items or amounts reported, contact the number included with the report.

Tenant Data (tenantdata.com)

This is another rental data agency that reports resident history and a tenant profile of rental prospects. If you do not rent a home, this would not apply to you. If you would like to see the data collected about you and your rental history, complete the following.

- ✓ Navigate to the following website and print the form.

  tenantdata.com/downloads/AuthorizationforFileDisclos_new.pdf

- ✓ Complete this form and submit via postal mail to the following address.

  Tenant Data
  PO Box 5404
  Lincoln, NE 68505-0404

- ✓ Expect your report to arrive in approximately two weeks.

Experian Rent Bureau (experian.com)

Experian maintains their own database of rental history and creates profiles of renters.

- ✓ Navigate to the following website and print the form.

  experian.com/assets/rentbureau/brochures/request_form.pdf

✓ Complete the form with your real information. Fax the form to 972-390-4970 or mail the form to the following address.

Experian Rent Bureau
PO Box 26
Allen, TX 75013

Chex Systems (consumerdebit.com)

If you have been the victim of identity theft or any type of financial fraud, criminals may be attempting to write checks against your accounts. Many automated systems will stop this fraudulent activity, but may not notify you of the issues. You can request a report of any negative impact on your checking accounts from two sources.

✓ Navigate to **consumerdebit.com/consumerinfo/us/en/chexsystems/report/index.htm**. Click "Agree" to begin the online form submission. Complete all required fields and click "Submit". You should receive your report via postal mail within five days.

TeleCheck (firstdata.com)

The second company to request a checking report is TeleCheck. The request process is more demanding than the previous report, and the submission must be sent via postal mail.

✓ Open a copy of your custom opt-out form created in Chapter Three. Include your anonymous telephone number and your social security number. All other information can be removed from the document except the copy of your driver's license. Print the form when completed.

✓ Package the previous form, a copy of any utility bill or tax statement, and a voided check. Send the documents to the following address.

TeleCheck Services, Inc.
Attention: Consumer Resolutions-FA
P.O. Box 4514
Houston, TX 77210-4514

Retail Equation (theretailequation.com)

When you return a product to a retail or online store, your information is recorded and shared with several companies. This includes the location, product, amount, and reason for return of the product. This database was created to combat exchange fraud, and you are likely in it. If you are curious about the information being shared about your shopping habits, you can request a copy of your report.

✓ Create an email addressed to **returnactivityreport@theretailequation.com**. Include your name and anonymous telephone number in the message.

✓ You will be contacted by the company to process your request. If you are asked for a transaction number, state that you do not have that information.

Medical Information Bureau (mib.com)

When you apply for medical insurance, the provider will seek your report from the Medical Information Bureau. This report will include information such as height and weight, and identify any noteworthy gains and losses. Depending on your medical history, the additional information will vary. This report can influence the amount of money that you pay for medical insurance. Verifying the accuracy of this report is important when seeking new coverage.

Navigate to **www.mib.com/disclosuretransfer/disclosureservice/formrequest** and complete the online request form. Select "For Yourself" on the first screen and click "next".

✓ Provide only the following information. The additional fields are optional.

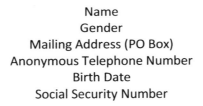

Name
Gender
Mailing Address (PO Box)
Anonymous Telephone Number
Birth Date
Social Security Number

✓ Confirm the information and expect a report within two weeks.

Milliman IntelliScript (rxhistories.com)

This company stores information about your prescription drug history. These reports are shared with insurance companies that determine your insurance rates. If you are seeking new insurance quotes, inaccuracies in this report can be devastating. You may obtain a free copy of your report.

✓ Telephone **877-211-4816**. Be prepared to disclose your name, mailing address, telephone number, date of birth, and last four digits of your social security number. Expect a mailed report within ten days.

National Consumer Telecom and Utilities Exchange (nctue.com)

This database is managed by Equifax. It provides fraudulent activity and delinquencies involving utilities and related services. These reports are obtained by companies before utilities are authorized for a building. If someone has fraudulently used your personal information, this report will disclose the details.

- ✓ Telephone **866-349-5185** to speak with a representative. State that you want to request a free copy of your "data report". Be prepared to disclose your social security number, name, and date of birth. While I usually never recommend providing this information, it is only used to verify your identity to the company. If you have ever had any utilities in your name, they already have this information. Supplying the details does not put you at additional risk.

- ✓ You will be placed on hold while your report is retrieved. After the report is generated, you will receive a confirmation number. The actual report will arrive within three business days.

- ✓ Visit www.nctue.com/Consumers and complete the Opt-Out request.

Social Security Administration (ssa.gov)

Beginning in 2012, the social security administration no longer sends reports via postal mail. This cost savings measure requires you to view your statements online. If you plan to conduct a credit freeze, be sure to complete this process first. The account creation on this website cannot be completed with a credit freeze in place.

- ✓ Navigate to **ssa.gov/myaccount** and click the button labeled "Sign in or Create an Account". Click the "Create An Account" button and provide the requested information. Choose a secure password and view this statement yearly. If anyone attempts to use your social security number for payments, this statement will disclose the fraud.

The reports in this phase of the chapter are optional and none of them will help you hide from the internet. Many will not apply to you. Only you can determine which companies are likely to possess information about you. If you find yourself continuously trying to figure out why you tend to pay more for various services than other people, your answer may be in one of these reports.

Chapter Three

Preparation

Before you attempt to remove any of your personal information from the internet, you must take several steps to prepare yourself for this journey. While most of this book can be read in any order, this chapter should be read in its entirety before proceeding. Failure to have these preparations in place will cause some of the methods described in this book to take longer than necessary. Even worse, it will make some of the methods ineffective. Before you prepare to start removing your personal information from the internet, you should evaluate how your information became accessible to the public.

Rule # 1: Stop Giving Out Your Information!

The first obvious thing to discuss is how you provide your personal information to the world. Every month, you provide many personal details about you and your family that get sold to numerous companies. Large databases are created that include a profile on you that is passed around and updated continuously. The following are three examples of the information that you provide unknowingly.

Reward Cards & Loyalty Programs

As a frugal person, I love these money saving cards. As a privacy advocate, I hate them. Many grocery stores, cafes, restaurants, and discount clubs offer them to save you hundreds of dollars every year. When you use these cards, everything you buy is associated with your name and address. When companies contact the rewards card provider looking for new customers, your information often gets sold if you fit a certain criterion.

For example, a shoe company wants to know all of the customers of a specific grocery store that purchased magazines associated with running or fitness. That grocery store can easily conduct a search and create a list of reward program customers that fit the criteria and sell that list to the shoe company. This list could include your name, home address, telephone number, email address, and shopping habits. Now, you may get bombarded with unwanted advertisements in the mail, spam in your email inbox, and telephone calls offering fitness themed vacations. This same information may then get passed on to another company. In one extreme scenario, The New York Times reported in February of 2012 that the department store Target began sending advertising for expectant mothers to a female high school student in Minneapolis. The package included coupons for baby items addressed to the minor. The father was furious and complained to the store. He accused Target of encouraging minors to become pregnant. He later was informed by the minor that she was indeed pregnant. This automated package was sent to her after analyzing other shopping habits of the minor.

I am not against the continued use of the loyalty cards and programs, but users should change the way that they apply for the program. The first step is to simply stop providing accurate information. Very few of these programs verify the information provided. If you sign up for one of these programs, change the spelling of your first and last name. If your last name is Laporte, use Lepurt. It is enough to confuse the system but still be accepted by you. More importantly, never provide your home address and telephone number. This chapter will discuss what to use as an address and phone number if you want to receive information from the company.

Many people use a completely false name. For programs that rely on the use of a physical card, such as a grocery store, there is little harm in providing a false name. The only purpose of the card is to save the money immediately at checkout. Be aware, however, that the debit or credit card you use will be associated with that loyalty card. Cash is king. For those programs that demand to see your identification before issuing a card, use your real name and tell them you recently changed your address.

Utility Bills

When you have your utility bills mailed to your residence, you are announcing to the world where you live. Your utility company will obviously know your address, as they are providing a service to the structure such as electricity or water. They maintain a database of the utility bills sent to the customer including home address and phone number. This is often passed around to other companies that may have an interest in providing other services, and you will be targeted with advertising. These details are also made available to data mining companies that can be searched online. If you have a utility bill in your name mailed to your home address, internet searches will eventually announce the location where you and your family sleep at night.

Credit Cards and Financial Accounts

In 2011, I conducted an experiment. I called my credit card provider and requested an additional card in another name completely different from mine. A new card arrived promptly with the alternative new name, and my original account number. I began using this card for purchases, which were charged to my account. In three days, I conducted a detailed online search for my address that I use for the bill, and the fictitious name I had provided was now associated with my address. I was astonished. More details on how to use this technique to your advantage are discussed in Chapter Five.

This is just the tip of the iceberg. Numerous other ways that you give out your personal information will be explained as well as solutions to stop the tracking.

Removal vs. Disinformation

Most of this book will focus on the techniques to permanently remove your information from internet searches and data-mining companies. There will be moments that will require you to provide information to companies in order to add or remove their products or services. Sometimes you will need to provide details about you that will be verified by the company. This may include utilities that insist on a working telephone number for you and your date of birth with social security number. It could also be a website that requires your mailing address, email address, and mother's maiden name before granting you access to the website. Both of these situations can be handled in two extremely different ways.

You could take the standard approach that most people take and supply all of your real information and allow those details to be passed on to dozens of companies that will pass it on to dozens more. Alternatively, you can use a combination of anonymous information and disinformation. In this chapter, you will learn how to create an anonymous email address and telephone number that can be provided to companies without jeopardizing your privacy. As for the other information requested, I prefer to use disinformation. Disinformation is basically falsifying or manipulating the data in order to cause so much inaccurate information that it becomes difficult for companies to know the real details. Chapter Fifteen will identify many ways to fool every data mining company in existence with disinformation.

Any time that someone requests your home and work address, you should evaluate whether that information is really needed for that scenario. If you are turning on water services at a building, that seems like a legitimate reason to disclose the address. You should not disclose your work address though, as it is not needed for that situation. If you are completing a membership form to join an association of bird watching enthusiasts, a post office box would be more appropriate. If you are making a purchase at a store that wants your address to add to the purchase history, you should be prepared to provide disinformation. One approach is telling them that you do not want to provide that information. This is usually met with hostility, and on rare occasion, refusal to sell the item or service. Instead, consider having a fake address ready to provide from memory. This should be an address that does not exist since you should not cause someone else to receive unwanted advertisements and mailings. Eventually, databases will start to associate you with this fake address, which is better than having no record in the database.

Many companies will want your date of birth and social security number for their records. Unless you are requesting some form of credit from the business, there is no need for them to have these details. Again, simply refusing often results in a difficult situation. Instead, consider providing a different date of birth. If it is something you will need to remember, reverse the month and day of birth and add 10 to the year. If your date of birth is 5/9/1970, provide 9/5/1980. Most people will avoid questioning your age, especially if you look older. The social security number is a little stricter. Usually, the company does not have anything in place to verify if the number is valid or assigned. Using someone else's number can be a crime. Instead, use one of the ten numbers reserved by the government to be used in advertisements. None of these special numbers will ever be assigned to a human and they do not look false as does 000-11-2222. Here is the complete list.

987-65-4320	987-65-4324	987-65-4328
987-65-4321	987-65-4325	987-65-4329
987-65-4322	987-65-4326	
987-65-4323	987-65-4327	

One scenario that provides a unique situation is when applying for employment. I do not recommend providing any disinformation on the application. Instead, use a post office box, the anonymous email address you will learn about here, and your real date of birth. The risk of this data being entered into a public database is minimal. Providing your social security number will probably be safe, but you could also fill in this space with "Upon hiring".

Whenever a company wants your personal details, stop and consider where this information may be copied or sold. In order for the rest of the techniques in this book to work, you must change the way that you provide your personal information. You could take every step in the book and eliminate everything out there, but signing up for a great credit card offer or filling out a form to win a new car with all of your information will re-introduce the details to the web based companies. You must change your habits.

Providing disinformation is not identity theft. Providing these small "errors" is not the same as creating a new account under another person's name. The disinformation that you provide will only be enough to meet the collection requirements while masking your true information. It should never cause any fraud or financial gain to you.

Anonymous Email Address

Many of the websites that will be discussed throughout this book will require an email address to remove information. The email address provided to them will be stored by the company that it is submitted to and possibly sold to other businesses. If you use your real personal or business email address, this is counter-productive to the idea of eliminating personal information online. Therefore, you should never provide your current personal email address to any online website from which you want your information removed. To get around this, you will create two anonymous email addresses.

Gmail (gmail.com)

First, you should create a new account with a free email provider. Personally, I have many Gmail accounts from Google. Most privacy advocates hate Gmail and refuse to use their services. I agree that Gmail is invasive and scans all of your email for advertisement delivery. They are very open about that. However, we will not be using them for our personal email. For the purposes of this book, we will only use Google services as part of our effort to remove personal information and provide disinformation. We will not be using it for personal messages or "real life" content. Therefore, I recommend Google services for the methods discussed in this book. The services are reliable and free. After you have completed the removal process, you never have to use their service again if desired. Alternatively, you could choose any other email provider.

Navigate to gmail.com and click on "Create an Account" in the upper right corner. Provide any name that you want and create a password. For the gender and date of birth, you can also provide any data that you want, including false information. This will not be verified by Google. Gmail will ask you to pick an email address. I recommend choosing something with your real name in it. This address will be used to request removal of your personal information from select companies that demand an email response. If your real name is Mike Smith, but your email address is BillJohnson@gmail.com, this looks suspicious. It may delay your request for removal. This email address should only be used during the removal methods described in this book. It should never be used for any other personal or business communication. The book will refer to this account as your new personal email address.

Many services that allow for information removal from their systems do not require you to email them. Instead, they will ask for your email address and will send an email directly to you. For these situations, you should use a completely anonymous forwarding email address that cannot be associated with you. You could create temporary forwarding accounts online, but after a short period of time, the email account is automatically terminated. My preference is to forward email from a permanent anonymous account to a personal account. This is different than the many providers that will give you a temporary account that works for a limited time. The next technique will give you a permanent email address that will always forward to any real email address of your choice.

Not Sharing My Info (notsharingmy.info)

This is an anonymous email forwarding service. Not only does it provide instant email delivery and a superb privacy layer, it is also free. Obtaining a permanent email address is immediate.

Navigate to **notsharingmy.info** and type in your actual personal email address. This can either be the new Gmail account that you created earlier, or a personal account that you check frequently. This may be the free Gmail, Yahoo, or Hotmail account that you use for your everyday email. I do not recommend using your business account since you probably have very little control over the account and access. Figure 3.01 displays the screen to enter your personal email account. When you click on "Get an obscure email", the site will give you your permanent forwarding email address. In Figure 3.02, you can see that my new email address is: dhd9j@notsharingmy.info.

Figure 3.01: The email entry form for NotSharingMy.info.

Figure 3.02: An anonymous email address provided by NotSharingMy.info.

From now on, any time a person, automated service, or verification procedure sends an email to dhd9j@notsharingmy.info, the email will be forwarded to test@computercrimeinfo.com. This is all done behind the scenes and the original sender of the message will have no idea of what my real email address is. However, if you respond to an email received from this account, the email will be sent from your actual personal account, not the anonymous account. This method should only be used for receiving emails.

For people I correspond with, I do not use this type of address. I save this type of address for use with verification techniques during information removal. Many websites that require a profile on the site also require a valid email address. As an example, when you sign up for Facebook, you must provide a valid email address. Once you do, Facebook will send an email to that address which you must read and click on a link within the email. Clicking on this link verifies to Facebook that they have an email address that belongs to you. By using the anonymous method described here, Facebook would only know your anonymous address, and not your real personal address. This also allows you to continue to receive messages from them without disclosing your personal account. Facebook occasionally restricts new accounts from Not Sharing My Info addresses, but the next service that will be discussed is always allowed.

The email address that is created for you from this service is rather generic and may be hard to remember. If you want a more custom email address, such as MikeBazzell@notsharingmy.info, you can do that as well. This will require you to sign into your Facebook account and convince a friend to sign up for the free service. I do not recommend this for two reasons. First, attaching this service to your Facebook page eliminates a layer of privacy that this service provides. Also, picking a custom address, such as your name, helps attach you to your anonymous account. For the purposes of this book, both are a bad idea. I recommend accepting the default address created for you. It is wise to write down the address immediately for future use. If you do decide to create a custom address, the instructions are on the same page as your new address.

According to the notsharingmy.info website, once an email message is delivered to the recipient, the message is not stored on their servers. This means that if you are using a service such as Gmail, Yahoo, or Hotmail, this company only has the content of your message for a short period of time. The site states that they do collect your IP address when you create your account, but that it is not associated with the email address or kept permanently. It should be noted that the service will always know your real email address, there is no way around that. The only way that this would be disclosed is through a legal request such as a subpoena or search warrant. For the scope of this book, the only concern is keeping this information away from the general public. For the remainder of this book, any technique that mentions providing an email address should be given your new anonymous address created on this site.

Over the past few years, readers have advised the Not Sharing My Info would occasionally not work reliably. They reported outages for short periods of time. For a brief period, they were not accepting new accounts. At the time of this writing, the service appeared stable. However, if you would like more reliable experience with many additional features, I have a superior service to consider.

33 Mail (33mail.com)

This is my new favorite email forwarding service. Similar to Not Sharing My Info, it will transfer any incoming email from your anonymous account to your real personal email address without the sender knowing. However, this service provides three additional features that make it superior to other email forwarding companies. It provides unlimited forwarding email addresses within one account, the option to reply from these addresses, and the ability to disable a forwarding address if desired. The following steps will explain how to create your new account and use the free service.

✓ Navigate to **33mail.com** and create a new account at the "Get Started!" button.

✓ Provide your personal email address, choose a user name, and provide a password when prompted. Your user name should not have any association with you. It will be visible on all of your new forwarding email addresses. Somehow, I was able to obtain "NSA" as my user name.

✓ Choose the "Free" service plan when prompted. This is not selected by default.

✓ Check your personal email account and confirm the email from 33 Mail to verify your personal email address.

✓ You now have a new domain that you can use for any email address. Figure 3.03 displays my new email domain of nsa.33mail.com. Any email sent to that domain will be forwarded to my real email address. If an email was sent from anyone to removal@nsa.33mail.com, it would forward to my real email address.

✓ The next time you visit a website that asks for your email address; do not give it to them. Instead, make one up especially for them. For example, if the website spokeo.com demanded an email address for removal of my content, I might give them spokeo@nsa.33mail.com. Obviously, replace my domain listed here with yours.

You do not need to create any alias addresses on the 33 Mail website. This will happen automatically when incoming mail is received at their server. In order to demonstrate the service, I sent an email message to the following three accounts.

test@nsa.33mail.com
spam@nsa.33mail.com
removal@nsa.33mail.com

I immediately received the three messages in the inbox of my personal email address. Additionally, 33 Mail created the three aliases of Test, Spam, and Removal. Figure 3.04 displays the aliases page of my profile. If I were to start receiving a lot of unwanted email addressed to spam@nsa.33mail.com, I could click the "block" link next to that account, and that address would no longer be forwarded to my real account.

This service helps you identify how companies share your personal information. While writing this book, I encountered a service that required an email address before I could access any potential personal information about me on their website. I provided the email address of shady@nsa.33mail.com. I received an immediate email verification link at my personal email address that was forwarded by 33 Mail. One week later, I began receiving several spam messages from various clothing retailers. They were all addressed to shady@nsa.33mail.com. I now know that this web service shares their email database with online marketers. In one click, I could block all future email from that address. You can use this technique to monitor how your information is shared. I recommend a unique email address through 33 Mail for every removal process mentioned in this book.

As a free user, you can reply to one message per day from the anonymous address that you created. This is still in beta, and not extremely reliable, but worth testing. Figure 3.05 displays an email received from the 33 Mail forwarding service. If you reply to this message, it will be delivered to a unique email address only used once for each message. In this case, it was 0735c09e9b0001a31dd6bbcba1f669a72f31a9dd@reply.33mail.com. When 33 Mail receives your reply, it will forward your message back to the original sender. However, instead of your real email address being visible, the recipient will see your 33 Mail address.

I am excited to see this new service. I have been using it successfully for several weeks. While many social networks and other services have begun blocking addresses that end in notsharingmyinfo.com, I have found very few that are blocking 33mail.com. I encourage you to create, test, and maintain addresses through both services.

HOME
MANAGE ALIASES
ACCOUNT INFO
How to use 33Mail
Your 33mail domain is: @nsa.33mail.com

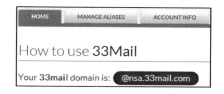

Figure 3.03: A 33 Mail domain ready for use.

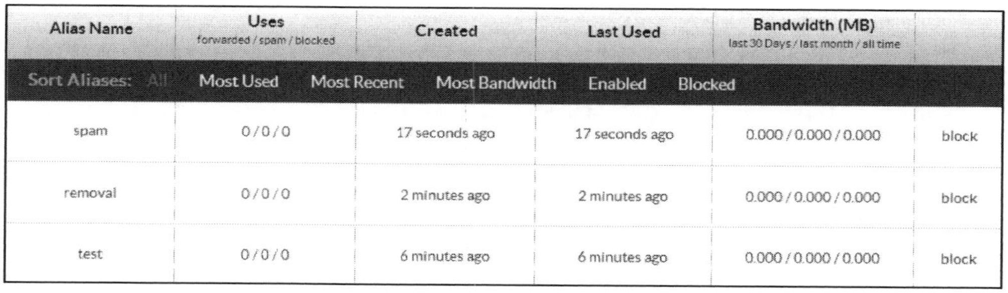

Alias Name	Uses forwarded / spam / blocked	Created	Last Used	Bandwidth (MB) last 30 Days / last month / all time	
Sort Aliases: All	Most Used	Most Recent	Most Bandwidth	Enabled	Blocked
spam	0 / 0 / 0	17 seconds ago	17 seconds ago	0.000 / 0.000 / 0.000	block
removal	0 / 0 / 0	2 minutes ago	2 minutes ago	0.000 / 0.000 / 0.000	block
test	0 / 0 / 0	6 minutes ago	6 minutes ago	0.000 / 0.000 / 0.000	block

Figure 3.04: The 33 Mail panel displaying existing email accounts.

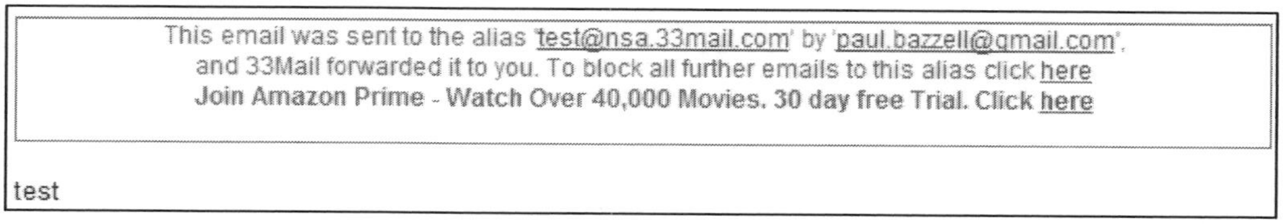
This email was sent to the alias 'test@nsa.33mail.com' by 'paul.bazzell@gmail.com',
and 33Mail forwarded it to you. To block all further emails to this alias click here
Join Amazon Prime - Watch Over 40,000 Movies. 30 day free Trial. Click here
test

Figure 3.05: The 33 Mail email banner displaying a blocking option.

Anonymous Telephone Number

Having an anonymous telephone number to provide to various sites and services that demand one is very important. Years ago, this would be difficult and expensive. Today it is easy and free. There are several services that will issue a telephone number to be used over the internet. This is called Voice Over Internet Protocol (VOIP). Some of these services have a small fee, and some are free and advertiser supported. One of the most common is Google Voice. This free service will assign you a new telephone number in your area code and let you make and receive calls. This service is free but has many drawbacks. You must associate the account with an actual telephone number and email address. All of your incoming voice mail will be transcribed and analyzed. You will then see advertisements based on the conversation recorded by the service. I believe all of this is invasive. As a privacy advocate, I do not recommend daily personal use of the Google Voice service. However, it is the only stable free option currently available. It is adequate for the techniques described in this book. However, the way that you create the account is very important.

Google Voice (google.com/voice)

Most users of Google Voice create an account on their home computer, provide their real name, associate their cellular telephone number with the account, and use the associated Google Mail account for all of their personal email. We will do none of that. You should have already created a Google Mail (Gmail) account. When you log into this account and navigate to google.com/voice, you will have the option to create a new telephone number. You will be prompted to enter a valid telephone number before you can choose your new number. This must be a number where you can receive a text message or telephone call in order to verify your access to the number. This can be tricky. You do not want to associate your real cellular or landline telephone with this service. If you do, your new "anonymous" number is not anonymous at all. Instead, you only need a telephone number where you can receive one telephone call. There are many options.

✓ Many hotels allow guests free unlimited incoming calls. If the hotel you are at provides a direct line to your room, you could use this. Google must be able to dial a ten digit direct number, and not dial an extension.

✓ Your place of work probably has several direct telephone lines that you have access to. You can tell Google to contact you at one of them.

✓ Your local library probably has a fax machine for patron use. The direct phone number of this device is likely written on the machine. These machines are usually set to not accept an incoming fax. Therefore, if it rings, you could answer.

Use your imagination and position yourself at a location that provides both wireless internet access and an incoming telephone line. You can use a laptop computer to complete the setup. Provide the telephone number that you have access to and allow it to call you. When you answer, you will be given a two digit code. Type that code into the Google Voice window that is requesting it. You have now activated your Google Voice account and can choose your area code and new number.

By default, Google will want to forward all incoming calls from your new number to the number associated with the account. In the settings menu, under the phones tab, uncheck any options for call forwarding. This will force any incoming calls to go straight to voicemail. You can create a custom voicemail message, but I recommend leaving the default generic message. In the "Voicemail & Text" tab, you can choose to have all messages forwarded to your anonymous email address. You now have a new telephone number that you can receive incoming calls and the caller can leave you a message. That message will be forwarded to your email inbox. Figure 3.06 displays a few of the voicemail and text options.

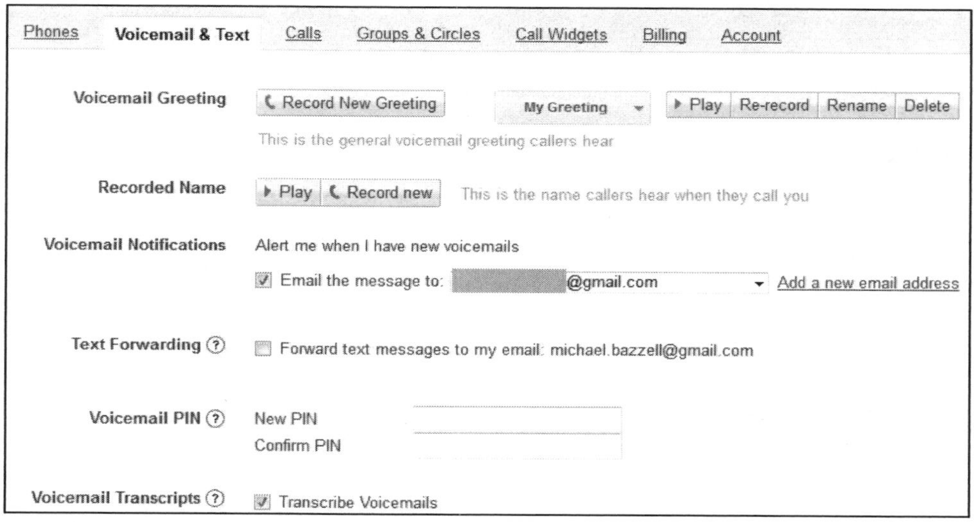

Figure 3.06: A Google Voice telephone number options page.

Mailing Address

Most services, memberships, and publications that you sign up for are going to want a mailing address. Using your personal residence is one of the worst practices when trying to stay private. For much of this book, you will focus on removing any trace of your home address from several databases. Occasionally, you may need a real address where you can receive mail. I recommend a post office box at your local post office. These are associated with your real name and personal address, but only the post office will have access to that information. It will not be passed on to any public databases (unless you do it!). I like to have a post office box address available for various services such as utilities, medical, or any organization that needs to send a bill or invoice.

You can print an application from the USPS website or receive one in person at your local post office. Chapter Eleven will discuss how to start sending all of your mail to your post office box, and eventually no mail designated for you and your family will arrive at your residence. This may sound like overkill, but all of those magazines, coupon packs, and advertisements sell your information to many online services. You will never eliminate this information from the public internet until you stop receiving items at your home. The only mail that should continue to arrive will be generic items addressed to "Current Resident".

Driver's License Image

In order to complete the data removal process with some companies, they will want to verify that you are indeed the person requesting the removal. Most companies do this by demanding a copy of your driver's license. Many of you are probably skeptical of this request, but there is no way around it. Fortunately, you can mask most of the personal content on the license before you send a copy.

The first step is to create a digital image of your license. There are two ways to do this. The easiest way is to use a digital camera or the camera on your cellular telephone to take a close-up image. Try to get good detail and fit the license perfectly into the border of the photo. An alternative to this method is to use a scanner connected to a computer. After you have created the image, use photo editing software to mask some of the information. For those of you that use Microsoft Windows, which is most of you, there is a free tool for this already installed. Click on the start menu, then "Programs", then "Accessories", then "Paint".

This program will allow you to manipulate the digital image that you created of your license. The only information that the companies need from this image is your name, address, and date of birth. Therefore, you should give them nothing more. You could use the paintbrush feature of this program to mark over the additional information, but that looks messy and is more time consuming. Instead, use the "Shapes" tool to easily draw filled blank boxes around all other sensitive information.

If you are using Windows 7 and 8, follow these instructions:

After starting the program, open the file that contains the photo or scan of your license. In the center of the menu bar, click on "Fill" and choose "Solid Color". Now click on the square icon in the shapes box directly left of the "Fill" menu. You are now ready to draw boxes around all sensitive information which will mask the data. Figure 3.07 displays this menu bar.

If you are using Windows XP, follow these instructions:

After starting the program, open the file that contains the photo or scan of your license. Click on the grey square icon in the first column toward the bottom on the left menu bar. This will present three wide rectangles below the square icon. Click on the last rectangle. You are now ready to draw boxes around all sensitive information which will mask the data. Figure 3.08 displays this menu bar.

With your mouse, draw a box around every piece of information except your name, address, and date of birth to mask the data. This should include your photo, license number, signature, expiration, and any other information not vital for our purpose. Save this new file with a new name, such as license2. Figure 3.09 displays the final version of my altered license. Please note that I have masked my address and date of birth for my own privacy for this book in the color grey. Everything masked in white would also be masked on your version. Your version should have your name, address, and date of birth visible. You will now use this saved image on your Opt-Out Request Form.

Figure 3.07: A Windows 7 Paint menu bar.

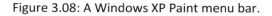

Figure 3.08: A Windows XP Paint menu bar.

Figure 3.09: A redacted copy of a driver's license for submission.

Opt-Out Request Forms

You are now ready to prepare your generic Opt-Out Request Forms that will be used for submission to several companies. By creating one form that has all essential information, you will not need to create a new form for each company from which you want your information removed. I recommend using Microsoft Word for this, but you can use any word processing program you prefer. If you do not use Microsoft Word, you will need to save your document as a PDF file, which will be discussed later.

The first form will be referred to as the "Basic" form, which will contain the following information.

Date: This should be the date of the submission of the form.

Company: This should be the official company name that owns the database containing personal information.

Request: A brief statement identifying the request. I recommend "I request to have my name removed from your public and non-public databases. Here is the information you have asked me to include in my request."

Name: Your full name as it appears in the online database. This should reflect any shortened or misspelled names as they appear online.

Mailing Address: Any addresses that appear in the database that you want removed.

Social Security Number: This should only be included when specifically requested. The few sites that demand this will be identified in this book.

Date of Birth: This will be necessary for all requests that require this form.

Direct URL(s) of personal information: This will be direct links to information that you find online that you would like removed from the internet. A "URL" is the "Uniform Resource Locator". It is the address of a web page. Examples of URLs are google.com, facebook.com/user/johndoe, and pipl.com/opt-out. It is the information that you type into the address bar to get to a specific web page.

Driver's License / State Issued ID: This is a copy of the image that you created in the previous step.

The second form that you should create will be referred to as the "Extended" form. This form will only be used for a small number of companies, and will not be necessary for everyone reading this book. These companies include data brokers such as Westlaw, Accurint, and LexisNexis. The data in these databases includes several pages of information about you including every place you have lived, every car you have owned, your SSN and DL numbers, all of your family members names and locations, your neighbors names and phone numbers, limited financial information, marriage and divorce information, court cases you are involved in, and much more. Law enforcement relies on these companies for information, but the data is not limited to the government. This information is also shared with businesses that are willing to pay for it.

The profile created about you includes information from both public and private sources. While the government customers get access to all of the information available, private business is issued a redacted view. This usually only removes a person's Social Security Number and Driver's License Number. The rest of the personal details are available to any commercial customer with a few bucks. This can include lawyers, private investigators, hiring firms, and anyone else that has an affiliation with a business. Most organizations pay a monthly premium for unlimited data requests about individuals. The wide scope of people that can access these personal details is disturbing to me. Removing your information from these databases is more difficult, but possible.

Since this data is much more valuable than public information from websites, the removal process is stricter. The companies that sell this data are bound by the rules of the Fair Credit Reporting Act (FCRA). All companies must allow people to have their information removed as long as the person requesting the removal meets the any of following criteria:

✓ The person is a judge, public official, or member of law enforcement; or

✓ The person is the victim of identity theft; or

✓ The person is at risk of physical harm

At first glance, you may read this and think that you would not meet these requirements. The criterion is actually quite broad and will be explained later. The only instances that you will need this form will be during the removal processes explained in Chapter Ten. You will learn how to complete this form there and do not need this step completed until then.

Once your basic form is complete, save it and have it available when needed throughout the rest of the book. Each technique in this book that requires this form will explain which information to complete on the form and where to submit the completed form. Note that the printed version of the driver's license in this book masks the name, address, and date of birth in grey. This information should be visible on your copy. The information masked in white should also be masked on your version. Figure 3.10 displays my own from used during these techniques.

Facsimile (fax) Service (GotFreeFax.com)

Several companies demand that requests for removal from their databases be sent via fax. This outdated and wasteful technology is seldom used by the general public. Fortunately, several online websites assist with this function free of charge. I believe the best free service is Got Free Fax at www.gotfreefax.com.

When a section of this book instructs you to send a fax to a company, navigate to this site. Enter your name and new email address into the "Sender" section and the company details provided into the "Receiver" section. This should also include the subject line of "Data Removal".

The next section of this website will allow you to send a free fax using two different methods. The first method allows you to enter text directly into the site and send that text. The second option will allow you to upload a document to be sent. You should use this second option to send the Opt-Out Request Form mentioned earlier. This site will only accept documents with a DOC or PDF extension. If you are using Microsoft Word, the DOC extension is usually the default. If your version of Word is newer that 2007, this default extension may be DOCX. You may need to open the form and select "Save as" and change the file type to DOC. If you are using a free word processor such as Open Office, you will have the option to save any document as either DOC or PDF.

Select the option to "Upload a PDF or DOC file to fax". This will display a "Browse" button. Click on that button and select the document you created from the window that opens. In the section directly below this option, choose the "Send FREE Fax Now!" button. You will receive an email that will include a confirmation link. When you click this link, the fax will be delivered. Each time that this method is required in this book, you will have complete instructions on what information to include with the fax.

This chapter probably takes more effort on your part than any other chapter in the book. It is for good reason though. If you followed all of these steps, you are ready to begin eliminating your private data from the internet.

Date_____   Company_____

I request to have my name removed from your public and non-public databases. Here is the information you have asked me to include in my request:

Name: _____

Mailing Address: _____

Social Security Number (If Required)   _____

Date Of Birth (If Required)   _____

Direct URL(s) of personal information online:

http://_____

http://_____

Thank you for your prompt handling of my request. I have also included a redacted copy of my driver's license below to prove identity.

Figure 3.10: An example of an Opt-Out Request Form.

Chapter Four

Online Protection

Much of the private information that you share with various companies originates with your internet traffic. Before you begin the process of eliminating your data online, you need to properly protect any computer that you will use on the internet. Entire books have been dedicated to true online privacy and staying anonymous. This chapter will focus on the core concepts that should be followed to stay invisible.

Some of these techniques can require a high level of technical skill. I have separated the chapter into three specific groups. The chart below should help you identify which group you fit in.

Privacy Level	Protection Level	Skill Level
Basic	The bare minimum of effort that anyone reading this book should perform. This provides basic protection to block a lot of personal data.	If you can point to the computer in your home, you will have no problems here. Knowing what operating system you have will help.
Intermediate	The next level of protection for true privacy seekers. This will be the suggested level for most readers that want to stop sharing personal details.	You know what a web browser is, the difference between Mac and Windows, and worry about the "cookies" on your computer.
Advanced	The highest level of protection designed for those that want to eliminate any unnecessary trace of personal information from leaving their computer.	You know how to boot your computer from a CD, you already clear out your cookies weekly, and you understand how an IP address is used.

Basic Protection

Too many computer users purchase a desktop or laptop, plug it into their home internet connection, and mistakenly believe they are ready to start browsing the internet. Within moments of starting the system, you are vulnerable to viruses, malicious software (malware), and tracking data. My book *Personal Digital Security* walks you through all of your options for configuring your systems and devices. Here, I will summarize the basics for Microsoft Windows users.

Antivirus

There are dozens of popular antivirus solutions for Windows based systems. Many are not free and can cost over $100 annually. Only free solutions will be discussed in this book. Antivirus programs run continuously and monitor all activity. This includes any time you open a document, launch a program, or download a file from the internet. The program scans all new files and quarantines any files that are suspicious. It should then prompt you for action. There are two very important things to consider when configuring your antivirus program. The first is to make sure that your program is receiving updates. I have seen computers that possess an expired version of premium software that is no longer receiving any updates. This is the same as having no antivirus software at all. The second important detail is to make sure you only have one antivirus program installed on the computer. This is a situation where more is actually less. If you have more than one antivirus program, they will battle each other for authority over your system. If you have an expired premium software package, such as Norton or McAfee, and you do not plan on renewing the service, you should uninstall it completely. If you currently have a paid or free version of premium software, and you have verified that it is functioning and receiving updates, you should leave it on the computer and disregard installation steps for the next two programs, Microsoft Security Essentials and AVG Free Addition. However, if you believe, as I do, that some of these premium software packages slow your computer down, you may want to consider replacing your current program.

Microsoft Security Essentials

If you want to stick with Microsoft created security programs, Security Essentials is your only option. This free program is provided and maintained by Microsoft and will work on any version of Windows (XP through 7). This software is not included with any version of Windows and must be downloaded and installed. The following steps will complete the installation.

✓ Navigate to:
  http://windows.microsoft.com/en-us/windows/security-essentials-download.

✓ Click on the "Download now" button.

✓ Execute the downloaded file and allow the default choices.

If successful, you should see a green window when launching the program from either your start menu or the status bar in the lower right portion of your screen.

AVG Free Edition

Personally, I prefer AVG over Security Essentials. In my experience, AVG protects from the newest threats before Microsoft and is more responsive in interfering with malicious files before they can damage anything. Since AVG also offers a premium version that is not free, finding the completely free version can be tricky. The following steps will aid in obtaining the absolutely free version of AVG.

✓ Navigate to free.avg.com and click the "Free Download" button.

✓ Scroll to the bottom of the next page and click the orange "Download" button. Do not click the "Free Trial" button.

✓ Click the green "Download Now" button on the page hosted by CNet.

✓ Execute the downloaded file and allow the default choices. Be sure to only select the "Free" version" during setup.

System Updates

Securing your operating system is vital to protecting your computer from online threats. Thousands of hackers are constantly scanning Internet Protocol (IP) Addresses looking for vulnerable computers that do not possess specific security patches. No matter which version of Windows or Mac OSX you use, even if the computer is brand new, you should apply security patches weekly. Most versions of Windows will conduct this patching automatically by default if you allow it. The following instructions will demonstrate how to make sure that your computer system is automatically updated when a new security patch is released. Your computer must be connected to the internet to download any updates.

Windows XP

Click on the "Start" button in the lower left portion of the screen and select "Settings" and then "Control Panel". If you do not see the "Automatic Updates" option, you are missing Service Pack 3, a free update from Microsoft. Open Internet Explorer and click Tools and then Windows Update. Alternatively, you can look for "Windows Update in your start menu. Either way, apply all default updates possible until you have installed Service Pack 3.

You should note that Microsoft ended support of Windows XP in July of 2014. This means that there will be no more updates for this operating system and it will be unsecure. I recommend upgrading to Windows 7, which is more secure and will be supported for several years.

Windows 7

Click on the "Start" button on the lower left portion of the screen. In the right column, click "Control Panel". Click the last option, "Windows Update". Click on "Change Settings" and review the options. For optimum results, make sure that all boxes are checked. Figure 4.01 displays these options.

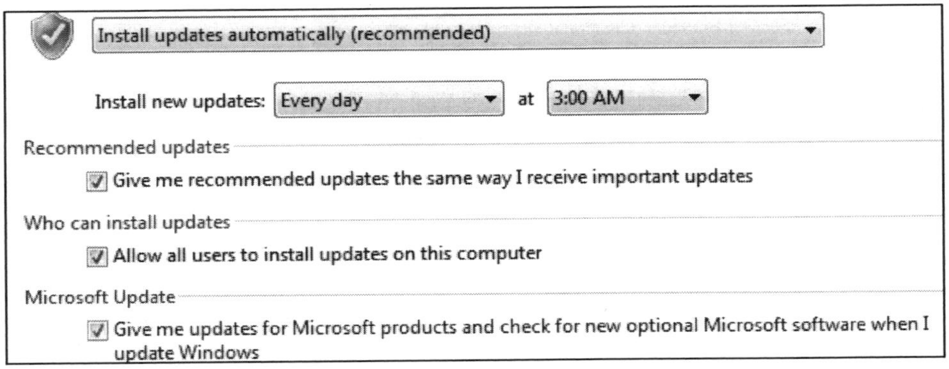

Figure 4.01: A Microsoft Windows Update options screen.

Click "OK" to close this window. If you made any changes, you may want to click "Check for Updates" to manually download any pending security updates for your system. If this automatic setting was disabled for some time, or you are setting up a new computer, it may take up to an hour to retrieve and install all of the updates. Many updates will require you to reboot your system. After reboot, you should check for new updates. After you have your system completely updated, you will probably only notice updates once a week. Your computer will conduct the updates automatically and finish the process upon restarting.

Windows 8

Windows 8 computers are set to download updates automatically. It is important to shut your computer down completely on occasion to allow the updates to be applied.

This brings up a common question that I receive during my presentation. Many people ask whether they should turn their computer off at night or just leave it on all of the time. There are many different opinions on this, but I firmly believe that you should turn your computer off at night, or when it will not be used for an extended period of time. The reasons are listed below.

✓ Specific hardware in the computer, including the standard hard drive, has a limited life. Since it has moving parts, every standard hard drive will fail eventually. The less time that your computer is on, the less time that the hard drive is spinning at 7200 revolutions per minute (RPM).

✓ When a computer is turned off, it cannot respond to digital attacks.

✓ Turning off your wireless router and internet connection device when not in use will provide even more protection.

✓ Turning the computer off when not in use will save energy.

Mac OSX

The default configuration for the many versions of Macintosh OSX is to prompt you when an update to the operating system is available, but not to apply the update without your intervention. Visit the "App Store" within your "Applications" folder. Click on the "Updates" tab in the upper right of the screen. You will be notified of any available updates. Select the updates and follow the instructions.

Anti-Malware

At this point, you are probably asking yourself why you would need additional protection than the products already discussed. You may also feel that adding more protection is too difficult and you may want to abandon installing more programs. Unfortunately, there is no one program that will catch and remove all malicious software. In fact, if you encounter a program that makes this claim, it is probably a virus in disguise. I would avoid any product that guarantees to stop all intrusions. If you have successfully downloaded the programs that were previously discussed, they are now monitoring your system and you need to take no additional action. The following two programs in this section do not necessarily monitor your system at all times. They are present on your system and waiting to be executed.

Malware Bytes

After cleaning out any temporary and unnecessary files, I recommend the first scan for malicious files on your computer. Overall, you will use three individual programs to make sure that you have removed everything, but I believe the Malware Bytes is the best.

✓ Navigate to http://www.malwarebytes.org/ and select the "For Home" option.

✓ Click the "Download" button, and then click the "Download" button again to install the file.

✓ Execute the downloaded file and accept the default installation options.

After you have installed the application, you must execute it in order to run a scan. Malware Bytes (and the remaining applications in this chapter) do not run in the background as an antivirus program does. I recommend that you perform a scan at least once monthly. The following steps should be taken every time you run the program.

✓ Click on the "Update" tab and choose "Check for Updates".

✓ If any updates are available, allow the program to install the updates.

✓ Under the "Scanner" tab, choose the default option of "Perform full scan" and click "Scan". Choose the drives you want to scan. I recommend that you check the C drive and any other hard drives attached to your computer. The program will automatically scan your computer and remove any threats. You will receive a report at the end.

Spybot

Spybot is another application that will identify and remove malicious software and unnecessary files. You will probably notice that it will identify files that Malware Bytes missed. This does not mean that either product is superior to the other. Each of the products discussed in this chapter have unique strengths that allow them to repair issues that other programs miss. While there are hundreds of programs that will clean your computer, I believe that a combination of the products mentioned will cover all of your needs. To install Spybot, complete the following tasks.

✓ Navigate to http://www.safer-networking.org and click the "Download" tab.

✓ Choose the option to download the free edition under the "Home Users" category. This will forward you to a download page. Choose any option under the "Ad-free" section of this page. You may need to click the "download" button on the next page.

✓ Execute the downloaded file and allow the default installation options.

Similar to the previous two programs, I recommend scanning your computer with Spybot at least once monthly. This can be on the same day that you scan with the other programs. I will later discuss the recommended order of events. To update and run Spybot, complete the following steps.

✓ Choose the "Update" button on the home screen. The updates will be applied automatically. Close the update window when complete.

✓ Click on "System Scan" on the home screen. Choose the "Start a scan" button and allow the program to analyze your system.

✓ When complete, click the "Show scan results" button to view all of the problems that were found. The items will all be selected and you only need to click "Fix selected" at the bottom to remove the threats.

CCleaner

CCleaner is one of my favorite programs ever created. It provides a simple interface and is used to clean potentially unwanted files and invalid Windows Registry entries from your computer. It was originally called Crap Cleaner, but I assume that someone in the marketing division demanded a better name. This software works on both Windows and Mac computers. The following steps will download and install the free version of the application.

✓ Navigate to http://www.piriform.com/ccleaner/download.

✓ In the "Free" column, click on the "Download" button to get the Piriform CCleaner version. This will ensure that you download the free version. The download should start automatically.

✓ Execute the program and accept the default installation settings.

After the installation completes, launch the program. You have several options under the Cleaner tab that will allow you to choose the data to eliminate. The default options are safe, but I like to enable additional selections. Figure 4.02 displays my choices. Clicking on the "Analyze" button will allow the program to identify files to delete without committing to the removal. This will allow you to view the files before clicking "Run Cleaner" to remove them. If you are running this program on a computer with heavy internet usage, you may be surprised at the amount of unnecessary files present. The first time you use this program, the removal process can take several minutes and possibly an hour. If you run the program monthly, it will finish the process much quicker.

The Registry tab of CCleaner will eliminate unnecessary and missing registry entries. This can help your computer operate more efficiently. The default options on this menu are most appropriate. Click on "Scan For Issues" and allow it to identify any problems. This process should go quickly. When complete, click on "Fix Selected Issues" to complete the process.

The Tools tab provides an easy way to disable specific programs from launching when your computer starts. These programs can slow your computer down when they are running unnecessarily. Figure 4.03 displays four programs scheduled to launch when my computer starts. These can be found by clicking the "Startup" button in the left column. I have selected the Adobe and Java programs and applied the "Disable" button. They are now marked as "No" and will not launch the next time my computer starts. If I want to reverse this, I can select the entries again and choose "Enable".

Use a better browser

Most people settle for Internet Explorer as a web browser, which is included with Windows operating systems. I do not recommend using that browser for safe browsing. There are many free web browsers from which to choose. They all have strengths and weaknesses. These browsers do not look much different from the browser you are currently using. My recommendation is the free Firefox browser.

Firefox (mozilla.org)

The Firefox browser has several features that are missing from some default browsers. It can be configured or tweaked for privacy and allows third party software called "add-ons" or "extensions" to be installed. These are small applications that work within the browser that perform a specific function. They will make private browsing much easier. Firefox also has some optional features that you can customize to enhance the privacy of your web browsing. Some of Firefox's privacy features are enabled by default, however there are a few that need to be configured.

With Firefox open, select "Tools" and then "Options" in the toolbar. This will open a new window with many options. The top row of menu options includes an icon titled "Privacy". Selecting this option will display three categories of configuration options. The first section is titled "Tracking" and has only one option which is unchecked by default. Checking this option will prohibit some websites from tracking your internet usage. The next section, titled "History", tells Firefox how much of the history of your internet usage that you would like it to store. I recommend the "Never remember history" option. With this selected, every time that you close the browser, it "forgets" your internet history. Launching the program will present a fresh session without any memory of the previous session. Finally, the last section titled "Location Bar" will instruct the browser on what information to store and display when a new website address is entered ("Bookmarks"). This way, when you type in a website address, Firefox will only look into your stored bookmarks for information about the site to navigate to. Figure 4.04 displays these custom options for this menu item.

When installing and executing Firefox, choose not to import any settings from other browsers. This will keep your browser clean from unwanted data. The extensions detailed here will include a website for each extension. You can either visit the website and download the extension or search for it from within Firefox. The latter is usually the easiest way. While Firefox is open, click on "Tools" and then "Add-ons" in the menu bar. This will present a new page with a search field in the upper right corner. Enter the name of the extension and install from there.

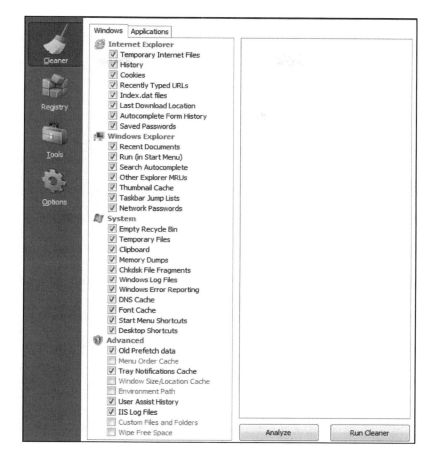

Figure 4.02: The CCleaner cleaning options recommended for most installations.

Figure 4.03: The CCleaner startup options with two services disabled.

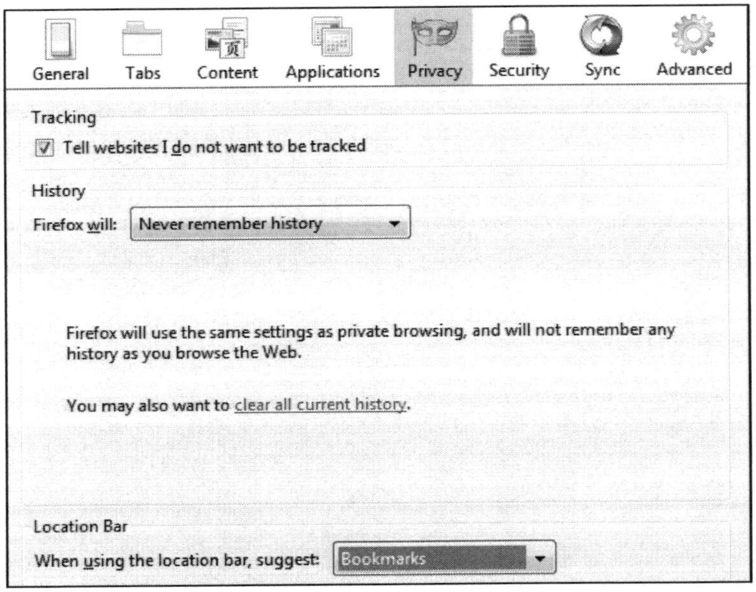

Figure 4.04: The Firefox Options menu.

Firefox Extensions

There are thousands of extensions available for Firefox. Some are helpful, some are worthless, and some are just fun. This chapter will discuss two of these extensions, Ghostery and AdBlock Plus.

Ghostery (ghostery.com)

Many sites that you will visit will be using website analytics. These free services monitor the visitors of a website and identify the IP address, location, business name, search terms, and site navigation of the visitor. This can be very invasive and personal information can be analyzed and distributed without your knowledge. While you are using the methods in this book to eliminate your personal information from online databases, it is important not to provide more information in the process. Ghostery can be of help. This extension will identify any analytics and other intrusive software running on a website when you visit it. With some configuration, it can be set to block these services and prevent the website from tracking you.

After installing the extension, click on "Tools", "Ghostery" and then "Manage Ghostery Options". Inside the new window that will open, scroll down to the "Blocking Options". Click on the checkboxes next to "Advertising", "Analytics", "Privacy", "Trackers" and "Widgets". This will stop over 1000 different types of intrusive software from monitoring and tracking your internet habits. Click "save" below the options and now click on the "Cookies" tab. Similar to the last screen, select the checkboxes next to "Advertising", "Analytics", "Trackers" and "Widgets". Click "Save" and then close this entire tab. This will block an additional 500 scripts that can collect private information about you. When you visit a site with analytics, the owner will no longer capture any information about your visit. Figure 4.05 displays this blocking feature in action. Any time you visit a website that is using a service blocked by Ghostery, you will be presented with a purple window displaying all services running on the page. When a service has been blocked, the service name will be stricken and faded. In Figure 4.05, you can see that the Google Analytics and Woopra were blocked, but the Twitter Button was not. Since the Twitter button does not collect your information, there was no need to block it.

Figure 4.05: A Ghostery notification.

Some versions of Firefox and this extension will not display the purple popup window. This is normal behavior and does not mean that the extension is not working. You can also obtain the details of the blocked items in either the lower right corner of the browser or the upper right portion of the menu bar in the browser. In Figure 4.06, Ghostery blocked nine services on wired.com. Clicking the ghost icon in the upper right portion of the browser displays the details of the services blocked. In Figure 4.07, this same information could be found by clicking the "9 trackers" link in the status bar in the lower section of the browser.

Figure 4.06: The menu bar identifying Ghostery notifications.

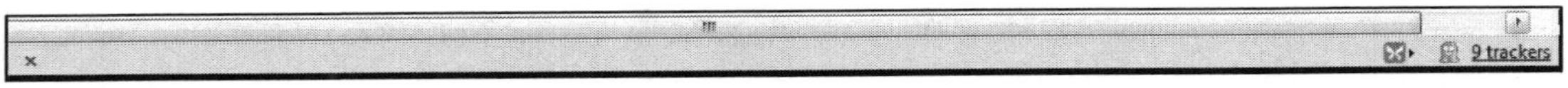

Figure 4.07: The status bar displaying a Ghostery notification.

It should be noted that in the display above, the services were intentionally not blocked in order to display the services in a readable format. When successfully blocked, the items appear light grey.

AdBlock Plus (adblockplus.org)

Similar to Ghostery, AdBlock Plus is a free extension for Firefox that blocks services on a website. Configuration is much easier than Ghostery though. After you install the extension, the default configuration is appropriate for most users. AdBlock Plus will allow you to tweak the settings, but it is unnecessary for our use. The following was copied from their website which explains the purpose of the extension.

"Adblock Plus is an extension for Firefox, Thunderbird, and several other applications with the primary goal of removing advertisements. For that, it will look at all requests made by web pages and block the request if the address the request should go to matches a filter in Adblock Plus."

In Figure 4.08, you can see that AdBlock Plus blocked 24 advertisement services on the home page of CNN.com. While you are removing your personal information throughout this book, these extensions will prohibit websites from delivering malicious code that tracks you while you browse the internet. There is nothing stopping you from using this browser with extensions for your entire daily internet surfing. The only downside is that occasionally, a service that you want to use may be blocked. One example of this is that a few websites will not display their content unless you allow them to place a tracking "cookie" on your computer. Personally, when I find a site that does this, I quit using that site.

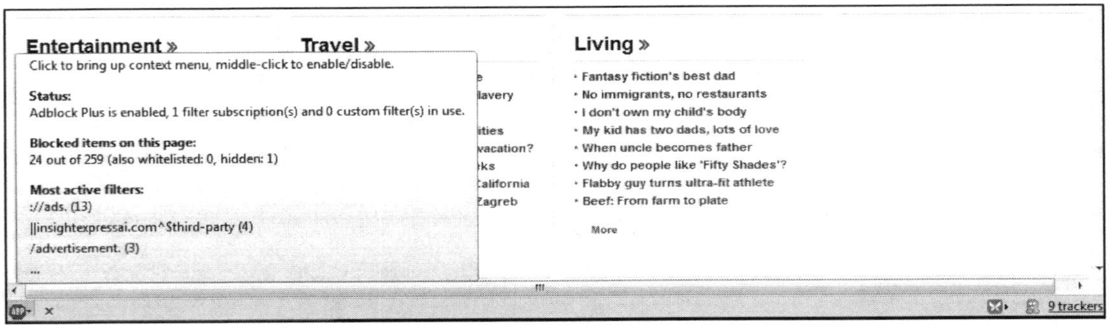

Figure 4.08: An AdBlock Plus report of identified items.

Intermediate Protection

The techniques explained here will involve a slightly higher understanding of technology. Anyone can apply these methods to their daily internet use and I encourage you to consider this next step in privacy protection.

NoScript (noscript.net)

This extension for the Firefox browser provides superior protection from malicious Java, Javascript, Flash, popups, and other web-based programming code. The default configuration of this software will block practically any script programmed to execute when you load a web page. This will include advertisements, tracking cookies, applications, and anything else that is not native to the display of the web page. The reason that this is listed in the intermediate area is because the protection can often block core content required to properly view the website. The following instructions will explain how to properly install and access NoScript.

- ✓ Within your Firefox browser, click on Tools and then Add-ons in the menu.

- ✓ In the search field, type NoScript and install the first result. Restart your browser and notice the new "S" icon in the upper left. Clicking this icon will present the NoScript menu for the website currently loaded.

Figure 4.09 displays the NoScript menu expanded while on a website. The extension identified and blocked five scripts from launching within this website. This includes Facebook data, advertisements, and tracking programs. Allowing these programs would have jeopardized your privacy by collecting data about you, your computer, your browsing history, and your Facebook profile (if logged in).

There are options within this menu if you want to enable scripts. If NoScript is blocking something on a website and is preventing it from displaying the content you want, use the following guide to correct the issue. I recommend taking action in the following order which starts with minor changes and ends with disabling NoScript completely from the website.

- ✓ Click on the "S" icon to launch the NoScript menu. Attempt to identify the blocked script that is desired. If you can identify the specific script, select "Temporarily allow" next to the script name. This will allow the script to load one time. However, the next time you load that website, the script will be blocked again. In Figure 4.09, clicking "Temporarily allow Facebook.com" would allow any Facebook script within the website.

- ✓ If you decide that any allowed script should not run in the future, you do not need to take any action. If you want to block the script right away, you can click the "Forbid" option next to the script name.

✓ If you decide that the temporarily unblocked script should always be allowed, select the "Allow" option below the "Temporarily" option next to that script. It will now always allow that specific script on any website. This may be beneficial to always allow a desired login or social network.

✓ The "Temporarily allow all this page" option near the bottom of the menu will reload the current website and allow any scripts as if NoScript were not installed. This can be beneficial when you cannot access the desired website appropriately and do not know which script is the culprit.

✓ The "Allow all this page" option will always allow all scripts to run on the current website. This can be beneficial when you commonly visit a trusted website, such as your bank or other financial service. Enabling this setting will advise NoScript to never block scripts on that page.

✓ If you are currently only using trusted websites and are frustrated with NoScript blocking desired content, you can choose "Allow Scripts Globally". This completely disables NoScript and you are not protected. You can reverse this action by selecting "Forbid Scripts Globally".

If you choose to use NoScript, you do not need to use the Ghostery and AdBlock extensions mentioned during the basic protection section of this chapter. I believe that NoScript is a superior service and provides more protection. In exchange for this security, you sacrifice convenience in your daily internet browsing. I hope that you find this inconvenience worth the reward of a safer online experience. The following describes my NoScript settings.

✓ I have a default NoScript installation and configuration within Firefox. I block all scripts while browsing and searching the internet.

✓ If I encounter a website that I cannot view properly, and it is a reputable website, I will select the "Temporarily allow all this page option" for a single use allowance.

✓ The first time I connect to trusted websites such as my bank, financial services, email, or educational site, I choose the "Allow all this page" to permanently allow the scripts.

✓ When I am conducting important business, such as financial transactions or creating accounts on business websites, I select "Allow Scripts Globally". As soon as I am finished, I choose "Forbid Scripts Globally". My individual settings are still maintained.

Figure 4.09: A NoScript menu for a loaded website.

Google Search Settings

Companies like Google make money from your internet browsing. Most of this revenue is from advertisements placed within your search results. You may have noticed that the ads that you see are directly related to your interests and shopping habits. This is not a coincidence. Google monitors your activity in order to deliver ads to you that you are likely to click. Some of this is based on cookies downloaded to your computer and some is from your search history.

If you use Google's free email service Gmail, you are targeted even more. Google scans through each email to deliver ads that are relevant to your conversation. While this tactic provides a great business strategy, many feel that it is intrusive. It is impossible to use Google's free services without giving them some of your information. However, completing the following steps will disable some of the most intrusive methods conducted against you.

  ✓ Activate Google Opt-Out by visiting the website **www.google.com/ads /preferences/plugin**. Click on "Download the advertisement cookie opt-out plugin". Depending on your browser, the installation method will vary. This will install a small file that will prevent a company called DoubleClick from installing files that monitor your activity. DoubleClick is the company that Google relies on for this type of data collecting. This file will not be deleted when you manually clear your cookies or when you use a program to clean up your computer.

✓ Turn off Google's web history. This service archives all of your Google search activity. To view this history and settings, navigate to **www.google.com/history**. You will need to be logged into your Google account, such as Gmail, in order to see this page. Once logged in, click on the gear icon and select "Settings". If desired, check the box to include history from other web and app activity, and then click the "Pause" button. In the next popup, click the "Pause" button. Go back to "Manage History" to manually delete any searches made up to this point. Click on the gear icon and select "Remove Items". From the drop down menu, select "from the beginning of time" and click the "Remove" button. This will stop Google from capturing your search history. Figure 4.10 displays these options as well as the interactive calendar that will show your search history. Parents that want to monitor their children may want to leave this enabled.

✓ Opt out of Google's Ad Preferences. While logged into your Google account, navigate to **www.google.com/ads/preferences/**. Click on the "Opt out" button which will stop the interest based ads from appearing.

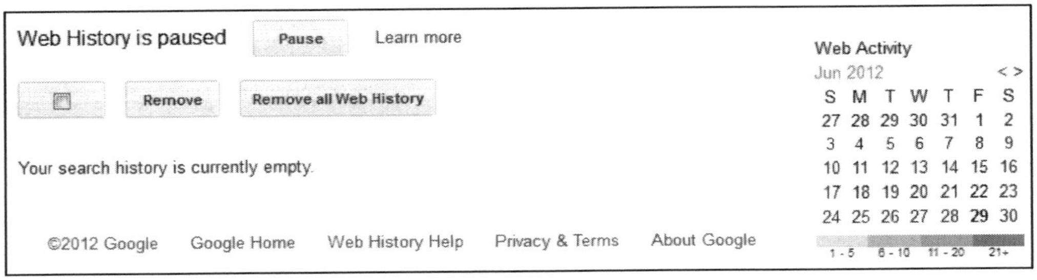

Figure 4.10: The Google Search History settings page.

Microsoft Search Settings

Microsoft has their own rules for their delivery of advertisements to your desktop. Disabling customized ads based on your internet history can be accomplished on the following website.

https://choice.microsoft.com/en-us/opt-out

Choose the option "Off" within the box "Personalized ads in this browser". This will not stop you from seeing advertisements from Microsoft's services. However, these ads will be more random and not based on your internet activity. If you are signed into a Microsoft account, such as one of their email services, you can disable this personalization across all browsers. Finally, selecting the "Data Dashboard" on this page will allow you to see the data about you that Microsoft uses for advertisement delivery.

Advanced Protection

If you have reached this point of the chapter and you still have an appetite for more online privacy, this section will take you to the next level. These techniques are not recommended for everyone. Familiarization with computer hardware and software will be required.

Tor

Tor, an acronym for the onion router, is a network and a software package that helps you anonymously use the Internet. Specifically, Tor hides the source and destination of your Internet traffic. This prevents anyone from knowing both who you are and what you are looking at. Tor also hides the destination of your traffic, which can circumvent some forms of censorship. Tor has been in development for many years and is very stable and mature. It is regarded as one of the best privacy tools currently in existence and it does not cost you anything.

Tor encrypts the data you send across the Internet in multiple layers, like an onion. Then it sends that data through multiple relays, each one of which peels a layer off the onion, until your packet leaves the final relay and arrives at its destination. This is called 'onion routing' and it is a fantastic method for keeping privacy on the web. Proper use of tor can be one of the best ways to ensure your browsing will remain anonymous.

For the purposes of a simple and incomplete explanation, consider the following to describe the actions of Tor. You connect to a Tor computer which routes your internet traffic through several other computers. This traffic is then sent to the "web" and returned to you through the same route. These computers are often in other countries and the traffic is encrypted. When you navigate to google.com, Google actually receives the request from another computer, in another country, from another IP address. Therefore, Google does not know who you are, where you are, or what other actions you are performing on other websites. Your IP address assigned to you from your internet service provider (ISP) is not disclosed to the websites that you visit.

The easiest way to apply this security is to use the Tor Browser Bundle. It is a version of Firefox that comes preconfigured with Tor. It is set up to use Tor the right way so that you will avoid a lot of the common pitfalls that can pierce your veil of anonymity. The following steps will help you download, execute, and properly browse the internet anonymously with Tor.

   ✓   Navigate to torproject.org and download the Tor Browser Bundle.

   ✓   Execute the downloaded file. This will extract all of the files necessary for the bundle. This software is "portable" and is not intrusive into your operating system. All of the settings are contained within the folder where the software exists. After the extraction is complete, allow the software to launch.

✓ You will receive a Tor Network Settings window that will configure the appropriate settings for your situation. Most users will select the first option which will connect you directly to the Tor network. The second option is only for advanced users that are behind a proxied or censored connection. Click the "Connect" button to launch your Tor session.

✓ You should receive a "Congratulations" notification when you have successfully connected. You can now use this browser for anonymous online activity.

This phenomenal layer of security does not come without costs. Your overall internet experience will likely be somewhat slower. However, the speed of the Tor network has increased substantially over the past couple of years. Some websites that you visit will detect that you are coming from a Tor connection and may refuse whole or partial service. Several websites that require an account to access content, such as Gmail, Facebook, and others, will often require additional steps in order to create or access an account while connected through Tor. Many will require a valid telephone number when detecting Tor connections. This is likely due to abuse of the Tor network by cyber criminals.

Tails

The Tor bundle will provide adequate privacy protection for the majority of users. Because Tor is installed on your computer within your operating system, there can still be vulnerabilities within the data stored on the computer. Your operating system possesses many details about your computer use and retains a record of further actions that you take. You would need to use a brand new computer every day and destroy the last used system in order to stop this type of vulnerability. The Tails live system provides a better solution.

Tails is a live operating system that you can start on almost any computer from a DVD, USB device, or SD card. You could use this operating system without a hard drive present in the computer. When using the DVD option, absolutely no details of your internet session are saved. It ultimately preserves your privacy and anonymity by routing all connections through the Tor network. Further, it leaves no trace on the computer you are using unless you ask it explicitly. It will also use state-of-the-art cryptographic tools to encrypt your files, emails and instant messaging. The following steps will help you launch your own private Tails system from DVD.

✓ Navigate to tails.boum.org and download the latest version of Tails ISO image.

✓ If using a Windows computer, right-click on the ISO image and choose "Burn disc image". Select your DVD recorder and select "Burn".

✓ If using a Mac OSX computer, launch Disk Utility from Applications-Utilities-Disk Utility. Insert a blank DVD and drag and drop the ISO file to the left pane in Disk Utility. Select the ISO file and click on the Burn button in the toolbar.

✓ If you are using Linux, you likely already know how to burn an ISO image.

✓ Put your new Tails DVD into the DVD drive and restart the computer. You should see a welcome screen prompting you to choose your language.

You can now perform basic internet tasks such as web browsing, email, and instant messaging. Your activity is only being stored in the computer's memory (RAM) and disappears when you shut down the computer. If you find this limiting and inappropriate for daily use, consider the following option for a virtual machine.

Virtual Machines

I currently use virtual machines every day. These are full computer operating systems that can be launched on top of your current operating system. The activity performed within a virtual machine is not associated with the main operating system of your computer. If you become infected with a virus or malware in a virtual machine, it does not infect your main operating system. These are often referred to as "sandboxes" that allow you to play inside of them without risk to your important data on your main computer. I will describe how I use virtual machines.

When I am conducting an investigation on the internet, I currently use a Windows 7 virtual machine while on a Macbook Pro laptop. If anything goes wrong during the investigation, my laptop is not compromised. This is not limited to viruses and malware. A website might capture details from my computer which could identify me. A virtual machine helps protect you in several ways.

✓ A virtual machine can use a full version of Windows. This can be beneficial because you can install any software that you need for daily use such as Microsoft Office, Adobe products, or custom browsers. Additionally, this avoids the learning curve involved with Linux based operating systems such as Tails.

✓ At the end of a session on a virtual machine, you can choose to delete any changes made to the system. This would eliminate any details that were left behind from your internet activity.

✓ You can possess multiple virtual machines for various operating systems. You can also have several copies of the same operating system that can be used for different purposes.

✓ Using a fresh operating system every time ensures that excess details about you and your activity are not visible to any websites or services.

✓ In the event of a virus or corruption that causes the system to not function, you can either return to a previous state or delete the entire virtual machine and start over.

Your need for virtual machines will vary from mine. You should create only those machines necessary for daily use. This may just be one machine with Windows or Tails that you use when you want to be private or have additional protection. I encourage you to attempt at least one virtual machine. Before I can explain the process, virtual machine software must be chosen.

There are many choices for virtual machine software. Most are commercial and cost money for a license. Some only work on specific operating systems, such as Parallels for Mac OSX. For the purposes of this book, I will explain how to use Virtual Box. This software is free and works on Windows, Mac, and Linux. The following steps will help get you started. These are simplified instructions and an understanding of operating systems will be required to complete this process.

✓ Navigate to www.virtualbox.org/wiki/Downloads and download the appropriate version for your operating system. Install the downloaded file with the default options.

✓ Execute the software and click "New" at the top of the window to create a new virtual machine. Default configuration options are usually sufficient for most systems. You will need a valid installation disc and license for the operating system that you choose. Complete the installation process and refer to the Virtual Box website for troubleshooting.

✓ Once you have your virtual machine running, configure any custom settings. This may include software installation such as office suites or custom browsers and extensions. Do not conduct any web browsing yet. You want to keep this system clean.

✓ When your virtual machine is configured the way that you want it, create a snapshot. Click on the menu then select "Take Snapshot". Provide a name and description to help remember the configuration. Your name might be "Windows 7 Pro" and the description might be "Clean install with Microsoft Office and Firefox". You now have a recorded point in time that you can revert to if necessary.

✓ The purpose of creating a snapshot is so that you can go back to a particular state. In our case, we want to return to the state that existed just after we installed the operating system. Any time that you shut the virtual machine down, you can now revert to the snapshot that was created right after the install of a clean image.

✓ When you want to revert to a snapshot, select your virtual machine from the list and switch over to the snapshots view. Here you will see a list of the various snapshots you have taken. To restore to a snapshot, simply right click on it and choose "Restore Snapshot" from the context menu. You have now eliminated any data written to the virtual machine since the snapshot was taken.

Now that you have a basic understanding of virtual machines and snapshots, I will explain how I use them on a daily basis. I currently use VMWare Fusion as my virtual machine software. It is not free, but I find it to be superior for my needs. I have five virtual machines installed and configured on my laptop.

Windows XP Demonstration: I use this standard installation of Windows XP during all of my presentations and training events. It is configured with all of the software that I need and has a snapshot of the image before I performed any demonstrations with actual data. When I turn it off after use, I revert to the snapshot.

Windows 7 Working: This updated and patched copy of Windows 7 opens any Windows only applications that I may need. I do not conduct any investigations on this image and do not expect total privacy. This is ideally for official business.

Windows 7 Investigations: This machine has minimal software installed. It possesses a custom version of Firefox which has many extensions that I use while browsing. Reverting to the snapshot after each session eliminates data about the investigation that I was conducting.

Tails Privacy: This is a standard installation of Tails as described with the DVD option earlier. Since my laptop does not have a DVD drive, and I find booting from USB too slow, this option works best for me. I always revert to the original snapshot after every use.

Windows 7 Privacy: I use this machine when Tails is not appropriate for my work. It has the Tor Browser as well as a custom Firefox browser with NoScript. It has also been configured to eliminate as much tracking as possible. This is not as secure as Tails, but much more user friendly. It suffices for the majority of my private browsing.

This selection of virtual machines will be overkill for most users. Much of my need for all of this is a combination of paranoia and enthusiasm for technology. You may also find that possessing multiple isolated operating systems can become addictive.

Chapter Five

Credit Companies

Credit companies collect a lot of information about you. They obviously know your name and personal details. Since they are providing you with a line of credit, they are entitled to know where to find you if you do not pay them. Unfortunately, they do not keep this information to themselves. They share their data with other creditors and various data mining companies.

Earlier, I mentioned an experiment that I conducted with a secondary credit card in a different name. The only company that I provided with this new name was my credit card company. After a few days, I requested my personal data from Thomson Reuters (CLEAR). This report included the new name as an alias to me. It identified my address as being used by this "person" and associated the name with my activities. This same report is available to anyone that has an account with one of the data mining companies. This report would cost under $6.00.

My point is that anyone can track you on the internet through your credit. The following methods will not replace the privacy of cash, but will eliminate much of the information available to the general public. This chapter is important for other concerns besides privacy. These methods will offer a new layer of security to protect you from identity theft and fraud.

Credit Opt-Out (optoutprescreen.com)

Under the Fair Credit Reporting Act (FCRA), the consumer credit reporting companies are permitted to include your name on lists used by creditors or insurers to make firm offers of credit or insurance that are not initiated by you. These are the pre-approved credit and insurance offers that you receive in the mail. The FCRA also provides you the right to opt-out, which prevents consumer credit reporting companies from providing your credit file information to businesses.

Through this website, you may request to opt-out from receiving these offers for five years. If you want to opt-out permanently, you can print a form that you must send through postal mail. If you choose to opt-out, you will no longer be included in offer lists provided by consumer credit reporting companies. The process is easy.

✓ Navigate to **optoutprescreen.com** and click the button at the bottom of the page labeled "Click Here to Opt-In or Opt-Out". On the next page, choose the second option of "Electronic Opt-Out for Five Years"

✓ Complete the online form and click "Confirm". You will receive an immediate confirmation. This action will need to be repeated every five years.

Fraud Alert

A fraud alert is an action that you can take to protect your identity from being used by criminals for financial gain. You can place an initial fraud alert on your credit report if you think that you have been the victim of identity theft. This is a good idea if you see any suspicious activity on your credit report. It can also be used if your wallet or purse has been stolen, if you've been a victim of a security breach, or even if you revealed too much personal information online or over the telephone. A fraud alert means that lenders must take extra precautions to verify your identity before granting credit in your name.

Anyone can place a 90-day initial fraud alert in their credit report. This alert can be renewed in 90-day intervals indefinitely. To request the alert, you need to contact only one of the three credit bureaus. The chosen bureau will notify the others. The following links forward to the online forms to complete to request a fraud alert. While you only need to complete one of these, I recommend completing all three if you are a victim of identity theft. In my experience, Experian provides the smoothest process. If you decide to pursue a credit freeze, which will be discussed in a moment, do not complete the fraud alert process.

✓ Experian: **https://www.experian.com/consumer/cac/FCRegistration.do?alertType= INITIAL_ALERT**

✓ Equifax: **https://www.alerts.equifax.com/AutoFraud_Online/jsp/fraudAlert.jsp**

✓ TransUnion: **https://fraud.transunion.com/fa/fraudAlert/landingPage.jsp**

The alert should be activated within 24 hours. You should receive a confirmation in the mail within a few days. If you do not receive this confirmation within one week, place another alert. When activated, your name will be removed from all pre-approved credit and insurance offers for two years. Instructions for removing the fraud alert will be included with the documentation sent to you via postal mail.

You can also obtain an extended fraud alert which stays on your credit report for seven years. To qualify, you must provide a police report or other official record showing that you've been the victim of identity theft. You will receive two free credit reports from each of the credit bureaus every 12 months in addition to the free copies anyone can obtain yearly.

Fraud alerts are not fool proof. A lender can see the fraud alert when a query into your credit is conducted for the purpose of opening a new line of credit. When the lender observes this alert, the lender should contact you by phone to verify that you really want to open a new account. If you are not reachable by phone, the credit account should not be activated. However, a lender is not required by law to contact you even if you have fraud alert in place. Many criminals that will open new fraudulent accounts will seek friends and family that are associated with lending companies to process the request. When this happens, the fraud alert does nothing. Most criminals will not attempt to open an account with a reputable institution that would acknowledge the fraud alert and take extra precautions. If you would like to have real credit protection, you should consider a credit freeze.

Credit Freeze

During my training sessions, people often ask about paid services such as Lifelock and Identity Guard. They want to know how effective they are at protecting a person's identity. These services can be very effective, but you pay quite a premium for that protection. A more effective solution is a credit freeze. This service is easy, usually free, and reversible.

A credit freeze, also known as a credit report freeze, a credit report lock down, a credit lock down, a credit lock or a security freeze, allows an individual to control how a U.S. consumer reporting agency is able to sell his or her data. This applies to the three big credit bureaus (Equifax, Experian, and TransUnion). The credit freeze locks the data at the consumer reporting agency until an individual gives permission for the release of the data.

Basically, if your information stored by the three credit reporting bureaus is not available, no institution will allow the creation of a new account with your identity. This means no credit cards, bank accounts, or loans will be approved. If someone decides to use your identity, but cannot open any new services, they will find someone else to exploit. I can think of no better motivation to freeze your credit than knowing that no one, even yourself, can open new lines of credit in your name. This does NOT affect your current accounts or credit score.

A credit freeze also provides a great layer of privacy protection. If companies cannot gain access to your credit report, they cannot identify you as a pre-approved credit recipient. This will eliminate many offers mailed to your home. This will also remove you from various databases identifying you as a good credit card candidate. Credit freezes are extremely easy today thanks to State laws that mandate the credit bureaus cooperation. This section will walk you through the process.

The first step will determine whether your credit freeze will cost you any money. The fee for the freeze is $10 for each of the three bureaus. While this is well worth the protection, most states have a law that entitles identity theft victims a waiver of this fee.

Currently, each of the three credit bureaus voluntarily waives this fee for victims of identity theft. A large portion of this book's audience has had some type of fraudulent financial activity. This may be an unlawful charge to a debit or credit card or something more serious such as someone opening an account in your name. If you have had any fraudulent charges or activity, contact your local police to obtain a police report. Request a copy of the completed report including the case number.

Complete three packets that will be sent by certified mail. One will go to each of the three credit bureaus. Each packet will include the following:

✓ A letter requesting the credit freeze. Figure 5.01 displays a sample letter. This letter should include the following information:

Official Request
Full Name
Full Address
Social Security Number / Date of Birth

✓ A copy of your police report if you have one.

✓ A recent pay stub or utility bill.

✓ A photocopy of your driver's license or state identification.

Send this packet to each of the following credit bureaus:

Equifax Security Freeze
PO Box 105788
Atlanta, GA 30348

Experian Security Freeze
PO Box 9554
Allen, TX 75013

TransUnion
Fraud Victim Assistance Department
PO Box 6790
Fullerton, CA 92834

If you do not have a police report and do not want the $10 fee waived, you can complete the entire process online at the EACH following three sites:

- ✓ Equifax: https://www.freeze.equifax.com

- ✓ Experian: experian.com/freeze/center.html

- ✓ TransUnion: freeze.transunion.com

TransUnion
Fraud Victim Assistance Department
P.O. Box 6790
Fullerton, CA 92834

08/01/2011

To whom it may concern,

Please accept this letter as an official request for a Security Freeze on my TransUnion credit file. Per your instructions, I have included a photocopy of my driver's license and a recent pay stub. Below are my details.

John Patrick Doe
1234 Main, Town Name, IL 62xxx
225-xx-xxxx
01/01/1970

I further request waiver of any fees due to my recent status as an identity theft victim in the state of Illinois. I have attached a photocopy of my police report.

Figure 5.01: A sample credit freeze letter.

Within a few weeks, sometimes sooner, you will receive a package from each of the bureaus confirming your credit freeze. This confirmation will include a PIN number that you need to keep. This number will be required if you ever want to temporarily or permanently reverse the credit freeze. After sending my requests via certified mail, and receiving the confirmation of delivery, I received a response from Transunion within three days, Equifax within four days, and Experian within eight days.

If you want to reverse the credit freeze, you can do so online at the previously mentioned websites. A temporary freeze would be done to establish new credit such as a credit card or loan. Be sure to generate this temporary reversal prior to the loan request, otherwise your loan may be denied. A permanent reversal will completely stop the freeze, and your account will be back to normal.

Unless you are constantly opening new lines of credit or using your credit to purchase real estate often, I highly recommend a credit freeze. It is the most effective way of stopping people from using your identity for financial gain. Lately, people are reporting that their under-age children are becoming Identity theft victims. A freeze could be applied to them as well. Generating a credit freeze on your child now will protect them until you request removal. This could protect your children from the temptation in high school and college to open new lines of credit.

After your credit freeze is in place on all three credit bureaus, you may want to test the system. In May of 2013, I decided that I was overdue for a test of my own credit freeze. The following are details of what I had to go through while attempting to obtain a new credit card with an active credit freeze in place.

May 27, 2013: I navigated to a website that was offering a great rewards point bonus for new members of a specific travel credit card. It was a very legitimate company that I have held credit with in the past. Even though I had a credit freeze in place, I thought that this company may use our previous relationship as a way around the freeze. This seemed like the best company to test my freeze with. I completed the online application and was told that I would receive an answer via postal mail soon.

May 29, 2013: I received a letter from the credit card company stating that they could not offer me a card. They advised that I had a credit freeze in place and that I would need to remove the freeze before my application could be processed. They identified TransUnion as the credit bureau that they ran my credit through. The freeze worked. This would stop the majority of criminals from accessing your credit. In order to continue the test, I contacted TransUnion and conducted a temporary credit freeze removal over the telephone. It was an automated system and I only had to provide the PIN number provided earlier.

May 30, 2013: I contacted the credit card company via telephone and advised them that the credit freeze had been removed and that I would like to submit my application again. I was placed on hold for a few minutes. The representative stated that she could still not offer me the card. While the freeze had been removed, there was still an extended alert on my credit file and there was not a telephone number for me attached to the account for verification. Basically, TransUnion automatically added this extended alert to provide another layer of protection when a freeze was ordered due to fraud. The representative advised that I should contact Transunion. I contacted them and was told that I should add a valid telephone number to my credit profile. Before I was allowed to do this, I had to answer four security questions about historical credit accounts, addresses, vehicles, and employers. After successfully answering these questions, I was able to add my cellular number to my account. I was told the changes should take place within 24 hours.

May 31, 2013: I contacted the credit card company and advised of my actions taken. She advised that she would not be able to pull another copy of my credit for 14 days. This was policy and there was no way to work around this due to the fraud protection rules in place.

June 15, 2013: I contacted the credit card company again and requested a new pull of my credit report. The credit freeze was still temporarily disabled until the end of the month. The new credit request was successful, and the representative could see the extended alert and a telephone number for contact. She placed me on hold while she dialled the telephone number on file. My cellular phone rang and she verified with me that I approved of the new credit request. I approved and switched back to the other line with her.

June 19, 2013: My new credit card arrived.

This was an interesting experience. I had never tested the system with the intent of actually receiving the card. I had occasionally completed credit card and loan offers in the past for the purpose of testing the freeze, but I was always denied later in writing. This enforces the need to have a current telephone number on file for all three credit bureaus. This entire process took just over two weeks. Any criminal trying to open an account in my name would have moved on to someone else. This same chain of events would have happened if I were trying to buy a vehicle, obtain a personal loan, or purchase real estate. Even routine tasks such as turning on electricity to a home or ordering satellite television service require access to your credit report. A credit freeze will stop practically any new account openings in your name. While I became frustrated at the delay in obtaining this card, I was impressed at the diligence of the credit card company to make sure that I really was the right person. My credit is now frozen again and I am protected at the highest level.

Credit Options

There are some techniques regarding credit cards and lines of credit that you can apply to further protect your privacy and security. Credit companies do not promote these methods because the actions make it difficult for them to make more money from you. You may get resistance as you apply these techniques, but do not give up. You have every right to control your information.

Unused Accounts

When you obtain your free credit report as outlined earlier in this chapter, you should pay special attention to each line of credit. If you observe an old account that you have not used in years, consider closing the account. Usually, these dormant accounts do not cost you any money, but they do not help you either. This open account contains your personal information that can be sold and traded to other organizations.

Closing unused accounts will generally not affect your credit score. The only time this would apply is with your oldest credit account. One way that your credit score is determined is by the amount of time that you have had a line of credit in good standing. If you have had an unused credit card for ten years, that would help your credit score. If you close this account, and your next oldest account is two years, this may hurt your credit score. If you have any open account that is older than the accounts you are closing, your score should not be negatively affected.

Closing these unused accounts will also add security to your credit. Any accounts that you have open make you vulnerable to identity theft. The fewer accounts you possess, the fewer accounts can be compromised. Criminals often target dormant accounts that may not be watched as thoroughly as current accounts. Having multiple unused accounts can make it difficult to monitor for unauthorized transactions.

Account Information

Credit companies share your home address to other companies. I highly recommend changing your address with your credit companies to your post office box or commercial mail receiving agency (CMRA). These mail drops can include commercial chains such as The UPS Store or locally owned mailing shops. This can be done by calling the number on the back of the card, but I suggest completing the process online. Calling the company and giving them the information may not help. The operator may simply add a new address to the account and not actually change the address of the account. If you have a login to access your account online, there should be an option to update your account. You then want to change your mailing address. If you do not have online access to the account, you can request access through your credit company's website.

Secondary Credit Card

Credit card companies will issue additional cards at your request. These cards possess the same account number as the primary card and all charges will be applied to the primary account holder. These cards are often requested by parents to give to their children for emergencies. Any time the secondary card is used, it is processed as if the original card had made the purchase. Since the secondary card is part of an account that has already been verified, there is no verification process to obtain the additional cards.

To request an additional card, you should contact the credit card company by calling the telephone number on the back of the card. Tell them that you want a duplicate card in the name of a family member. You can request an additional card in any name that you want. You will be warned by the credit company that you are responsible for any charges, and the new card will be sent out immediately to the address on file for the account. If you do not want this new name associated with your home address, be sure to update your address on file with the credit company as explained previously. I recommend confirming that the new address is active before ordering additional cards.

Many readers of the first edition of this book reported difficulty in obtaining a secondary card from traditional banks, such as Bank of America or U.S. Bank. I have found this technique to work best with traditional credit card companies. I have had great success, even recently, with several Chase cards. This technique will usually not work with debit cards.

There are a few ways that you can take advantage of this additional card. I have a credit card in an alternate name that I created for this single purpose. Notice that I do not refer to it as an alias. The term alias is used by criminals and those that deceive for fraud or financial gain. You will do neither, and the term alias will not appear again in this book. I keep the card with me next to my card with the same account in my real name. I now have a choice of which name to use when I make a purchase. I try to pay with cash whenever possible, but many scenarios exist where cash is not accepted. The following are examples of how this technique can keep your personal information private.

Hotels

Obtaining a hotel reservation is very difficult without a credit card. Some will reserve the room without a guarantee that it will be available. Some will refuse the reservation without a valid card number. Lately, many hotels apply the entire charge for the visit at the moment of the reservation. When you arrive, you must provide the card at the front desk to be scanned. This collects the data about the cardholder and attaches it to the sale. There are two main reasons for applying this technique while at hotels.

When you stay at a hotel, there is a lot of information that the business can analyze about you and your stay. The amount you paid, the length of your stay, any amenities you purchased, and the distance you travelled from home will be stored in your profile. This will all be used to target you for future visits. Worse, it will be shared with other hotels in the chain that can benefit from the data.

A more serious concern is for a person's safety. If you are the victim of a stalker or targeted by someone crazy in your life, it is not difficult for them to find out the hotel where you are staying. The easiest way would be to contact every hotel in the area where you will be traveling. The following conversation with a hotel operator will usually divulge your chosen hotel:

"Hello, I made a reservation there a while back and I need to add an additional day to my stay. I may have put the reservation under my wife's name, Laura Smith. If not, it could be under my name, Michael Smith. I'm afraid I do not have the reservation number; can you find the reservation without it? It is for next week."

The operator will either be unable to locate your reservation or confirm that an extra day was added. The call that gets the confirmation will identify where you are staying. A more high-tech approach could be conducted through the hotel's wireless internet. Many hotels require you to log into the wireless internet before you use it. This usually requests your last name and room number as verification that you are a valid guest. Some amateur programming can create a script that will attempt to log in with your last name and each room number of the hotel until the attempt is successful. This not only identifies the hotel you are staying at, but exposes the room number you are in. This can be a huge security concern.

You can use your new alternative name to create your hotel reservation. Since you are not committing any type of financial fraud, this is legal. You will be providing your legitimate credit card number and will pay the charges through your credit statement. Upon arrival at the hotel, hand this card to the receptionist. You may be asked for identification. In my experience, stating that your wallet was stolen and you only have the credit card because you keep it in the car is sufficient. If this does not work, have your travel partner show identification to meet the requirement. This information will most likely not be added to the reservation. I recommend persistence that you do not have an ID. Very few hotels will turn down a paying customer with a credit card in hand. I find that being polite and understanding always works better than acting agitated.

In 2014, I encountered a hotel chain that has made it absolute policy that the customer supplies both a valid credit card and photo identification in order to rent the room at check-in. I have found that the following two scenarios bypass this requirement almost every time.

First, create a rewards card with each of the hotel chains that you plan to use. When I check in, I immediately give both my credit card (alternative name) and my rewards card (also in my alternative name). Since I travel often, and I have an elevated status on my rewards card, I have encountered no resistance upon check-in. If I detect a stubborn receptionist that appears determined to follow the corporate rules, I will act like I am in the middle of a very important call on my cell phone. Usually, the receptionist will continue with the process just to get rid of me.

When I arrive at a hotel, I always hold the door open for anyone else entering and allow them to check in first. This is not me being polite, it allows me to determine what resistance I will be up against when it is my turn. Knowing the attitude of the employee may aid you in creating the most appropriate pitch.

If the previous trick does not work, I have found that having an identification card in your alternative name to be very helpful. I would never condone obtaining a real or fraudulent government identification card in your alias name. Not only is that illegal, but completely unnecessary. Instead, I create my own "club", which I am the founder (as my alternative name of course).

For example, you may be very interested in rock climbing. You could start your own organization titled "The Greater Houston Rock Climbing Gym". Maybe you have some steps on your back porch that you use to "climb". Your definition of climbing might be different than others. Now, you may choose to create an identification card for the members of your backyard gym. This could be completed in Microsoft Word and may include a photo of you. Your local print shop will happily print this on a nice paper stock and laminate it for you. The following should work well at the check-in of your hotel.

"I'm sorry, I left my license at the gym, can I show you my gym membership card until I go back to get it?"

Events

Many events, concerts, and various forms of entertainment now require a credit card for attendance. Most events allow the purchase of tickets through a single vendor. The tickets must be purchased either online or via telephone and mailed or picked up at the ticket area of the event. When you purchase tickets, you are usually required to give all of your personal information including full name, home address, home telephone number, and date of birth. With your secondary credit card, you should only provide the name on the card, and your post office box if the tickets will be mailed. There is no verification on any additional information. Ultimately, the company just wants to be paid for the tickets. Any other information they collect gets passed on to databases for the marketing division.

Utilities

In 2011, I assisted a colleague that was receiving very serious death threats to him and his family. It was serious enough that he moved his family to a new home that he purchased in a business name. He was having issues obtaining services to the residence without providing his complete personal information including a social security number for a credit check. He had reached a dead end with the cable company responsible for internet access in the area. They refused to provide internet service to a business name in a residential area. With his permission, I contacted the cable company on his behalf and reached a fairly polite customer service representative. My friend had already obtained a secondary credit card in another name on his primary account.

I advised the representative that I wished to initiate new service at my residence. I provided the address and the name on his new card. When she asked for a social security number, I informed her that I had been advised to never give that out over the telephone and requested an alternative way to verify my identity. As expected, she stated that I could place the monthly charges onto a credit card and warned me that the charges for the entire month would be applied immediately. I agreed to that and provided the card number. This eliminated the need for them to conduct a credit check. They now had a credit card number on file for automatic billing for the upcoming month. If the charges failed to go through, they would be able to disconnect service.

This method will not always work. I have been declined by one representative only to be approved by another with an immediate second call. Persistence often pays off. Power providers and water companies are less likely to accept automatic credit card payments. Fortunately, they are usually willing to bill the customer in a business name. This will be further explained in the next chapter.

Legalities

You may be reading this and thinking that there is no way that this could be legal. It is absolutely legal as long as you are not using this method to commit fraud. The card is attached to your account, and you are paying the bill. It is not identity theft because you are not claiming to be a specific person. If you were using someone else's social security number and opening credit lines with their information, then this would be illegal. You must only apply this to your own account that you have authority over. Additionally, you must always follow these rules:

✓ Never provide your alternative name to any law enforcement or government official.

✓ Never open new credit lines with your alternative name.

✓ Never generate any income with your alternative name.

✓ Never associate any social security number with your alternative name.

✓ Never receive any government or community benefits in your alternative name.

✓ Only use this name to protect your privacy in scenarios that a credit card is needed.

Prepaid Credit Cards

If you are not ready to jump into using an alternative name, a prepaid credit card may be better for you. A prepaid credit card is not a true credit card. No credit is offered by the card issuer. Instead, the customer purchases the card by paying the entire balance of the card upfront. A prepaid card with a balance of $500 would cost the customer $500 plus a small fee. This card can now be used anywhere that traditional credit cards are accepted. When the balance of the card is spent, the card is no longer accepted. These cards can be purchased at many retail stores. For the best value, I recommend the American Express prepaid cards. They occasionally offer to waive the fee associated with the card and I stock up.

A benefit of this card is that there is no name associated with it. You can provide any name you want when making a purchase. When the company you are dealing with applies the name to the card for the purpose of charging the account, the prepaid card company disregards any name submitted. The card company knows that this is a prepaid card and allows any name to be used. If you purchased your prepaid card with cash at a store, the card company does not know your identity. If you need a card with an alternate or real name printed on it, Green Dot offers a solution.

Green Dot (greendot.com)

If you do not mind paying convenience fees, you can have a pre-paid credit card with any name printed on the card. If you only plan on using the card for one month, you can obtain one for free. At the time of this writing, the drug store Walgreens provides Green Dot pre-paid cards without charging a load fee. You can purchase the blank card in the store for $5.00, and add $10 to $500 to the card balance with cash. There is a small fee for the original purchase, but no fee for re-loading money to the balance. You can complete a form included with the card to request a duplicate card printed in any name you want. No credit check is conducted, and the information will not be verified. You can have your new card mailed to your PO box. You should supply your anonymous email address and telephone number when required. If you do not spend the entire balance of the card within 30 days, Green Dot will withdraw $5.95 each month as a monthly fee. This will be waived if your load $1000 per month to the card. This can be a free solution to situations that require a single use credit card in an alternate name.

I often use these cards when traveling. If one gets lost or stolen, I do not need to worry about access to my true credit accounts. If the card information gets "skimmed" by a dishonest employee of a business I visit, the damage will be minimal. Any purchases I make will be completely anonymous and I will not be subject to future marketing attempts.

Virtual Credit Cards

When you make purchases online, you are at risk of your credit card getting compromised during a database breach. These thefts are so common that they rarely make the news. A criminal can obtain thousands of card numbers at one time by breaking into a business's servers. If your number is in the database, you will probably be a victim within hours. To avoid this, you can use virtual credit cards.

A virtual credit card, sometimes referred to as a temporary credit card or throw away credit card, is a credit card number that is generated by your credit card issuer on your behalf for temporary use. You don't actually get a physical credit card with this number. You simply use the number for an online transaction and then it expires.

Any time that I need to order something on the internet from a questionable source, I use this option. Some people have been known to provide these numbers for free trials that require a credit card. If the company tries to apply an unauthorized charge, it will be declined. Citi and Bank of America offer this free virtual number service. You should contact you credit card company to find out the options available to you.

Utilities and Residential Services

As a reminder, you can have all of your bills delivered to your post office box. I recommend contacting each credit and utility company that you have service with and request a mailing address change. The service will still be provided to your home, but the database of customers will list your address as your post office box. If this database is sold, traded, or compromised, the information will not identify your home address and landline telephone number. This can help keep you off marketing lists. It will also hide your residence from public view of data mining company reports.

Confidential Online Information

If you find a page in a Google search result that displays personal information about you, such as your social security or credit card number, you can request immediate removal. Google will review the request and remove the information from their search results. This will not remove the information from the website that is displaying it, but it will take the link off of Google to make it more difficult to find. Even if Google removes the link from their search results, you should contact the offending website directly and request removal of your information. The following are the three scenarios that will force Google to remove a link to personal information:

✓   Your social security number is visible on a website.

✓   Your bank account or credit card number is visible on a website.

✓   An image of your handwritten signature is visible on a website.

Each of these situations can be reported through the following three specific websites:

Social Security Number: **support.google.com/websearch/contact/government_number**

Bank or credit account: **support.google.com/websearch/contact/bank_number**

Signature: **support.google.com/websearch/contact/image_of_handwritten_signature**

Each page will instruct you to complete an online form which requires your name, anonymous email address, the URL of the website that is exposing the information, the URL of a Google results page that displays the information, and the information being exposed. Fortunately, Google offers detailed help on these pages explaining how to obtain the required information. Figure 5.02 displays a portion of a removal page. The underlined links offer instructions for each task.

Bing does not offer an automated removal request. Instead, you must complete an email support request that includes your name, email address, and URL of the exposed information. You must also choose "Content Removal Request" as the reason for contact. This form can be found by navigating to the following website.

support.discoverbing.com/eform.aspx?productKey=bingcontentremoval

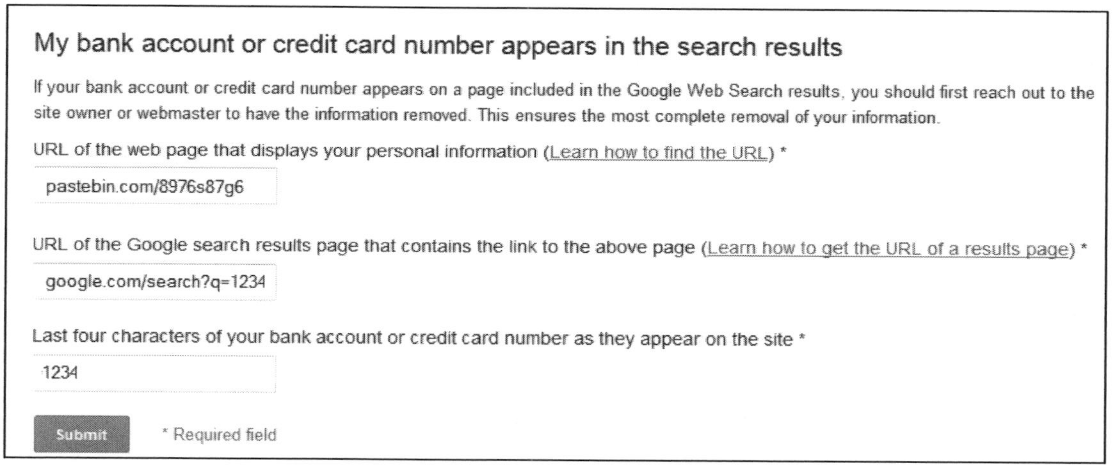
My bank account or credit card number appears in the search results

If your bank account or credit card number appears on a page included in the Google Web Search results, you should first reach out to the site owner or webmaster to have the information removed. This ensures the most complete removal of your information.

URL of the web page that displays your personal information (Learn how to find the URL) *

pastebin.com/8976s87g6

URL of the Google search results page that contains the link to the above page (Learn how to get the URL of a results page) *

google.com/search?q=1234

Last four characters of your bank account or credit card number as they appear on the site *

1234

Submit * Required field

Figure 5.02: A Google removal form for sensitive information.

Locating Vulnerabilities

If you want to know whether your signature, social security number, credit card number, or bank account information is visible on a public website, you will need to conduct specific searches. The easiest way is to occasionally conduct a search of your account numbers and view any results. Keep in mind that your searches will only be successful if the exposed data is in the same format of your search. You should conduct several searches of this type of data including spaces, without spaces, and only the last four or eight numbers alone. This also applies to searches for account numbers and social security numbers. If you do not want to continually conduct the same searches, you could set up a Google Alert as instructed in Chapter Sixteen.

Chapter Six

Purchases

The previous chapter explained the importance of a credit card in an alternate name. I rely on this technique during all of my travels. This is no longer reserved only for traveling. On a daily basis, we all make purchases that require credit cards and personal information. The days of living on cash only are gone. While it is still possible, and many people do it, it has become increasingly difficult. This chapter will explain various ways to protect your privacy while maintaining the convenience of making non-cash purchases online and in person.

Online Purchases

Do you remember a day when you would go to the grocery store for all of your food, the hardware store for replacement parts, and the department store for household goods? For many people, this has all been replaced by online retailers such as Amazon and Ebay. Even specialty crafts and artwork is now sought through websites such as Etsy. You can avoid these types of companies and still get what you need with cash at physical stores. However, you will miss out on the convenience and affordability of online shopping. This section will guide you on maintaining your privacy while using these services.

Amazon

I begin with Amazon because it is one of the largest online retailers. I place orders through Amazon weekly and never jeopardize my privacy during the process. If you are already using Amazon and have an account created, I recommend that you stop using that account and create a new one. The following steps will mask your real identity from your purchases. Create a new account with the following information.

- ✓ **Name**: Use the name on your alternate credit card.

✓ **Email Address**: You must provide an email address for your new Amazon account. I do not recommend a forwarding email service such as NotSharingMy.Info as discussed earlier. If this service was not available and you needed to reset your Amazon account, you would have no way of doing so. You could easily become locked out of your Amazon account. I recommend a specific Gmail or similar account only for Amazon purchases. Yours may be something similar to "amazon.email.123@gmail.com". Many privacy advocates will cringe when I say that because of Google's policy on scanning your email. However, I only use this account for this purpose, it is never associated with my real name, and it will not be connected with any of my real email accounts.

✓ **Credit Card**: Use your alternate credit card number, expiration, and security code. This number will be the same number on your real credit card, so be sure that this number is not in use on any existing profiles.

✓ **Address**: Provide the P.O. Box that you used for your credit card billing address. You can alter this information after the account has been verified. In the settings of the account, you can add a new address for shipments. I have used my real home address in the past for my deliveries. Because the name on the shipment is not my real name, I do not see this as a privacy concern. I believe it helps establish that someone else lives at your residence, and provides great disinformation.

Ebay

Ebay and Paypal, which are owned by the same company, can be trickier. Ebay will apply some minor validation to the data that you enter and will require a valid form of payment to simply create the account, such as your alternative name credit card. Paypal will also require this valid form of payment and will request a social security number that will only be used for income reporting.

Everything Else

For the most part, any online retailers simply want to be paid. If the credit card that you use is valid and matches the shipping name and address of the purchase, the order should go through. There is not much other validation when you complete the sale. There is no reason that you should not be able to use your alternate name credit card for all of your purchases. Eventually, your UPS, FedEx, or USPS delivery person will start to believe that you are named the alternate name on your card. Some have called me this name during deliveries.

Store Purchases

In 2012, I purchased a new refrigerator. The large home improvement store that had the best price won my business. They also offered free delivery to my home. I sat down to complete the purchase with the salesperson when the questions began. In order to sell and deliver a refrigerator, I had to provide my name, home address, telephone number, cellular telephone number, work telephone number, credit card information, and a secondary contact person. Obviously, my address was necessary, but I am hesitant to provide the rest. Later in the book, you will read about the ways that data marketing companies learn information about you and resell the data. This is one of the primary ways that you are targeted for future purchases. As soon as you provide this information, it is added to an internal database and resold to other companies. The following is how I handled the situation.

- ✓ **Name**: I advised that this purchase was for my father, so I would like the delivery in his name. I then provided a very specific name such as John Coolman. Why Coolman? The last name Coolman will remind me of my "cool" refrigerator. I choose a name like that because I want to monitor where the data provided to the salesperson is sent. In a few weeks, when I receive a mailing from an advertiser to John Coolman, I will know where that company received the information.

- ✓ **Address**: I provided my home address for the delivery. Because this was not associated with my real name, and I needed to tell them where to go, this was acceptable.

- ✓ **Telephone Numbers**: I advised that there is no telephone at the house but I will be available on my cellular number at any time. I then provided my Google Voice account.

- ✓ **Payment**: I used my alternate name credit card.

- ✓ **Secondary contact and work number**: I assured the salesperson that I would be available and a secondary contact or work number was not necessary.

This may all seem very basic and like common sense, but think about what took place. I kept the purchase anonymous with my alternative name credit card. I added another layer of privacy by placing the delivery in a generic name. That generic name will never be used by me again and will help me identify where that store shares my information. I will not personally be targeted with offers of extended warranty protection. My real name will not be added to the database of large product purchases that will receive future promotional offers. Finally, I have a receipt that will suffice for any issues with the product.

Any time that I make a purchase that requires delivery; I never use my real name. Doing so would add my name and address to various online websites from which I have previously removed them. The additional benefit is that this disinformation that I provided will now be associated with my home address. It will confuse data marketing companies about the actual tenants. The next chapter will expand on this concept.

Remember, we are keeping everything legal because we are not causing any financial fraud. All of our purchases are billed to a credit card number that is assigned to us. We will pay the bills as agreed with our credit card company. These transactions will not financially affect anyone else.

Purchasing a Home

If you are planning on purchasing a home, this is a huge opportunity to make it practically impossible to be located from an internet search. Chapter Twelve explains how your publicly visible property tax record will inform dozens of data mining websites of your home address. This data will be acquired by many websites and you would need to remove the data from each site. Instead, consider starting life in your new home without attaching your name to the residence.

This method is only for those that are truly committed to being invisible from the public. The general idea of this process is credited to J.J. Luna, the author of the book *How to be Invisible*. The basic premise of this specific method is the following:

- ✓ Purchase an official LLC from a registered agent in New Mexico. These are never publicly associated with your real name, but you own the business. These are very affordable.

- ✓ Purchase your new home using the LLC as the owner. The LLC can also purchase vehicles and other property.

- ✓ Never associate your name with the house you live in. Personal mail should be delivered to a PO Box. Utilities should be in the name of the LLC.

If you are at all intrigued by these possibilities, purchase Luna's book immediately. The methods are completely legal. Mr. Luna provides recommended services in New Mexico that will make the process easy. If you are in any way targeted by someone, such as police officers or victims of harassment, this will guarantee that you will have a home private from the internet. For more information, visit jjluna.com and select the New Mexico LLCs tab.

Over the past few years, I have spoken with several readers that were not ready to make the jump into invisible LLC's. I completely understand and agree that the idea of placing your largest asset into the name of an LLC that is not registered to you can be overwhelming. Additionally, this can be difficult when there is a lien on the home. The following option does not provide the same level of privacy as an invisible LLC. However, it will help shield your real name from public records.

Many people choose to make the owner of their home a revocable living trust. This is usually not associated with privacy protection. A living trust is a legal entity that many people use for the distribution of wealth when they die. A will can be beneficial, but it is subject to probate. This means that your wishes detailed in your will are not executed until approved by the probate court. This can take years. A living trust avoids the probate process altogether.

To create a revocable living trust, you (the grantor) transfers ownership of some or all of your property to the trust. Because you make yourself the "trustee," you don't give up any control over the property you put in the trust. If you and your spouse create a trust together, you will be co-trustees.

In the trust document, you name the people or institutions you want to inherit trust property after your death. You can change those choices at any time if you wish. You can also revoke the trust completely. When you die, the person you named in the trust document to take over, called the successor trustee, transfers ownership of trust property to the people you want to get it. In most cases, the successor trustee can handle the whole thing in a few weeks with some simple paperwork.

Essentially, you can create your own revocable living trust by completing a form. There are numerous versions online or you could create one using a word processor. This printed trust identifies the name of the trust and the assets that are owned by the trust. This document should be notarized and witnessed by at least two trusted subjects.

Trusts are extremely common with home owners. Often, a retired person will transfer any property, including a home, into a trust as part of estate planning. If you are buying a new home, you should consider taking this step now instead of later. This will keep your name out of many public databases.

Before you purchase the home, you should have your revocable trust complete and active. You do not need to generate an EIN number with the IRS. You will need to give your trust a name. Most people choose something obvious such as "The Michael Bazzell Living Trust" or "The Bazzell Family Living Trust". Using personally identifiable information is not mandatory or recommended. Instead, consider something generic such as "The Private Life Living Trust" or "The Partners Living Trust". These names do not associate you with the trust.

Once you have created the trust, you need to add your assets. You cannot add cash, but you can add property, real estate, collectibles, and financial accounts. Many people that I consult have all of their wealth in the name of their living trust. Financial accounts will still be associated with your real name and social security number. This is important to prove ownership.

When you close on your new home, consider allowing your real estate agent to sign the paperwork on your behalf. Make sure he or she understands your desire to place the title for the home in the name of your living trust, and not in your name. Financial institutions are familiar with this process and should allow this during your loan process. Obviously, any loan will still be in your name.

If you already own your home, and moving is out of the question, you can transfer your home into the trust. This will require filing a quitclaim deed at your county assessor's office. This is a very standard practice that should not raise any suspicion. Your home address will still be associated with your real name on several websites, but new information that is collected will replace your name with the name of your trust. This will eliminate a lot of new entries associating you to your home address.

I want to stress the importance of consulting with a lawyer when creating your living trust. I also recommend reading any books by Nolo on the living trust creation process. The minor expense that you spend to make all of the documentation correct will pay off tenfold when you die and your heirs are left with your assets. Additionally, having the correct and accurate paperwork will aid in a smooth process when placing a home in the name of the trust.

Renting a Home

Renting can have advantages and disadvantages in regard to protecting your privacy. Some places include all utilities which is a huge privacy layer. If the utilities are already in the landlord's name, you never need to provide your information to the utility companies. Unfortunately, most rental agreements will require your full details for a background check. You may also be asked to obtain an occupancy permit. The following suggestions will get you through these roadblocks.

Avoid large complexes. Apartments and condominiums that are maintained by larger businesses have strict rules on processing applicants. You will need to pay a fee to have them conduct a complete history, criminal, and financial background check on your real information. If you pass, you will then be required to use your details for all utilities and permits. Look for homes and apartments owned by individuals. They will be more willing to accommodate a good renter.

I recommend applying Luna's method of obtaining an invisible LLC for renting. Your LLC can rent the place and pay the bills. Many renters welcome this arrangement. Receiving money every month from a business is more reliable than from an individual. People that I have consulted in similar situations have had the best results with the following techniques.

Find an apartment or home that is a prospect for rental. Notify the owner right away that the company you work for is relocating you and will be paying the rent. Provide the name of the LLC and your post office box address. Offer to pay a month in advance and have a check from the

LLC ready for the deposit. Be polite and look professional. Refer to Luna's book for information about LLC bank accounts.

Another option is to notify the owner that you have been the victim of stalking or harassment and you are looking for a new safe place to stay. Explain your concern about making your information public. This tends to work best for females or families with children. Overall, be courteous and respectful. Offer to pay an additional month of rent in advance in order to demonstrate your ability to make the payments.

An entire book could be written of how to move into a home anonymously. The full techniques exceed the scope of this book.

Vehicle Purchases

The preferred way to stay anonymous throughout a vehicle purchase is to pay cash to an individual. This is not always ideal depending on the type of vehicle that you want. I believe that vehicles should be the property of, and registered to, an invisible New Mexico LLC. At the very least, they should be attached to a revocable living trust. They should never be registered to your real name. This is based on years of monitoring criminal behavior and erroneous lawsuits. Consider the following true scenario.

Several years ago, I was interviewing a criminal that had brutally attacked the driver of a vehicle that unintentionally cut him off in traffic. The victim had a faster car than the attacker and sped away before anything bad could happen. Though the victim had gotten away and felt safe in his own home, the attacker showed up at his door. A fight ensued and the victim was left permanently disfigured. During the interview, I learned that the attacker had received the home address of the victim through his license plate registration. These queries are only available to law enforcement and a handful of companies, so I was intrigued by how he was able to do this. He gave the following account.

After the road rage incident, the attacker was at home and furious about the event. He wanted revenge. He had written down the license plate of the victim and wanted to know where he lived. He turned on his police scanner and monitored the channel of his local police. He then called that police department and reported a drunk driver all over the road at a nearby location. He provided the actual license registration of the victim. He then listened to the police scanner as the dispatcher advised patrol units of the reported reckless driver. At the end of the dispatch, the patrol units were told the name and address of the victim according to the registration. The attacker had now heard what he needed to confront and beat the victim.

Having your vehicle registered to either an LLC or trust would save you from this type of attack. The offender would only know the name of your LLC or trust and a PO Box that receives mail. However, a trust will provide you no protection from erroneous lawsuits. Having your vehicle owned and registered to an invisible LLC will provide you an additional layer of protection. Nothing will make you 100% lawsuit-proof, but every layer can help. Consider the following.

Within 30 days of purchasing a new vehicle, data brokers know every detail about you, the vehicle, and how it was financed. If you have any doubt about this, request your personal report from LexisNexis and others as instructed in the next chapters. You should see the details of every vehicle at your residence and information about the licensed drivers. Figure 6.01 displays a portion of one of these personal reports. The entry identifies the full name and home address of the owner. The vehicle information includes the year, make, model, VIN, weight, wheel base, base price, and size of the vehicle. Figure 6.02 displays all of this and adds the vehicle's registration, title number, and lien information (redacted). If you are still not convinced that this is an invasion of your privacy, consider the following:

Accident attorneys, sometimes referred to as "ambulance chasers", make a lucrative living from suing people involved in traffic crashes. Some of their clients come to them seeking damages, but an overwhelming number of lawsuits are generated by the attorney. Lawyers can go to a police department and request a copy of every traffic crash report for an entire month. These redacted reports include the names of the vehicle owners and the insurance companies providing insurance on the vehicles. The reports are modified to mask the name and home address of the subjects involved. This request must be allowed because the attorney filed a Freedom of Information request. The police department must comply. I have personally witnessed teams of lawyers sit in the police lobby and look through the reports for traffic crashes involving expensive vehicles owned by the driver at fault. They then conduct a quick internet search on the vehicle owners and respond to the victim's home to encourage a lawsuit.

If you are involved in a traffic crash, you cannot keep the vehicle owner's name from appearing on a public report. You also cannot hide the details about your vehicle. You can keep your name from the public version by purchasing the vehicle with your new LLC. When you buy a new or used vehicle, notify the sales person that you will be purchasing the vehicle on behalf of a business and that the registration and title should identify the business as the owner. This technique is explained in J.J. Luna's book, *How To Be Invisible*. With this method in place, the nosy lawyer will only know that your LLC owns the vehicle, and will not have a name to associate with the vehicle. If a lawsuit is filed, the attorney can make a new request for the complete report, which will identify you. However, the mass search will mask your details. Please note that this does not hide your details from the other party involved if they request a report. It also does not hide your details from the police department investigating the incident.

2004 CHEVROLET VENTURE

Registered Owner:	▮▮▮▮ (Business)	Secondary Owner:	
VIN:	1GBDX23▮▮▮	Valid VIN:	Y
Make/Model/Series:	CHEVROLET VENTURE	Model Year:	2004
Full Body Style:	INCOMPLETE CHASSIS	Country of Origin:	UNITED STATES
Body Type:	Incomplete Chassis	Base Price:	$23,225
Fuel Type:	Gas	Drivetrain:	Front Wheel Drive
Shipping Weight:	3838	Cubic Inch Displacement:	207
Wheel Base:	120.0"	Tire Size:	

Figure 6.01: A portion of a data broker's personal report identifying vehicle information.

```
2004 CHEV PARTIALLY BUILT FROM FACTORY (Possible Current Vehicle) (Missouri)

    2004 CHEV - Series: BASE MODEL - Model: PARTIALLY BUILT FROM
    FACTORY
    VIN: 1GBDX23         [ Copy ]
    Body Style: VAN - Vehicle Type: Unknown
    Most Current Tag #: MO  SF       Valid from: (09/15/2010 to 09/30/2012)
     Map All Addresses

Most Current Owner/Registrant/Lien Information - 09/15/2010 to 09/30/2012

Title Holders                                          Registrant
          [ View Person Record ]                                 [ View Person Record ]
                 SAINT LOUIS, MO 63114-2810 (SAINT    Registered: 09/15/2010 to 09/30/2012
LOUIS COUNTY)                                          Addresses Registered to While owned by
Title Number: TTE7                                            SAINT LOUIS, MO 63114-2810 (SAINT LOUIS
State Titled In: MO                                    COUNTY) (09/15/2010)
Original Title Date: 09/17/2010
Title Transfer Date: 09/17/2010                        Vehicle Tag History
                                                       License Plate: MO SF    Valid from: (09/15/2010 to 09/30/2012)
Lien Holders
```

Figure 6.02: A portion of a data broker's personal report identifying vehicle information.

Senseless acts like these are reasons why I recommend purchasing and registering any vehicle as an entity and not an individual. The idea of an invisible LLC discussed earlier may not have been ideal for you when buying a home. However, you may be more comfortable with this tactic during a vehicle purchase. For many people, registering their vehicle to an LLC or trust is the gateway toward complete anonymity with all future purchases. There are several possibilities for this, and I will outline various scenarios here to give you an idea of the best formula for your needs. Each method identifies the type of purchase, payment used, and method of identity protection.

✓ Individual-Cash (LLC): If you possess an invisible LLC from New Mexico, this is the ideal way to go. Give the individual cash and obtain a valid title. Take the title and your LLC paperwork to a local vehicle title shop and have them complete the proper process for registering the vehicle. This type of business will be much more accommodating than the Department of Motor Vehicles (DMV).

✓ Individual-Cash (Trust): After you have created your revocable living trust, give the individual cash and obtain a valid title. Take the title and your trust paperwork to a local vehicle title shop and have them complete the proper process for registering the vehicle.

✓ Dealer-Cash (LLC): Staying anonymous at a dealership is not difficult, but it will take some diligence. Having the resources to purchase a vehicle without a loan will aid in this process. When you first meet the sales person, advise them right away that you are shopping for your boss and that the company (LLC) will be purchasing the vehicle. The dealership will facilitate the registration process and you should demand that all information is in the name of the LLC. While you cannot use a PO Box on your driver's license, most states allow the use on vehicle registration.

✓ Dealer-Cash (Trust): When you first meet the sales person, advise them right away that you are purchasing the vehicle in the name of your Grandma's trust. They will not know if this is true. The dealership will facilitate the registration process and you should demand that all information is in the name of the trust. Again, provide your valid PO Box and never give them your real address.

✓ Dealer-Loan (LLC): A dealer will not give you a loan in the name of an LLC or trust. This does not mean you cannot register the vehicle in the name of either. Complete the loan paperwork and demand that the vehicle is registered to your LLC. Inform the sales person that you will not complete the sale until you see proof that this is set up accordingly. I advise avoiding the loan process if at all possible.

✓ Dealer-Loan (Trust): Similar to the previous option, complete the loan paperwork and demand that the vehicle is registered to your trust. Inform the sales person that you will not complete the sale until you see proof that this is set up accordingly.

I can speak from experience that providing your real address when you purchase a vehicle is a bad idea. I purchased a new vehicle in 2003 and provided all of my personal information. I did not know better at the time. In 2005, I began receiving numerous advertisements referencing my vehicle and offering me discounted services. In 2008, I began receiving third party warranty options since my standard warranty was about to expire. My name, address, and vehicle information was in the hands of dozens of companies.

When you buy from a dealer, you cannot stop this information from being sold. However, you can control the information that is attached to your profile. When paying cash, always provide the name of an LLC or trust, a PO Box address, and nothing else. Have a check ready for the sale that is attached to an account for the LLC or trust. Be prepared to walk away when a sales person begins pushing you for more information. They will always stop you and do whatever it takes to make the sale.

Incoming Mail

After you complete the steps in this book, pay close attention to the mail that you receive at your home. Each piece should be categorized as either junk or important. If it is junk, refer to Chapter Eleven and eliminate the mailings through Catalog Choice or DMA. If the mailing is something important that you want to continue to receive, contact the sender and change your address to your post office box. If you have an online account for the company, attempt to change this yourself through their website. Any mail that you send out should always have your post office box address instead of your home address.

Package Deliveries

Internet shopping offers cheap prices and global access to products. You have probably ordered a product from an internet company such as Amazon or Netflix. When you supply your home address for these deliveries, the information will be added to marketing databases. These databases will probably only be used for internal marketing from one company, but the data may eventually be sold to other collectors. The best solution is to provide your post office box address for deliveries. Further, be sure to remove your residence address from your profile through the online retailer. If you have a mailbox that is not large enough for the delivery, you will receive a notification of a package available for pickup at the counter.

Another option is to have packages delivered to your workplace. This may not be appropriate for everyone. If you are a victim of domestic violence and you do not want anyone to know where you work, you should not choose this option. If you are a government employee, public official, or have a job with any public presence, there is probably no harm in using a work address. I choose to have everything delivered to my workplace. A package left inside a workspace is more secure than one left outside an empty home. Additionally, there will likely be someone available to sign for a package during business hours.

Food Deliveries

Ordering pizza or Chinese food does not necessarily compromise your privacy. You must disclose your address for the delivery, but you do not need to provide your real name. If you want to keep your home address private and unassociated with your name, always obey the following rules:

- ✓ Never provide your real name or telephone number. Always use an alternate name.

- ✓ Never call from your landline telephone. It will identify your name.

- ✓ Never rely on caller ID to protect your information.

- ✓ Order online through the company's website when available.

- ✓ Always pay with cash.

Chapter Seven

Social Networks

Social networks are mentioned early for a good reason. You now know that you must change your habits of providing personal information to the companies that request it. That will stop new data from entering the databases. With the explosion of social networks, many of these companies are collecting data from public profiles and adding it to a person's record. Before you learn how to remove the unwanted data from the companies that sell it, you must first clean up your social network profiles. Otherwise, the data companies will eventually collect the data from your profile and create a new database on you. The level of difficulty with this removal process will depend on how much information you have made available.

There are hundreds of social networks. The largest networks will be discussed in this chapter. You should visit any social network where you have created a profile. Even if you think that there was no personal information provided, take a look at the public page visible to anyone on the internet. Evaluate the information that could be gathered about you and then log into the social network and see what information was provided when you created the account. Make a note of all of this and consider the next three topics.

Privacy Settings

Most social networks provide an option to protect your personal details from the public. This is usually in the form of privacy settings that you can customize. These settings allow you to specify who can see the content of your profile. This can determine who can see your messages, photos, current location, employer and alumni information, friends and family, and other details. You can specify that either the public can see everything, or that certain details can only be viewed by people that you have classified as "friends". Facebook also provides another option of "Friends of friends". This means that people that you do not know can see your information if they know someone that you have classified as a friend. Modifying these settings to restrict who can see your data is advised. But, it can also create a false sense of security and encourage you to post sensitive content. Here are a few of things to consider about privacy settings.

These settings only prohibit the public from seeing the content. The content is still visible to the company that owns the social network. When you created the account, you agreed to a long list of legal terms called the terms of service. These terms probably discussed how the company that owns the social network can do whatever they want with the data that you provide. While these networks may be careful not to share your private data now, no one knows what will happen in the future.

It is common to read in technology news sources about people that break into other people's accounts to steal information. Celebrities are continually having their accounts compromised by self-proclaimed "hackers" for both fun and profit. If someone wants your data bad enough, and has the money to fund an expedition to retrieve your data, there is a criminal ready to complete the task.

Finally, there are many legal ways to retrieve data that is believed to be private. I have demonstrated during my law enforcement training how videos and photos from "hidden" MySpace profiles can be located through Google and how the Twitter API can reveal personal details that are not visible on a person's profile page including exact location. Many people take a quick glance at their profile and are satisfied that only those with approved access can see their content. They are often wrong.

I believe that any time you post anything to the internet you must assume it is for public view. Even if you have your privacy settings locked as tight as possible, you should accept that there is a possibility that someone else could get your data. If the content you are uploading to your private page would also be acceptable for public view, then you can proceed. However, if the photos of you drunk the night before would embarrass you if anyone but your friends saw it, you should not take the chance. Privacy settings will not always save you.

Content Removal

If you have looked at your profiles and have identified personal data that you no longer want on the internet, you can remove it. There are too many different social networks to provide instruction for the removal of specific information. The process is usually fairly easy. If you have trouble, conduct an internet search for the answers. Ultimately, any information that you provided to your profile can be removed. The exception may be your name on certain sites. If you find something that you cannot remove, choose to update the information and insert blank spaces or disinformation.

Most likely, it will not be your profile that contains information that worries you. It will probably be the profiles of your children and other relatives. Many teenaged children have no concern about privacy and the dangers of online information. Many will post hundreds of photos from their daily habits that will expose every intimate detail of their lives. There is nothing legal that you can do to modify this information on your own. Often, a calm yet stern talk with your children will start the process of cleaning up the profiles.

Delete Accounts

By now, you may be considering completely removing all of your social networks. This process is not as easy as you would think. Social networks want your profiles, and more importantly your eyes on their advertisements. Facebook's home page does not inform you how to delete your account. Actually, no social network does this. It is very important to delete your accounts in a specific manner to ensure that the data is removed. The process to do this on several popular networks will be explained here.

Facebook

Facebook is the most popular social network on the internet. If your content is public, there are several data mining sites collecting everything that you post including comments, photos, and friends. The first layer of privacy that you should implement is appropriate privacy settings. Recently, Facebook made this process much easier than before. After you login to your account, click on the "down arrow" in the upper right corner of the page. Choose the "Settings" option and select "Privacy". In the section "Who can see my stuff?", you can edit your desired settings. Figure 7.01 displays the settings option and Figure 7.02 displays the privacy options.

You will now have four choices of how you want to protect your data. The first choice, "Public", allows anyone to see all of your information. This is not advised. The second option, "Friends", allows only the people that you have identified as your friends to Facebook. This is a much more secure option. The third option of "Only me" allows you to make your posts completely private and only visible by you. The last option allows you to customize different areas of your profile so that different people can see different types of content. I only recommend this for advanced Facebook users. If you are going to use Facebook, select the "Friends" option. More importantly, make sure that the subjects listed on your friends list are people you really know and trust.

Many people have decided to completely delete their Facebook profile. They have discovered that this process is not as easy as it should be. Additionally, a Facebook account cannot be deleted right away. There is a "waiting period", similar to purchasing a gun. This period is fourteen days, but photos may remain on the Facebook servers for months. If you are ready to pull the plug, the following are the proper steps.

✓ Log into your account and delete all of the content that you can. This includes all photos, messages, and interests. If you find something that cannot be deleted, replace the current data with bad information.

✓ Navigate to the following specific address (URL)

http://www.facebook.com/help/contact.php?show_form=delete_account

✓ Click on the "Delete My Account" button. This will technically deactivate your account for two weeks. If you log into your account any time within that period, your account will be reactivated.

Figure 7.01: The Facebook settings option.

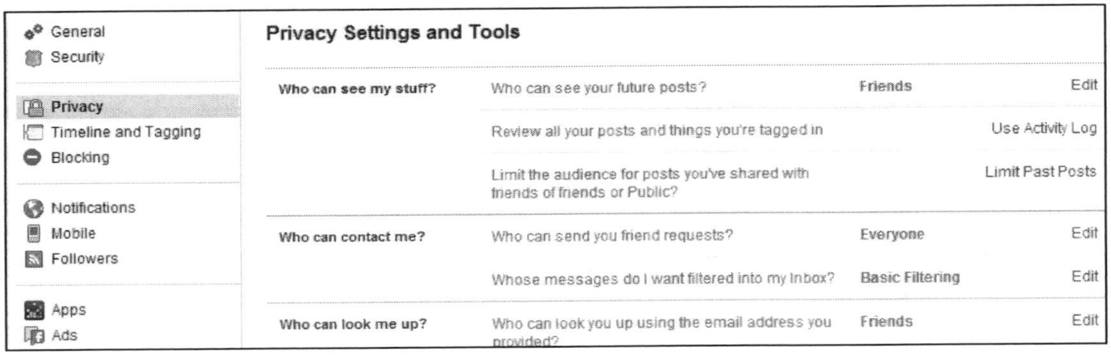

Figure 7.02: The Facebook Privacy Settings options.

Facebook Tagged Photos

If you possess a Facebook profile, anyone can post a photo of you to his or her own profile and "tag" you in the image. This will identify you in the photo by name and connect the viewer directly to your own Facebook page. Facebook gives you the ability to not only remove this tag, but you can also request removal of the entire photo. The following instructions will guide you through the process.

- ✓ Click on the down arrow in the far upper right of your profile while logged in to your Facebook account. Select "Activity Log".

- ✓ Click "Photos" in the left column. Select the images that you would like to remove the tag from.

- ✓ Click "Report/Remove Tags" at the top of the page and select "Untag Photos" to confirm.

- ✓ If you would like the photo completely removed, choose the option "I want this photo removed from Facebook". This will send a message to the user that posted the photo indicating your desire to remove the image. This is not mandatory to the user, but most people comply with this type of request. Figure 7.03 displays this option.

Figure 7.03: A Facebook tag removal request.

Twitter (twitter.com)

Deleting your Twitter account is fairly straight forward. Go to your settings page. On the bottom of the account tab, there is a "Deactivate my account" link. Click it, and confirm. Before you take the easy route, I encourage you to consider a few things.

If you have a Twitter profile with personal posts associated with it, there are dozens of websites that have collected all of your data and reproduced it. Deleting your account will not remove the posts that are replicated on third party websites. As an investigator, I am often presented a message on a suspect's account that says "Account deleted". This is usually due to the suspect learning that he or she is being investigated and the account is deleted out of panic. When I find this, I just go to a website such as Topsy (topsy.com) and pull up the user's posts. The next tactic will add an additional layer of privacy to hide your tweets.

Before deleting your account, remove every message that you have ever posted. Eventually, many of the third party websites that collect Twitter data will re-scan your profile and update the messages that are displayed on their site. Often, this will overwrite the information that is currently displayed with the current messages, which will be none. I prefer this over simply deleting the account. Also, when you delete your account, someone can open up a new account with your profile name after 30 days. With this method, you still have control of your account, there are no personal messages associated with it, and sites that collect your Twitter posts will collect your empty profile. Active Twitter users often have thousands of messages on their account. Removing each message individually can be very time consuming. Instead, consider an automatic message deletion option that will do the work for you.

Twit Wipe (twitwipe.com)

This service will remove all messages from your Twitter profile. In order to do this for you, the site will need your user name and password for your Twitter account. Before you provide this information, make sure that the password for your account is not associated with any other accounts. For example, if you use the same password for Twitter and your bank account, you do not want to provide anyone or any service that information. The chances of Twit Wipe disclosing this information are minimal, but do not take the chance. Change your password on Twitter to something unique. After you have a unique password for your account, navigate to **twitwipe.com** and log into your Twitter account. Confirm that you want the site to delete all of your messages and click the link for "Start Wiping". This can often take up to an hour. When the process is complete, and you have verified your messages are gone, change your password back to the original password of your choice on Twitter.

MySpace (myspace.com)

MySpace users are steadily leaving the service for more advanced networks such as Facebook and Twitter. These users leave behind an abundance of data that is being collected by dozens of data-mining companies. If you have ever created a MySpace page, you should consider completely deleting the profile to keep your photos, messages, and contacts from being passed around in public view. The official process is to log into your account, click on "Settings", and select "Delete Account". You can visit the MySpace privacy page at the following website.

https://myspace.com/pages/privacy

In my experience, this account removal process does not work. The request is ignored and nothing changes. However, I have found the following technique effective.

✓ Log into your MySpace profile and click the control panel and then "Profile". On this page, click on the "Basic" tab and change your year of birth to a year 12 years before today. This will make you appear to be 12 on your profile.

✓ The URL of the page that you are on will reveal your user number. It may look something like "http://www.myspace.com/4024450". Write down this number.

✓ Send an email to the law enforcement legal compliance division's account at **compliance@support.myspace.com**. Type "Underage User" in the subject line. Include a message similar to the following.

> "My 12 year old daughter has a MySpace profile stating she is 12. She is receiving unwanted contact from adults. Please remove this account immediately."

While this method is deceptive, it has worked. You are not breaking any laws by using this technique on your own profile. MySpace will delete the profile immediately without question as a precaution.

LinkedIn (linkedin.com)

Many people have successfully used LinkedIn to gain employment and communicate with others in their industry. Most people that use this social network supply personal information to their LinkedIn profile including employment history, education, contact information, and various details that are often placed on a resume. The following steps should remove your account from the internet.

✓ Log into your account. Hover over the photo or photo placeholder of the account and select "Privacy & Settings". Click the "Account" link near the bottom of the page and navigate to "Helpful Links" and then "Close your account".

✓ Complete the Account Closure form and confirm the account that you want to terminate. LinkedIn will try to convince you to keep your account open a few times. When you successfully complete this process, you will be notified that an email will be sent confirming the deletion of your account. This may take up to a week.

✓ Many people report that the account deletion confirmation never arrives. If this happens to you, submit a help center request. In a web browser, navigate to **help.linkedin.com/app/ask**. The website may automatically direct you to the help home page. If this occurs, you will notice access to the "Contact Us" link at the top of the page is blocked until you search for an answer. Simply search any term. Then after the results are displayed, you are allowed to click the link to "Contact Us". Complete this form with your information and an account deletion request as displayed in Figure 7.04.

Be sure to include your profile number, which can be found in the address (URL) of your profile. In the following address of a LinkedIn user, the profile number is 300972.

http://www.linkedin.com/profile/view?id=300972

First Name *	Joe
Last Name *	Wilson
Email Address *	kjh332@notsharingmy.info
Issue Type *	Account/Settings ▾
Subject *	Account deletion
Your Question *	I have attempted to delete my profile, but was unsuccessful. Please remove this account immediately. My profile number is 300972.

Figure 7.04: The LinkedIn account removal submission.

Public Photos

A combination of cheap digital cameras and free online storage of photographs has created an enormous amount of personal information available to the public. Social networks and photo sharing websites encourage you to upload all of your photos and send the links to all of your friends and family. Many people have a false belief that only people that possess the direct links to the photos can see them. This is not true. Every one of these sites has a search function embedded into all of the pages that allows anyone to search for pages that may contain photos. The obvious risk here is that your personal photos will be seen by complete strangers. These strangers often include internet predators looking for images of children. The next concern is called the Exif data.

Exif Data

Every digital photograph captured with a digital camera possesses metadata known as Exif data. This is a layer of code that provides information about the photo and camera. All digital cameras write this data to each image, but the amount and type of data can vary. This data, which is embedded into each photo "behind the scenes", is not visible within the captured image. You need an Exif reader, which can be found on websites and within applications. Keep in mind that some websites remove or "scrub" this data before being stored on their servers. Facebook, for example, removes the data while Twitter and Flickr often do not. If the image has been compressed to a smaller file size, this data is often lost. However, most photo sharing sites offer a full size view. The easiest way to see the information is through an online viewer.

Jeffrey's Exif Viewer (regex.info//exif.cgi)

I consider Jeffrey's Exif Viewer the online standard for displaying Exif data. The site will allow analysis of any image found online or stored on a drive connected to your computer. The home page, as seen in Figure 7.05, provides two search options. The first allows you to copy and paste an address of an image online for analysis. Clicking "browse" on the second option will open a file explorer window that will allow you to select a file on your computer for analysis. The file types supported are also identified on this page.

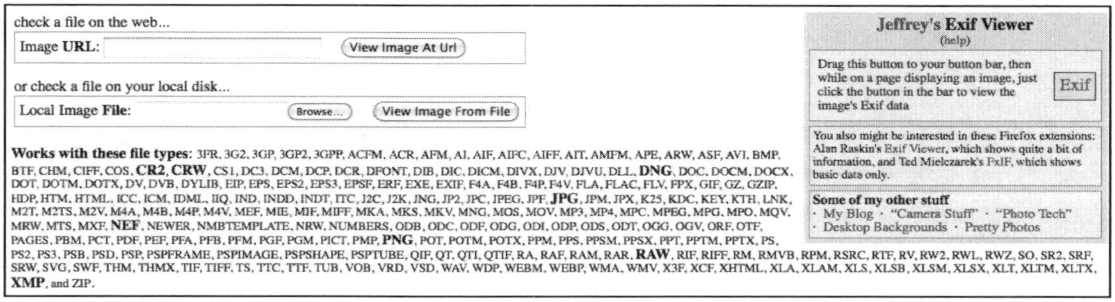

Figure 7.05: Jeffrey's Exif Viewer home page.

The first section of the results will usually provide the make and model of the camera used to capture the image. Many cameras will also identify the lens used, exposure settings, flash usage, date and time of capture and file size. In Figure 7.06, you can see that the camera used was a Canon EOS Digital Rebel with an 18 - 55mm lens at full 55mm setting. Auto exposure was selected, the flash was turned off, and the photo was taken at 2:30 pm on May 7, 2011. This is a lot of data to share with the world.

Scrolling down the analysis page will then identify the serial number field. This is most common in newer SLR cameras and will not be present in less expensive cameras. Figure 7.07 displays a serial number result. This camera will identify the make, model, and serial number of the camera inside every photo that it captures.

A serial number of a camera associated with an image can be valuable data. This can help someone associate photos that you "anonymously" posted to the internet directly to you. For example, if I found a photo that you posted on your Twitter feed that you took with your camera, I may be able to identify the serial number of your camera. If I then find a photo that I suspect that you took but posted anonymously, I can see if the serial numbers match. I bring this up to explain the next threat.

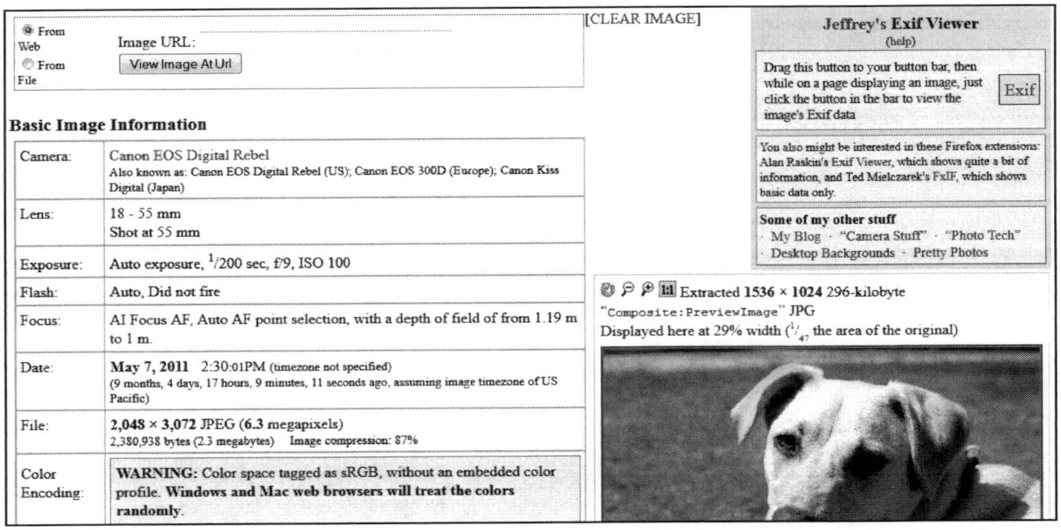

Figure 7.06: The top portion of a Jeffrey's Exif viewer result.

Color Space	Unknown (-1)
Serial Number	520201773
Lens Info	70-200mm f/?
Lens	EF70-200mm f/2.8L IS USM
Image Number	6

Figure 7.07: An Exif viewer result with a serial number.

Stolen Camera Finder (www.stolencamerafinder.co.uk)

This site was designed to help camera theft victims with locating their camera if it is being used by the thief online. For that use, you would find a photo taken with the stolen camera, and drop it into the site for analysis. This analysis identifies a serial number if possible. If one is located, the service then presents links to photo-sharing websites, such as Flickr, that contain photos with the same serial number. This can locate photos that you may not want to take credit for.

Camera Trace (cameratrace.com/trace)

An additional site that provides this service is called Camera Trace. Type in the serial number of a camera and the site will attempt to locate any online photographs taken with the camera. This service claims to have indexed all of Flickr, Twitter, Twitpic, Pnoramio, and 500px.

GPS

Many new SLR cameras, and almost all cellular telephone cameras, now include GPS. If the GPS is on, and the user did not disable geo tagging of the photos in the camera settings, you will get location data within the Exif data of the photo. Figure 7.08 displays the analysis of an image taken with a camera with GPS. The data is similar to the previous analysis, but includes a new "Location" field. This field will translate the captured GPS coordinates from the photo and identify the location of the photo. Further down this results page, the site will display an image from Google Maps identifying the exact point of the GPS associated with the photo. Figure 7.09 displays this satellite view map from another photo taken in Florida on a Droid cellular telephone. All Android and iPhone devices have this capability.

Cropped Photos

Another piece of information that can be located from the Exif data is the presence of a thumbnail image within the photograph. Digital cameras generate a small version of the photo captured and store it within the Exif data. This icon size image adds very little size to the overall file. When a user crops the image, this original smaller version may or may not get overwritten. Programs such as Photoshop or Microsoft Photo Editor will overwrite the data and keep both images identical. Other programs, as well as some online cropping tools, do not overwrite this data. The result is the presence of the original and un-cropped image within the Exif data of the cropped photo. An example of this is seen in Figure 7.10. A cropped photo found online is examined through an alternative Exif viewer, Camera Summary (camerasummary.com). The cropped full size large photo is seen on the left. The embedded smaller original photo was not overwritten when cropped. You can now see what the image looked like before it was cropped.

It is possible to delete or manipulate this Exif data. If you have a situation where it is necessary to upload photos to the internet, you may want to consider removing this metadata. This process is often referred to as "scrubbing" a photo. There are several ways to accomplish this.

If you have a computer that uses Microsoft Windows 7 as an operating system, you are ready to edit this data immediately. Locate an image on your hard drive and right-click the file name. Select "Properties". This will present a new window with a tab titled "Details". Click on this tab and review the information. If the data attached to this image contains information that you do not want to share with the world, click on the link "Remove Properties and Personal Information". This will allow you the option to remove specific data from the image. I recommend selecting the "Select All" button to be sure that all of the Exif data is removed. Figure 7.11 displays this window before and after the removal.

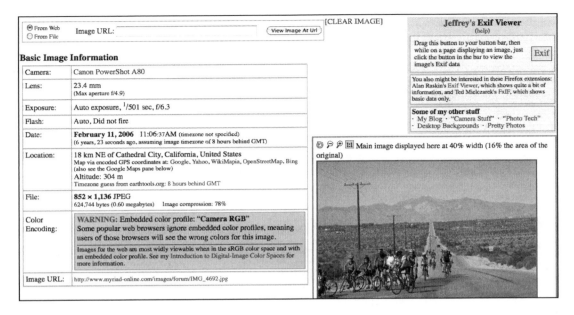

Figure 7.08: A Jeffrey's Exif Viewer result identifying location.

Figure 7.09: A Jeffrey's Exif Viewer result displaying a satellite view of the location data.

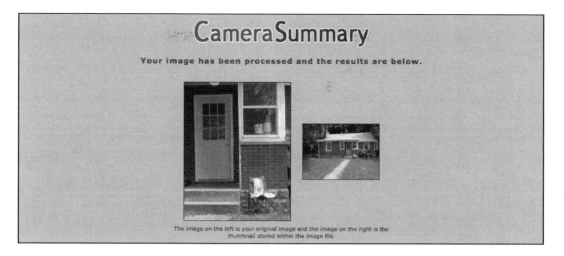

Figure 7.10: A Camera Summary result displaying an original un-cropped photo.

EXIF version	0220		EXIF version	0220
GPS			GPS	
Latitude	33; 52; 31.658935546875		Latitude	
Longitude	116; 18; 5.8305664062500...		Longitude	
Altitude	304		Altitude	

Remove Properties and Personal Information   Remove Properties and Personal Information

OK   Cancel   Apply   OK   Cancel   Apply

Figure 7.11: Exif data as seen in Microsoft Windows 7.

If you are using a different operating system, there are several free applications that will remove this data. Instead of downloading software, I recommend using a website to remove this data.

Exif Remover (verexif.com/en/)

This website allows you to upload a digital image and either view or remove the metadata attached to it. Click on the "Browse" button, locate the photo you want to edit, and click "Remove Exif". You will be presented with a new download that will contain your image without the Exif data embedded.

Deleting Photo Sharing Accounts

Has this information motivated you to delete your photos uploaded to photo sharing networks?

Figure 7.12 is a list of the most common services used in past years to upload and share photos. Many of these are no longer popular, but any content uploaded is still present today. The information to the right of each network is a brief summary of the account deletion process. If you do locate photos that need to be removed, you must log into the account that was used to upload them. If you did not create the account, you will need to contact the friend or family member that did.

Flickr	Log in and go to http://www.flickr.com/profile_delete.gne
Fotki	Log in and go to My Account > Account Information > Close Account
Fotolog	Log in > Edit My Parameters > Contact Information > Deactivate Account
Image Shack	Log in and go to My Images > Preferences > Delete Account
Jalbum	Log in and go to Settings > Close Account > Delete Me
Lockerz	Send email to change@lockerz.com with subject "Delete"
Panoramio	Log in and remove all photos > Settings > Delete
Photobucket	Log in and go to account page > Cancel Account > Delete My Account
Picasa	Log in and select album > Actions > Delete Album > Repeat for each album
Pinterest	Log in and select Edit Profile > Deactivate Account > Confirm
Shutterfly	Select each album > Delete Album
Skydrive	Log in and select Options > More Options > Edit > Account > Close Account
Smugmug	Log in and select Account settings > Me > Subscription > Close account
Snapfish	Send email to service@snapfish.com with subject "Cancel"
Webshots	Log in > delete online photos > Uninstall Webshots software on computer

Figure 7.12: The most common photo sharing services with removal instructions.

Google Maps (maps.google.com)

Unless you live in a very rural area or at the end of a mile long private drive, a street view of your house is probably on the internet. Google has been taking 360 degree photos from every street in the country for years. People can then use the Google Maps website to see images of a residence or business. This often identifies personal and work vehicles, physical security vulnerabilities, and occasionally family members standing in the yard. Many people assume that there is nothing that can be done about this. Removing these images is quite easy.

✓ Navigate to the Google Maps website and type in your home address. There will be a red marker on the map hovering over your house. Click on this marker and look at the options in the popup menu. If there is a street view of your house, this option will appear in this window. Figure 7.13 displays the street view option. Click on the Street View link to open a new view which can be moved and zoomed with the mouse.

✓ On this new view, manipulate the image so that you can see your house on the screen. On the lower left portion of the image, there is a link titled "Report a problem". Click on this link and view the resulting page. Figure 7.14 displays this links.

✓ The first section of this page asks "Why are you reporting this street view?". Select "Privacy Concerns", and then "My House", and then "I have found a picture of my house and would like it blurred". In the next section, enter your privacy concern which can be "I have found a picture of my house and would like it blurred". Enter your anonymous email address and make sure that the red box on the image below is surrounding your house. Complete the word verification and click "Submit". I have heard about success stories and failures. Some people have reported that they added one of the following lines in the description window to obtain immediate removal.

"Photo identifies a building used for home-schooling students". I like this one. Most likely, you have taught a child something in your home at some point. Technically, you were home-schooling.

"Photo identifies physical security vulnerabilities of the building". This one is a great catch-all as well. Every building has a physical vulnerability such as a door lock, windows, or attic vent. You would qualify for this.

"Photo identifies home of a covert police officer targeted by violent criminals". For the law enforcement community, this seems to get their attention. If you believe that you would not qualify as a covert officer, think again. Have you ever been involved in a work situation off duty or in civilian clothes? That sounds covert to me. If you have not, report some speeders on the highway to your immediate supervisor while off duty and "under cover". You now qualify. Be aware that this may raise sanity issues at your department. You will immediately receive an email confirmation from Google and a removal confirmation within 48 hours. Check and verify that the image has been removed or blurred. Figure 7.15 displays a portion of this form.

Figure 7.13: A Google Maps Street View option.

Figure 7.14: A Google Maps Street View of a building.

Figure 7.15: Selecting a building on Google Maps for removal.

Blogs

A personal blog is a website where a user can publish personal content. These are often compared to a diary kept in public view. They are very popular with teens and young adults. Often, the site will include text, photos, and videos. The text is usually personal and occasionally discloses information that is later regretted. The most common free blog services are provided by Blogger.com, WordPress.com, and Blog.com. The method of deleting a blog is different on each service and is outlined below.

Blogger (blogger.com)

Blogger, owned by Google, does not give you the option to delete your blog after it has been published. There are no options in your account settings that allow you to close your account. Instead, you must take a manual approach.

✓ Log into your Blogger profile. This will be the same credentials used to log into your other Google accounts, and you should be automatically logged in if you are already signed in to any Google service. You should be directed to your Blogger Overview page. If not, click on "My Blogs". Click on "Posts" on the menu on the left of the page. This will present every post published on the blog. Select each box next to each post and then click the trash can icon in the upper middle. Figure 7.16 displays this page with the posts selected.

✓ Edit your profile to remove any personal information stored there. For required fields, you can enter false information. To access this content, click on your user name in the upper right corner of any blog page. This will present a menu with an option of "Account Settings". Click this and remove or edit personal data.

✓ Change your user name on Blogger to something not related to you. I recommend random characters. This will prevent any traces of your old blog from being associated with you.

WordPress (wordpress.com)

Similar to Blogger, WordPress will not let you delete your account. They will allow you to delete any individual blogs though.

✓ Log into your WordPress profile page and click on the "My Blog" tab. This will provide a list of all blogs that exist in the account. Click on the "Dashboard" link under each blog.

✓ Highlight the "Tools" option on the left menu. This will present a link titled "Delete Site". The next page will ask for a reason for this action. Choose the last option of "Permanently delete the blog name and all content". Check the box to confirm this action and click the button to execute the removal. Figure 7.17 displays the request.

✓ Check your email account that was used to originally create the blog. You will receive a verification email that will include a link to confirm the removal. Repeat this process for any other blogs in the account.

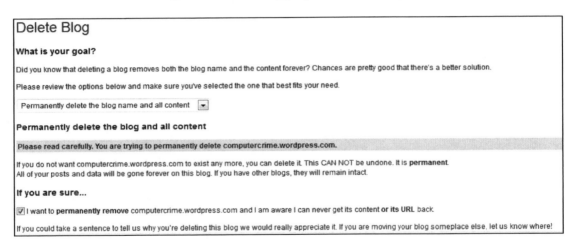

Figure 7.16: The Blogger post deletion page.

Delete Blog

What is your goal?

Did you know that deleting a blog removes both the blog name and the content forever? Chances are pretty good that there's a better solution.

Please review the options below and make sure you've selected the one that best fits your need.

Permanently delete the blog name and all content ▼

Permanently delete the blog and all content

Please read carefully. You are trying to permanently delete computercrime.wordpress.com.

If you do not want computercrime.wordpress.com to exist any more, you can delete it. This CAN NOT be undone. It is **permanent**. All of your posts and data will be gone forever on this blog. If you have other blogs, they will remain intact.

If you are sure...

☑ I want to **permanently remove** computercrime.wordpress.com and I am aware I can never get its content **or its URL** back.

If you could take a sentence to tell us why you're deleting this blog we would really appreciate it. If you are moving your blog someplace else, let us know where!

Figure 7.17: The WordPress blog removal page.

Blog (blog.com)

Until recently, the only option for removing a personal blog on this site was to submit a help ticket and request removal from customer service. You can now complete this on your own account.

✓ Sign in to your account on blog.com. On your dashboard, click "settings" and then "Delete Blog". This will present a large button titled "Delete My Site Permanently". You will receive an email at the address that you used when creating your account. Click on the verification link in this email to confirm the deletion.

Social Network Search Sites

Now that you have removed all of your social network presence, you may think that you are ready to move on to another topic. Unfortunately, there is more to discuss. While your personal information is no longer visible on the social networks where it was posted, it has been collected and archived by other companies. These social network aggregators maintain their own copy of the public data that was visible on your profiles from Facebook, MySpace, Twitter, and others. The methods described next will remove the data collected about you.

Infospace (infospace.com)

If you can locate your own personal information on Infospace.com, you can request it be removed by contacting their customer service via email. The link above will direct you to an online form. Supply your name, anonymous email address, and place "Removal" in the subject line. In the message box, type something similar to the following.

"I have discovered that my personal information is being displayed on your website. I request that all information associated with me at the following address be removed."

> Bob Wilson
> 1212 Main
> St. Louis, MO 63321

Peek You (peekyou.com)

Peek You has created a large database of personal information about millions of people. This was all collected from public sources including social networks. Removal is easy and can be completed online.

- ✓ Search for your personal information on peekyou.com and note the unique number assigned to your profile. This can be found in the address (URL) of the page that displays the information. An example may look like the following.
  http://www.peekyou.com/mike_bazzell/26918995

- ✓ Navigate to **peekyou.com/about/contact/optout**. Supply your name as it appears in your profile, your anonymous email address, and unique ID number. In the example above, this number would be 26918995. For "Actions", choose "Remove my entire listing" and for "reason" choose the most appropriate option. Supply a brief reason for removal, which can be as simple as "Please remove this page".

- ✓ You will eventually receive an email notification confirming removal. Search peekyou.com again to confirm the information was deleted. This can take three days.

My Life (mylife.com)

My Life does not offer any method to remove your own information. Instead, you must either call them at 888-704-1900 or email them at privacy@mylife.com. I have experienced better results through email.

- ✓ Create an email to **privacy@mylife.com** using a personal email account. It is best if you do this from the account that you originally created your social networks. My Life can use this as verification that you are indeed the same person as the person in the profile. This email should include a general removal request such as "Please remove any profile associated with my information as follows". Then list only your full name as it appears in a search on mylife.com and the city and state that you live in. If you live in a large city or have a common name, you may need to also include a street, but not the full address.

- ✓ My Life will contact you within 10 days via email. This will either confirm that the requested information was deleted or will ask for further verification. In my experience, I had to submit this request twice before I received any communication from My Life.

Spoke (spoke.com)

This free service has a reputation of providing accurate data about a person based on the person's online presence. The summary provided combines the results that would be obtained from a thorough search of public sources. Each profile can be removed individually.

- ✓ Conduct a search of yourself on **spoke.com**. Click on each profile associated with you. At the bottom of the profile is a link titled "Request Removal". This is in the footer section of the page. Clicking this link will open a new page.

- ✓ Complete the online form. Supply your name as it appears on the profile you want to delete and your anonymous email address. Select the option "I do not want to be searchable on the internet right now" and click submit. This appears to add you to an online spreadsheet of users that want to be removed.

- ✓ Within 48 hours, you should receive an email confirming the removal of your profile. Follow the directions in the email to confirm the request.

Email Finder (emailfinder.com)

This service relies on social network data to allow a search of an email address. This search can identify the information collected before you deleted your account. Removal is almost immediate.

✓ Navigate to **http://www.emailfinder.com/EFC.aspx?_act=Optout** and complete the online form. Supply your personal email address that was used to open any social network accounts. For your first and last name, your initials are enough. The next email address you provide should be your anonymous address. Click submit. Figure 7.18 displays a completed form with information.

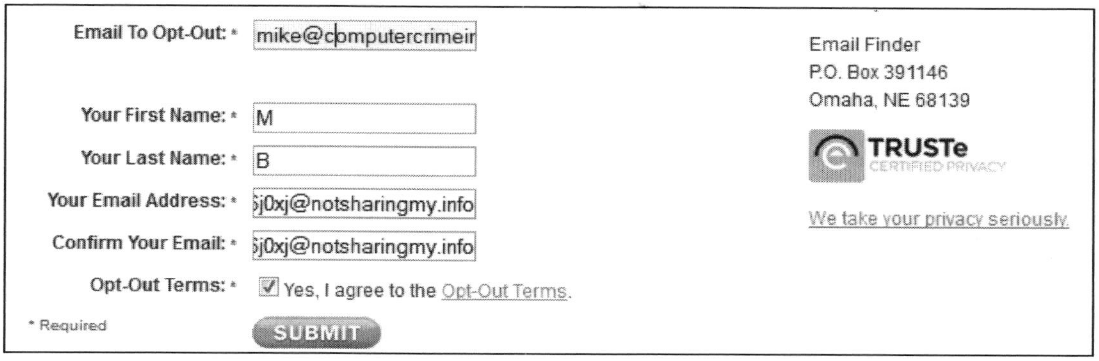

Figure 7.18: An opt-out form on emailfinder.com.

Everything Else

There are hundreds of social networking websites. They each have their own method for proper account deletion and few of them make these instructions easy to find. Two online services are available to help you discover the preferred way to delete a specific account. Account Killer (**accountkiller.com**) and Delete Your Account (**deleteyouraccount.com**) both offer detailed instruction on deleting hundreds of different accounts. Check these sites, enter the name of the website from which you want your data removed, and follow the instructions. If you have a rare site that is not mentioned here, conduct a search on a couple of search engines and you are likely to find everything you need.

Many of you will find that you have never opened a social network account, yet there are many personal details out there about your family. This is often posted by siblings and children. You will not be able to take direct action against an online profile that you do not have access to. If you want the data removed, you will need to approach the friend or family member that posted the content.

Chapter Eight

People Directories

When a person wants to locate your home address, telephone number, family information, or associations, he or she will probably visit an online people directory. These sites give anyone with internet access a view into your personal details. When I was young, I recall that the only option for this type of information was a phone book. If the subject of interest paid for an unlisted number, I was out of luck. Today, an unlisted number and address means nothing to the internet. Other sources, such as tax data, social networks, resumes, and marketing databases, fill in the gaps. These sites are mostly free to access and create revenue by enticing visitors to pay for premium data in the form of a complete background check. The removal process is usually easy, with a few exceptions. Many of the links that will connect you directly to the page that you need are long and easily mistyped. I encourage you to visit the "links" section of my website. As mentioned before, the link called "Hiding from the Internet" will have everything you need.

Spokeo (spokeo.com)

Spokeo is one of the most popular websites for locating free personal data about people. Fortunately, it also provides one of the easiest methods of information removal. After verification of an email address, the results are immediate. Here is how to eliminate your private information from this site.

✓ Navigate to **spokeo.com** and enter your full name. You will be presented with a list of any states that possess information about the name entered. Select your state and then select the city that you live in. The site will now identify any locations in the city that you specified, as seen in Figure 8.01. If any of these display your address, select the entry. You will now see the profile that Spokeo has collected about you. Select the entire URL of this page, as seen in Figure 8.02, and right-click and select "copy". This URL will start with www.spokeo.com and end with a series of numbers.

✓ Navigate to **www.spokeo.com/optout**. This will present a form at the bottom of the page with three fields. The first field requests the URL that you copied above. Right-click this field and select "paste". The next field requests an email address for verification. Enter the anonymous email address that you created in Chapter Three. Finally, the third field requests the captcha code that appears to the right of the field. Select "Remove This Listing" and check your email inbox. An example of this email can be seen in Figure 8.03.

✓ Complete the removal process by visiting the link included in the email. Figure 8.04 displays an example of the email received from Spokeo. This confirms your request for removal. You should now search your name again and confirm that the profile was deleted. Figure 8.05 displays a response indicating that no information was available. Complete this process for every entry on Spokeo that applies to you. If there are more than five entries, you may need to use a secondary email address for verification.

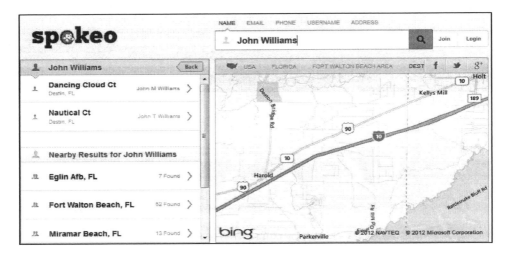

Figure 8.01: A Spokeo search selection result.

Figure 8.02: An example of a URL from Spokeo associated with a person.

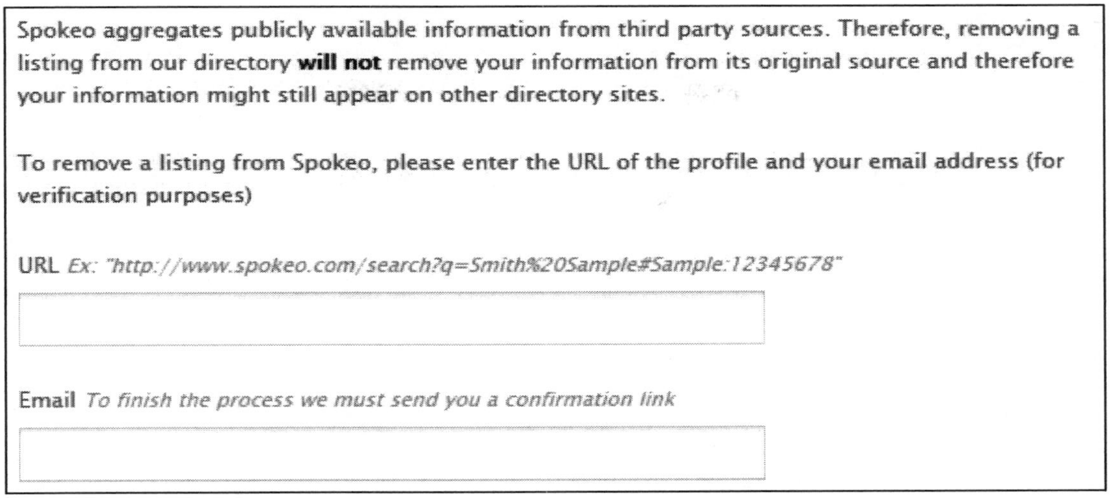

Spokeo aggregates publicly available information from third party sources. Therefore, removing a listing from our directory **will not** remove your information from its original source and therefore your information might still appear on other directory sites.

To remove a listing from Spokeo, please enter the URL of the profile and your email address (for verification purposes)

URL *Ex: "http://www.spokeo.com/search?q=Smith%20Sample#Sample:12345678"*

Email *To finish the process we must send you a confirmation link*

Figure 8.03: The Spokeo removal request page.

You have requested that the following url be removed from Spokeo searches:
http://www.spokeo.com/search?q=Michael+Bazzell&s2-   848664701

To complete the removal process, please click here.

If the above link is not clickable, please paste the following into your browser:

http://www.spokeo.com/privacy?c=32a2af2003c791fd9146f12e8116b2
0e9604faaa&dp=13848664701

Figure 8.04: An email received from Spokeo to verify deletion.

spokeo

👤 **Michael Bazzell**, Enter a City

👤 Michael Bazzell   Back

🚫 **No Results Found**

We could not find any profiles for **Michael Bazzell.**

USA   ILLINOIS   ALTON

Figure 8.05: A Spokeo response with negative search results.

Pipl (pipl.com)

Pipl has been one of my favorite people search websites for many years. As an investigator, I make this one of the first sites that I check when trying to locate someone. The information available includes home address, email address, social networks, online photos, and family members. The removal process is a little tricky, but possible. Next are the instructions for removal.

- ✓ Navigate to **pipl.com** and conduct a search on yourself. Include your full name and nickname. For example, I would search for both Michael Bazzell and Mike Bazzell. Insert your location by typing your city. Allow the website to display a list of all cities matching your request and select the appropriate city and state. Click on "Search" when done. Figure 8.06 displays a result identifying the best option for my city and state.

- ✓ If Pipl has generated a profile on your name, it will be listed on the results page. In Figure 8.07, you can see that a profile has been created on several people with my name. Selecting the link that describes me will give more details including my age, location, high school, and other data. You should find the link or links that match your information and click on them to see the full detail. Remember the exact full name that it displays on your profile.

- ✓ Navigate to **pipl.com/directory/remove**. This will allow you to enter the page address that stores your profile. Instead of entering the exact page that your profile is on, you must enter the path that stores profiles on all subjects with your name. The path should be structured like this:

  http://www.pipl.com/directory/name/lastname/firstname/

- ✓ For this example on my name, I entered:

  http://www.pipl.com/directory/name/bazzell/michael/

- ✓ Enter your anonymous email address and click "Submit". Figure 8.08 displays my entry for this screen before I entered my email address. The results page will list all profiles assigned to people with your name. It will also display various search results that are added to profiles. Find each entry that is associated with you and click on the "Remove" button. This will submit a request for removal. Figure 8.09 displays two profiles. The second profile, associated with me, identifies that a request was sent for deletion after I clicked the "Remove" button.

- ✓ Check your email for a confirmation from Pipl. You will receive a separate email for each page that you requested removal. Inside each email will be a link to click titled "please click this confirmation link". You will receive an immediate confirmation from Pipl that the information was deleted. While your profile was immediately deleted from the Pipl Directory, it will still appear in search results for a few days.

Mike Bazzell	Alton,	SEARCH
Name, Email, Username or Phone	Alton, IL, US	

Figure 8.06: A Pipl search form.

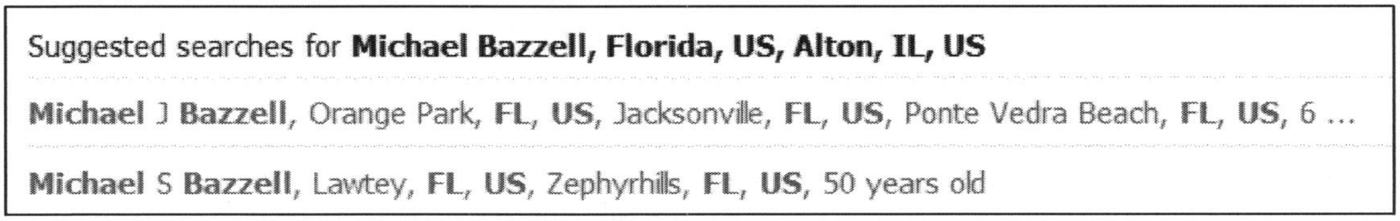

Suggested searches for **Michael Bazzell, Florida, US, Alton, IL, US**

Michael J **Bazzell**, Orange Park, **FL**, **US**, Jacksonville, **FL**, **US**, Ponte Vedra Beach, **FL**, **US**, 6 ...

Michael S **Bazzell**, Lawtey, **FL**, **US**, Zephyrhills, **FL**, **US**, 50 years old

Figure 8.07: A search result on Pipl.

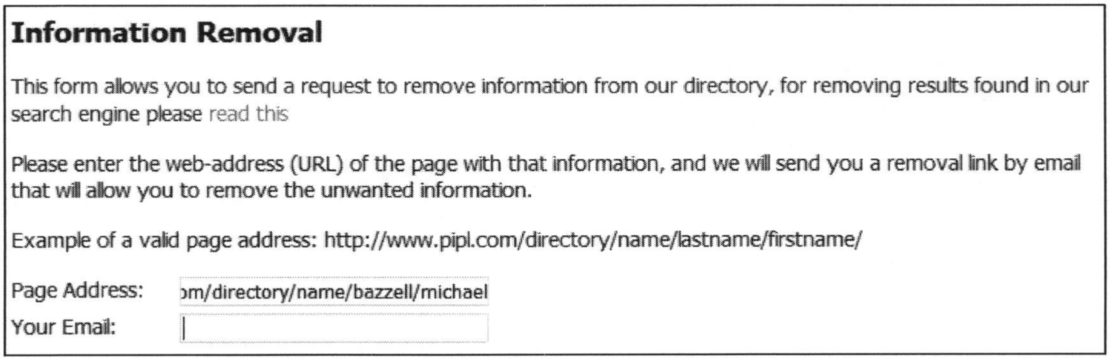

Information Removal

This form allows you to send a request to remove information from our directory, for removing results found in our search engine please read this

Please enter the web-address (URL) of the page with that information, and we will send you a removal link by email that will allow you to remove the unwanted information.

Example of a valid page address: http://www.pipl.com/directory/name/lastname/firstname/

Page Address: om/directory/name/bazzell/michael

Your Email:

Figure 8.08: A removal request form on Pipl.

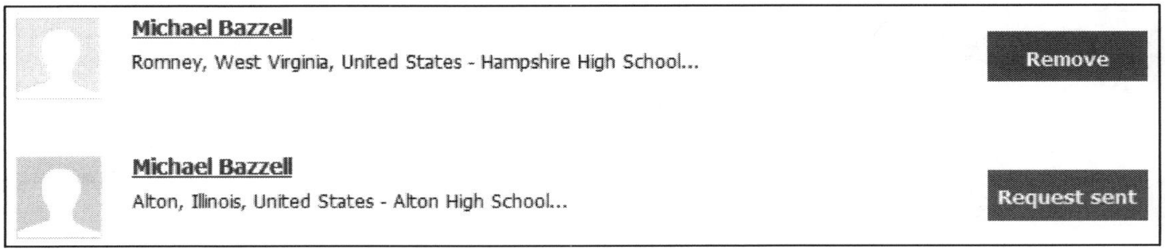

Michael Bazzell
Romney, West Virginia, United States - Hampshire High School...
Remove

Michael Bazzell
Alton, Illinois, United States - Alton High School...
Request sent

Figure 8.09: Profiles on Pipl ready for removal.

ZoomInfo (zoominfo.com)

This site focuses on a person's work history and career. It collects information from public and private sources. Removing information from this profile is possible. The method is different from most sites. The instructions follow.

✓ Navigate to **zoominfo.com** and conduct a search for your name. Select the profile that matches your personal information. This will open a new site that displays the information that has been collected about you. Figure 8.10 displays a portion of a profile that had been created about me which included the college I work for, my government employment history with titles, rank, and assignments, associations I belong to, news articles I have been mentioned in, and various references to my career from blogs.

✓ On the left side of this page, click the link "Is this you? Claim your profile". Clicking this link will prompt you to sign up for the free service. While this may sound strange, you will need to sign up for the service in order to eliminate the service. Supply your anonymous email address, pick a password, and check your inbox for a confirmation link. Click the link and you should be forwarded to your profile management page.

✓ Next to each piece of personal information that you want removed from the internet, you should see a link to either "Delete" or "Remove" the information. These changes will be immediate. Figure 8.11 displays a portion of my page with these options.

✓ In a few days, search for your information on ZoomInfo and verify that the personal information has been removed. If it has, you should now delete your account. Navigate to **zoominfo.com/lookupEmail** and provide your anonymous email address.

Figure 8.10: A ZoomInfo personal profile.

Employment History	Add
Part Time Instructor * Lewis-Clark State College	Edit Delete
Computer Crime Detective * Alton Police Department	Edit Delete
Detective *	Edit Delete

Michael ...
www.computercrimeinfo.com, 28 Feb 2011
[cached]
Michael Bazzell

Michael Bazzell is the Computer Crime Detective for the **Alton**, llinois Police Department. Since 1997, he has handled all cases involving any type of **Computer Crime** and Computer Forensic Analysis, including several State and Federal cases throughout the

Remove

Figure 8.11: A ZoomInfo profile that will allow content to be removed.

People Finders (peoplefinders.com)

Following Intelius' footsteps, People Finders offers their fee-based services to several websites that offer background checks on "anyone". This will usually include full name, date of birth, address history for 20 years, employment history, family members, associations, memberships, and more. My unwanted profile included all of this plus my mother's maiden name! People Finders is owned by Confi-Chek which also owns Private Eye, USA People Search, and Veromi. You only need to complete this process once for all four websites, but you must reference them in the submission form. Follow these steps:

✓ Navigate to **http://www.peoplefinders.com/manage/default.aspx**. Search for your name and location. Select a listing by clicking the "This is me" button. On the next page click the button "Opt out my info" as seen in Figure 8.12. Then on the next page, type the captcha code, check both statement boxes, and then click the "Continue" button. On the last page, click the button "No thanks, skip this step" to ignore purchasing your background report. The result should be removed within an hour. Repeat for additional entries.

People Finder (peoplefinder.com)

The name of this service sounds very similar to the previous site, but it is different. Unlike People Finders, People Finder allows for an online removal submission.

✓ Navigate to **peoplefinder.com/optout.php** and complete the online form. For the removal reason, select "General Privacy Concerns". Your entry must match the entry in their records exactly, so you may need to play around with your details until it matches. You should receive an email confirmation within 24 hours. Figure 8.13 displays a completed form with masked information.

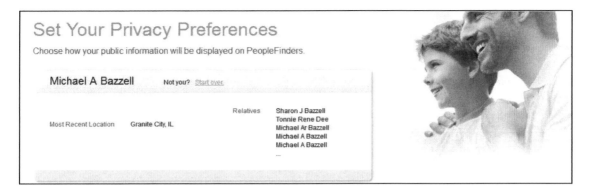

Figure 8.12: The printed removal request from peoplefinders.com

Figure 8.13: The online removal request on Peoplefinders.com.

Radaris (radaris.com)

Radaris is a popular people search service that provides a removal process that is difficult to complete. Radaris will allow you to remove up to five profiles at the same time. Many people have complained that Radaris bombards you with messages if you create an account to control your details. While you should proceed with caution, using an invisible email address and anonymous telephone number should stop many of the problems. The following instructions will guide you through this long process. Figures 8.14 through 8.22 will display each step of the process.

✓ Navigate to **radaris.com** and enter your name and state of residence. This will display all of the profiles built for the requested name. Click on the profile of interest, then click the down arrow next to the profile name, and select "Information control". Click the button "Hide Information / Remove mentions" and you can choose which to do first.

✓ The "Remove mentions" option will display a long list of references, address, phone numbers, social networks, and photos with a check box next to each entry. Review the list and place a check mark next to each entry that is relevant to you. When finished, select the "Remove selected record(s)" button at the end. Complete the form and provide a specific 33 Mail address such as radaris@(your-user-name).33mail.com. For the reason for removal, type "Privacy and security concerns". Submit the request.

✓ You will receive an email from Radaris. Confirm the removal request by clicking the confirmation link in the email message.

✓ The "Hide Information" option will require you to create a new user account with Radaris. Only complete this step if you have identified that Radaris possesses personal information about you such as your home address. Use your real name and the same 33 Mail address that you used previously. The next page will prompt you to enter your information including full name, full address, and date of birth. Provide the exact information that you see in the public profile that they display about you. If you provide inaccurate information, it will not allow you to proceed. While I always discourage providing accurate personal details, this is the only way that Radaris will allow you to remove your profile from their system.

✓ If you receive an error, it is because you are providing different information than that which is stored by Radaris. You may need to manipulate the details in order for Radaris to accept your submission. If the submission was successful and matches current data, you will receive a request for a cellular telephone number for verification purposes.

✓ Provide your Google Voice number that you created earlier. Do not provide a real cellular number unless it is an anonymous "minute" phone that is not associated with you and not used for personal calls. Radaris will send you a text message with a verification code to be entered on their page. Occasionally, Google Voice numbers will not work for this method and only an actual cellular telephone will suffice.

✓ Complete the form with your real name and anonymous email address. Confirm the code presented to the right of the third field. Uncheck the option titled "I'd like to subscribe for monitoring". This will prevent Radaris from sending you an email every time someone searches your name. Check the box next to "I agree with Advanced Removal terms & conditions" and click "Submit Request".

✓ You will receive an email from Radaris. Click on the first link in this email to complete the removal process. Search your name again and confirm that you have removed all of the information relevant to you. If you find more than five profiles, use an alternative anonymous email address to complete the removal process.

✓ The "Police / Government officers" option on the "Hide Information / Remove Mentions" page will allow officers, judges, and government attorney escalated removal. Follow the instructions and either submit a copy of your government credentials or an official request on department letterhead. I always choose the letterhead option for additional privacy. Either email the documents to police-removal@radaris.com or fax them to 800-861-9713.

✓ If you continue to receive unwanted email from Radaris, block the account that you used in your 33Mail settings.

Michael J Bazzell, 66
Orange Park, FL

More Results   Options ✔   Referenc
    ✎ Write a Review
    ☑ Information control
    🔔 Radar updates

Known also as: Michael Bazze · Mike Bazzell
Related to: Barbara Bazzell · Barbara Bazzell, ~61 · Sarah Bazzell, ~31

Figure 8.14: A Radaris person profile with Information Control option.

Control information on this page

Write your professional overview

Hide information / Remove mentions

Figure 8.15: A Radaris Information Control option page.

Hide information \ Remove mentions

≫ Hide information on your page
≫ Remove mentions

We have special program for police and government officers - Police / Government officers

Figure 8.16: A Radaris Information Control option page.

	Name	Address	Phone
☑	Michael Bazzell	ridge, Orange Park, FL 32065	(904) 376
☐	**Michael Bazzell**	ridge, Orange Park, FL 32065	(904) 375

Phone & Address

Figure 8.17: A redacted Radaris Remove Mentions option page.

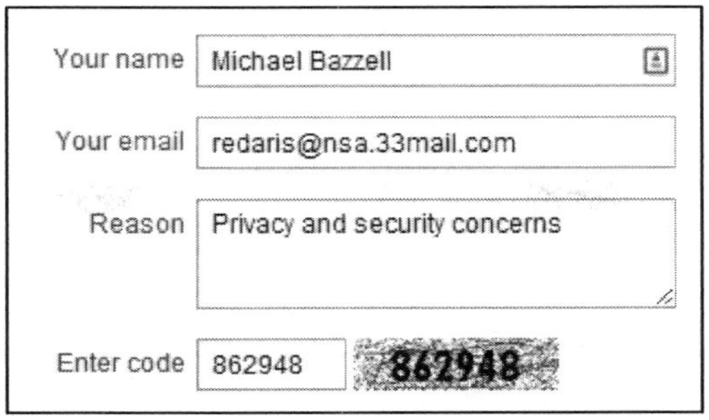

Your name	Michael Bazzell
Your email	redaris@nsa.33mail.com
Reason	Privacy and security concerns
Enter code	862948

Figure 8.18: A Radaris information removal request form.

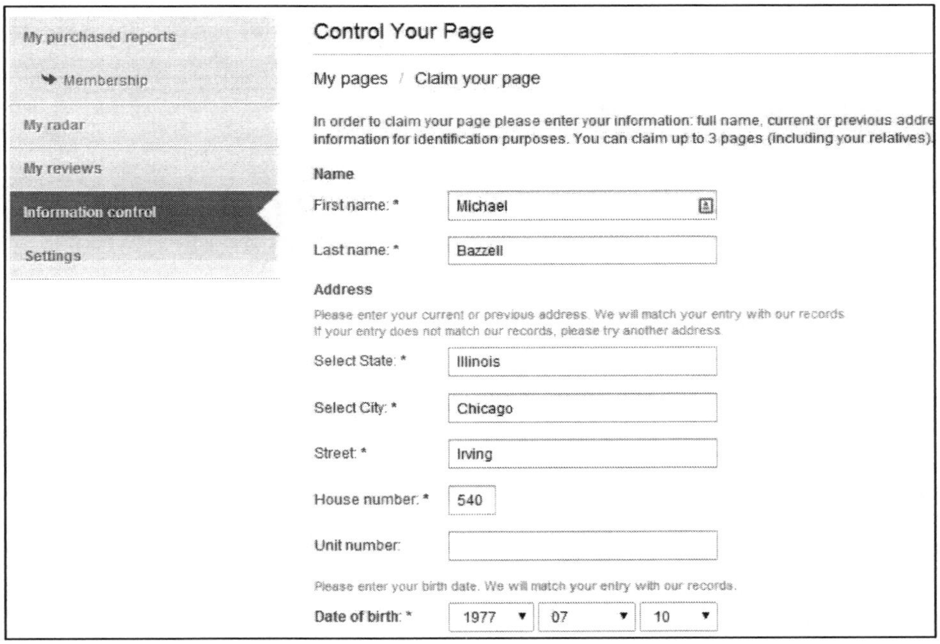

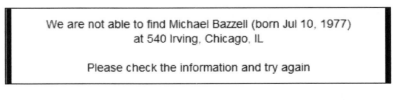

Control Your Page

My pages / Claim your page

In order to claim your page please enter your information: full name, current or previous addre
information for identification purposes. You can claim up to 3 pages (including your relatives).

Name

First name: *   Michael

Last name: *   Bazzell

Address

Please enter your current or previous address. We will match your entry with our records.
If your entry does not match our records, please try another address.

Select State: *   Illinois

Select City: *   Chicago

Street: *   Irving

House number: *   540

Unit number:

Please enter your birth date. We will match your entry with our records.

Date of birth: *   1977   07   10

My purchased reports
Membership
My radar
My reviews
Information control
Settings

Figure 8.19: A Radaris Information Control page for "Hidden Information".

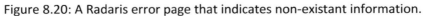

We are not able to find Michael Bazzell (born Jul 10, 1977)
at 540 Irving, Chicago, IL

Please check the information and try again

Figure 8.20: A Radaris error page that indicates non-existant information.

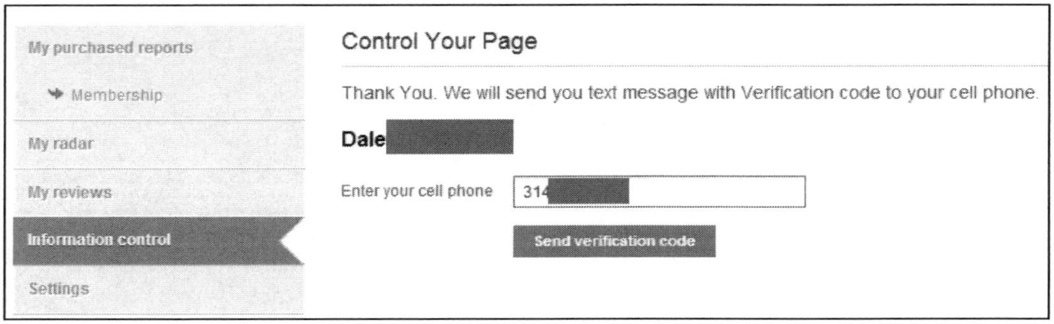

Figure 8.21: A redacted Radaris information removal from for a text message.

Dear customer,

Your information removal request is subject to approval by the administrator.
You will be notified by email when it has been reviewed. This may take up to 48 hours. Thank you for your patience.
Please confirm your request by clicking the link:

http://radaris.com/removal/confirm_request?rid=450110&p=25101B80A14DE084

Please note that Radaris works similarly to search engines. The information you see on Radaris comes from publicly available sources. Hiding information on Radaris does not remove data from its original source.

Figure 8.22: A Radaris information removal confirmation.

Yasni (yasni.com)

Yasni is another website that collects data about people and creates summaries about a specific person. This will often have personal information such as an email address or social network link. Previous to 2014, removing this information required no verification or email submission. The site allowed you to immediately eliminate details from a profile without logging in to the service. However, they no longer offer an option to remove your results.
Today, Yasni links a user directly to the live data that it identifies. This happens through the Yasni website, and any located content is displayed within a frame of the website. While you cannot remove this link from Yasni, you can use this service to connect you to the source of the unwanted data. Once you remove the content from the original source, such as a social network, Yasni will eventually stop linking to it.

Zabasearch (zabasearch.com)

Zabasearch is effective at identifying the unlisted home address and phone number of a person. The website does not offer an online form for information removal. Instead, you will need to send them a fax.

✓ Navigate to **zabasearch.com** and identify any profiles that contain your personal information by searching your full name. Any time you see a profile identifying you, click on your name to open the profile page. The URL of the page, otherwise known as the address of the page, will be a specific address that is associated with that profile. Make note of this address for later use.

✓ Print a copy of your custom Opt-Out Request Form with redacted driver's license as discussed in Chapter Three. Include your name and mailing address as it appears on a Zabasearch result. Include your date of birth but not your social security number. Finally, include the URL mentioned earlier that contains the exact address to a profile associated with you. It is common for Zabaseacrh to have several profiles with your information. Often, each contains a different address of a previous residence. Figure 8.23 displays a Zabasearch result while Figure 8.24 displays the URL of the result when clicked. Figure 8.25 is a portion of my fax submission that identifies the website addresses that I requested removed. Note that I masked the actual page numbers for privacy from a general book audience. You submission should include these numbers.

✓ Use the online GotFreeFax service discussed in Chapter Three to send your completed form. This request may take up to thirty days to be applied. The fax should be sent to:
Zaba, Inc. Fax: 425-974-6194

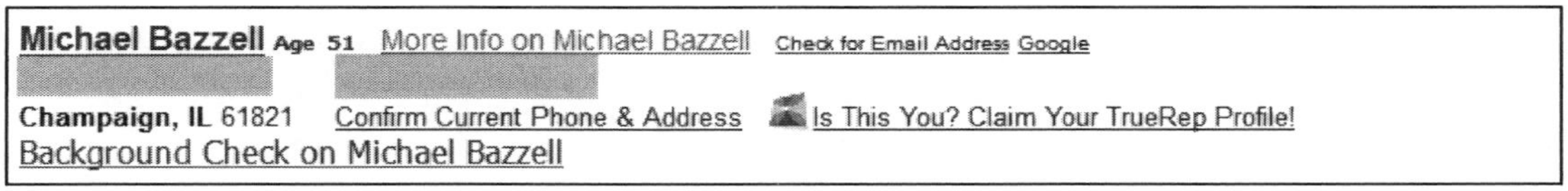

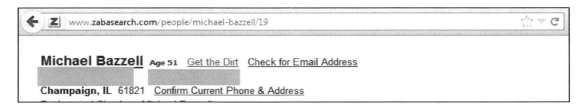

Figure 8.23: A Zabasearch result on a name search.

Figure 8.24: A Zabasearch URL of a profile page.

```
Direct URL(s) of personal information online:

http://zabasearch.com/people/michael-bazzell/XX _____

http:// zabasearch.com/people/michael-bazzell/XX _____

http:// zabasearch.com/people/michael-bazzell/XX _____
```

Figure 8.25: A portion of a Zaba fax submission identifying specific addresses.

People Lookup (peoplelookup.com)

Similar to many of the other people search sites, People Lookup allows a user to search for the home address, date of birth, and family members of a subject. The only option for removal is through fax.

✓ Conduct a search for yourself on **peoplelookup.com** and make note of the exact spelling of your name on the profile that appears.

✓ Use the online GotFreeFax service discussed in Chapter Three to send the basic opt-out form document that you created earlier. The form should include "People Lookup" as the name of the company and the fax should be sent to the following.
People Lookup Fax: 425-974-6194

People Search Now (peoplesearchnow.com)

In order to opt-out of People Search Now, complete the request form found at **www.peoplesearchnow.com/optout-form.pdf**. Alternatively, you can send them a letter including your complete name, any aliases or AKAs, your complete current address, your previous addresses, and date of birth to the following address.

PeopleSearchNow.com/Opt-Out
P.O. Box 29502
Las Vegas, NV 89126

People Smart (peoplesmart.com)

People Smart aggregates billions of records into a single interface and shares it with several companies. They provide personal details such as a home address, phone number, email address, and complete background checks. They also offer a reverse search service that will locate a subject based on a phone number or email address.

✓ Navigate to **peoplesmart.com/optout?** and supply your first name, last name, and state. Click on "Find my listing". This will provide a list of profiles that may be associated with you. When you find one, click on the green button labeled "This is me". The next page will display employment information that may be associated with you. If any of the information belongs to you, click the "This is me" button to the right of the listing. If not, click "Skip this step".

✓ Create an account. It may seem strange that you must create an account on the site to remove information. However, this is the only option. Only supply your initials and your anonymous email address. This will save the preferences that you provided and apply them to the following websites.

emailfinder.com   phonedetective.com   peoplesearchpro.com
freephonetracer.com   archives.com

That's Them (thatsthem.com)

This service appeared in late 2014. You will likely find a report of your personal details. Navigate to thatsthem.com/optout to immediately remove your entire collection of details. Enter only the details that you located about yourself from this site into the opt-out form.

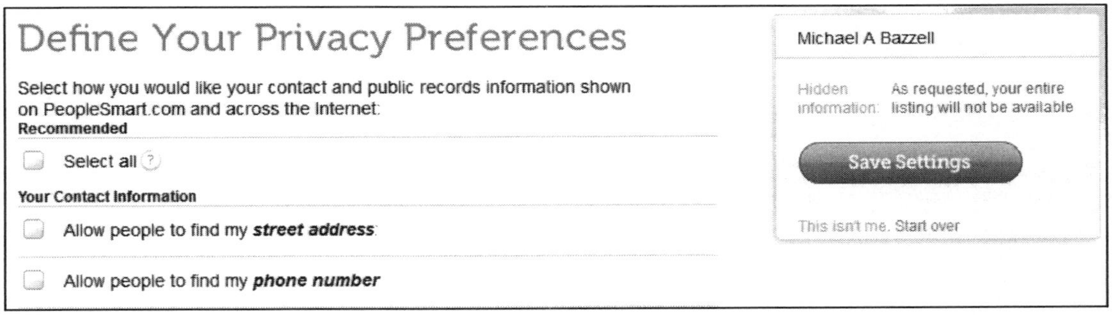

Figure 8.26: Privacy settings on People Smart.

Lookup (lookup.com)

The majority of the results on this site forward to Intelius. If you have already removed your information from Intelius, a user may not get information about you from Lookup. To be safe, an online removal request should be completed and takes only a few moments.

✓ Conduct a search on yourself on **lookup.com**. When you see a profile that matches your information, click on the link for that profile. The page you are forwarded to will want payment before seeing the data. Select the entire address (URL) of this page and right click the address and select "copy".

- ✓ Navigate to **lookup.com/optout.php** and complete the removal request form. Supply the first and last name as it appears on the profile, the URL that you copied in the previous step, your anonymous email address, your anonymous telephone number, and your current address that appears on the search of your name. Click "Submit".

- ✓ Allow up to 30 days. In my experience, you should receive an email verifying that the account was removed within one week. If you do not receive anything, contact them at optout@lookup.com.

Lookup Anyone (lookupanyone.com)

You may have noticed by now that a few of the companies that require a fax to be sent to them for data removal are using the same fax number. Add Lookup Anyone to this list. The fax number is owned by Intelius, which is most likely providing much of the data on the websites. It is possible that a single fax to this number would remove your information from all of the companies that it services. I doubt that this is the case. The only sure way to remove your data from each is a separate fax to each company, specifying the company that you want your data removed from. These multiple fax requests will ensure that Intelius has completely removed your information from their public database.

- ✓ Conduct a search for yourself on **lookupanyone.com** and make note of the exact spelling of your name on the profile that appears.

- ✓ Use the online GotFreeFax service discussed in Chapter Three to send the custom opt-out form document that you created earlier including a redacted driver's license. The form should include "Lookup Anyone" as the name of the company and the fax should be sent to:

    Lookup Anyone Fax: 425-974-6194

US Identify (usidentify.com)

By now, you may notice that some of the searches that you conduct on yourself are returning no results. If so, congratulations. This is a sign that your hard work is paying off. This may be the case at usidentify.com. However, if you do find your information present on the site, complete the following steps using the basic opt-out request form that you created in Chapter Three.

- ✓ Navigate to **http://www.usidentify.com/company/privacy.html**. Under section IV. Choice and Opt Out will be listed the information to include on the form. Include your full name, date of birth, and current city and state.

✓ Mail this form to the following address.

Opt-Out / USIdentify.com
9450 SW Gemini Dr. Suite #29296
Beaverton, OR 97008-7105

US Search (ussearch.com)

This company has been providing personal details about people via the internet since 1994. Beginning immediately, you can prevent them from offering your information to anyone else.

✓ Navigate to **ussearch.com/privacylock**. Supply your first and last name as well as state. Click on "Go".

✓ Review the profiles that were located and identify the profile that is associated with you. Click on "This is the record that I would like to block". A new page will be shown with a form that needs to be printed or saved. This form needs to be sent to US Search by either postal mail or fax. If you choose to send it through postal mail, print the form as well as a copy of the basic opt-out form created in Chapter Three. Mail them both to the following address:

US Search – PrivacyLock
PO Box 4145
Bellevue, WA 98009-4145

✓ For the tech savvy, save this page as a HTM or HTML file. Open the file with Microsoft Word. Save the page as a DOC file. Use GotFreeFax to send this new DOC file along with the basic opt-out form created in Chapter Three to the following fax number.

US Search – Privacy Lock
(425) 974-6242

Top People Finder (toppeoplefinder.com)

This site appears to have been acquired by another company, but an independent database still exists online. Removal is immediate through an online request.

✓ Navigate to **toppeoplefinder.com** and search for your information. If you locate a profile with your details, apply the next step.

✓ Navigate to **toppeoplefinder.com/remove.aspx** and complete the online form. Supply your full name and address exactly as it appeared in your search. Click "Search" and verify your listing.

PeepDB (peepdb.com)

The search field on this website does not always locate your information. You should attempt searching your name, but do not move on if you do not find any results. The following directions will ensure you remove your profile.

- ✓ Choose the link for the state where you reside. You will be prompted to click on a link for the first letter of your last name. This will continue, asking for the first two letters and then first three letters of your last name. You should then be presented with a long list of subjects that fit your criteria.

- ✓ Find your profile and click your last name. Click on the link "Get The Uncensored Listing". This will unmask your address and phone number. Click the link below the listing titled "Remove This Listing". This presents a new page with removal instructions.

- ✓ If you are a government employee, they require an email from your work email address that identifies the profile you want removed. I submitted my request at 4:00pm on 02/28/2013. The next morning, I searched for my name and the listing had been removed.

- ✓ If you are not a government employee, you can still request free removal. Follow the instructions on the removal page which includes sending a scanned copy of a photo ID. I recommend redacting everything on this scan except your name and street address that is visible on the PeepDB listing. If you want the listing removed immediately, you can pay them $3.95, however I do not recommend this based on their prompt response to a free request.

Sales Spider (salespider.com)

On its surface, Sales Spider appears to be a business search website. Searching your name within the site will likely not identify any personal results as a free user. However, there is a large database of personal profiles that probably contains information about you. Conduct the following steps in order to locate and eliminate your profile from this service.

- ✓ Navigate to google.com and conduct a search for your address on Sales Spider. If you live at 1212 Main and your last name is Bazzell, your search would look like this:

    site:salespider.com "1212 Main" "Bazzell"

- ✓ Research any results. If you locate a profile with sensitive information, find the section titled "Are You (Your name here)". Below that, you should see a link titled "Delete This Profile".

✓ Ignore any premium offers and click the link at the bottom titled "No Thanks – Just Remove". You should receive immediate confirmation.

W9R (w9r.com)

At first glance, W9R appears to be another people search website connected to the White Pages directory of user profiles. However, it possesses its own database of records from several public sources. In 2013, I was surprised to find a profile on me. Removal was easy and the following directions will guide you through the process.

✓ Navigate to **w9r.com** and enter your name. A custom Google search will present all matching results. If you have a common name, include a street name or address number.

✓ Click any accurate results from this search and then identify your name within the list of people on the W9R page presented. It will likely appear to be random names, and they will not be associated with you.

✓ Open any profiles associated with your name. Each profile will possess an option titled "Opt Out or remove" with a link titled "Click here". Click the link and complete the captcha that will be presented.

✓ You should be presented with a "success" notification. Attempt to refresh the profile page. You will receive an error notifying you that the page has been removed.

Poedit (poedit.org)

Poedit is a people search site that likely retrieves its information from other profile sites mentioned here. If you have found your details on other sites, they are probably here as well. Removal is easy.

✓ Navigate to **poedit.org** and search your name. You may find numerous results which can be displayed by state.

✓ Open your profile and copy the address (URL) of the exact page that hosts this information such as **poedit.org/person/MO/Springfield/John_W_Smith_113866.html**.

✓ At the bottom of the page, select the "Removal Request" link and complete the form.

Public Records 360 (publicrecords360.com)

Public Records 360 also appears to obtain information from other search websites. The removal process can be completed online and requires identity verification.

- ✓ Navigate to **publicrecords360.com** and search for yourself. Identify any profiles and note the address (URL) of each.

- ✓ Navigate to **publicrecords360.com/optout.html** and complete the form.

- ✓ Compose an email to optout@publicrecords360.com and attach either a redacted copy of your ID card, the completed opt-out form created earlier, or a notarized identity verification form available at the following online location. **p_pr360.commondatastorage.googleapis.com/images/notaryverificationform.pdf**.

Deleting Inaccurate Information

During your information deletion process, you are likely to locate inaccurate data. You may find a previous address or addresses where you no longer reside. Many privacy advocates encourage people to leave this information online to protect real addresses. This is an example of disinformation. I do not recommend leaving any information online that was ever accurate. While the expired data may not be a privacy issue, it can create a serious security problem.

Many online services will require you to complete a questionnaire to confirm your identity. Common examples would be when you open a new bank account online or request a credit report. The questions generated during this automated process are validated through your current credit report and personal profile. These questions are designed to be difficult to answer by anyone except you. The questions usually reference previous addresses and the precise amount of specific bills. The following example illustrates how leaving your previous addresses online can jeopardize your identity.

An identity thief decides to open a new credit line in your name. He has already obtained your full name, date of birth, and social security number from various sources. He completes a form on a credit lender's website and is asked two security questions to verify the identity. Figure 8.27 displays the security questions which include a previous residence street and current home mortgage holder. This type of verification is common on financial websites. The multiple choices make it easy to guess the correct answer, but an educated thief will conduct a quick search. Searching the victim's name on Spokeo identifies a previous residence addresses with the numbers masked. Figure 8.28 displays the results identifying Boyne Avenue as a previous street of the victim. A Google search of the four lender options identifies that only one of them is located in the area of the victim. Figure 8.29 displays this result with details of the location.

This scenario is far too common. This is why I recommend erasing all information from public view. An old address on a reverse search website can haunt you later. If you find information associated with you that has never been correct, you should leave it. If a people search website identifies your residence as a location where you have never lived, this can be beneficial. Misinformation is an effective privacy layer.

You have now made a huge dent in the amount of information that is available to anyone about you on the internet. This process will continue to be time-consuming, but will seem easier from this point forward.

---

1. Which of the following streets have you lived on?

  ◎ Wilmington Street
  ◎ Boyne Ave
  ◎ Washington Street
  ◎ Edwards Ave

2. Which of the following lenders do you have a mortgage through?

  ◎ Citizens Bank
  ◎ Connecticut Finance

Figure 8.27: Security questions from a financial website.

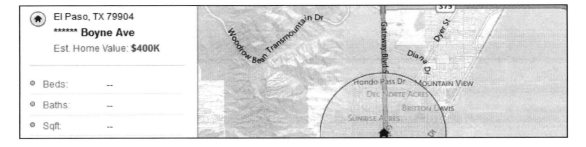

Figure 8.28: A Spokeo result identifying a street name.

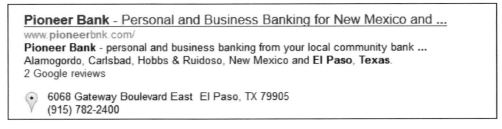

Figure 8.29: A Google result identifying the correct lender by location.

Chapter Nine

Data Brokers: Public Data

Data brokers collect public information like names, home addresses, purchase histories, credit card activity and other sensitive data. They create large databases and then sell copies to other companies. It's mostly marketing companies that are interested in this information, particularly those that do online targeting. But most will sell the data to anyone that will pay. Some of the companies mentioned earlier are technically data brokers. Since the primary focus was locating people, they were isolated from those in this chapter. The companies mentioned in this chapter collect and sell much more interesting data about you.

Aside from the basics needed to locate you, these data brokers, sometimes called information brokers, go deeper into your life to build a profile on you. Their databases include your DMV records, property records, voter records, weapon permits, internet search history, online comments, online aliases, shopping history, court history, and much more. Most of this is also geo-coded, which provides your location when the information was gathered. This is all done thanks to the advancements in technology and the internet. These companies take this data and package it into a profile that can be easily analyzed and used to target more products and services toward you. Removing your information from these databases will be similar to the previous methods discussed earlier.

Acxiom (acxiom.com)

This international data mining company has over 23,000 servers in Arkansas that are always collecting, collating, and analyzing your consumer data. With $1.1 billion in yearly sales, it is quite lucrative. Here is how you can remove your data from this collection.

- ✓ Navigate to **isapps.acxiom.com/optout/optout.aspx**.

✓ In the "Opt-Out" section, there are six categories that must be completed. Figures 9.01-9.03 display the recommended selections for these areas. Note that you can enter multiple entries on each field for additional email addresses, phone numbers, and mailing addresses.

✓ Click the "Submit" button and review the next page. Enter your anonymous email address for the verification address. This will be used to forward you to a final confirmation. When you receive this email from Acxiom, click the included link to finish the request.

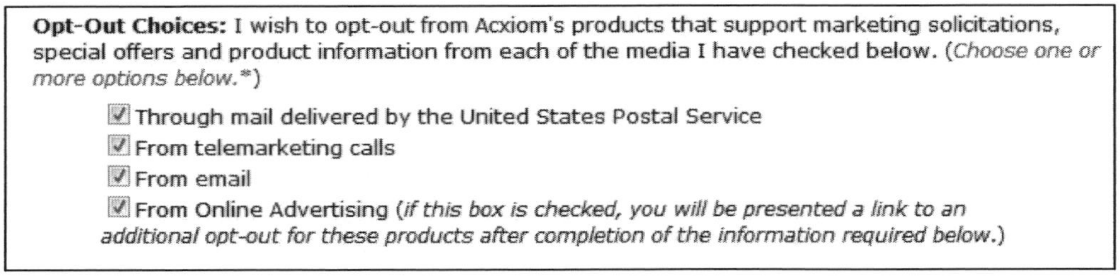

Opt-Out Choices: I wish to opt-out from Acxiom's products that support marketing solicitations, special offers and product information from each of the media I have checked below. (*Choose one or more options below.**)

- ☑ Through mail delivered by the United States Postal Service
- ☑ From telemarketing calls
- ☑ From email
- ☑ From Online Advertising (*if this box is checked, you will be presented a link to an additional opt-out for these products after completion of the information required below.*)

Figure 9.01: Opt-Out choices on Acxiom.com.

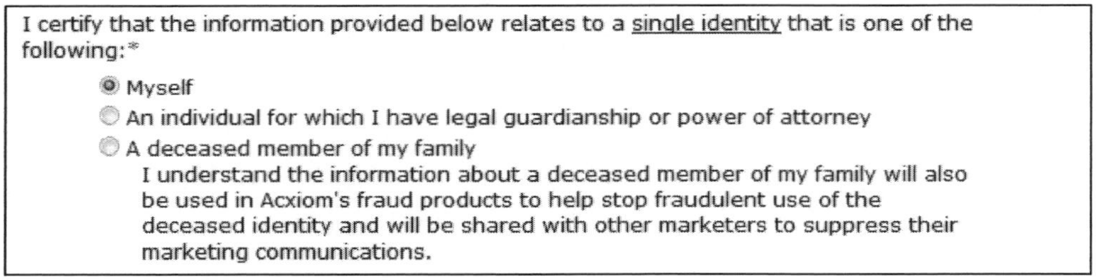

I certify that the information provided below relates to a single identity that is one of the following:*

- ◉ Myself
- ○ An individual for which I have legal guardianship or power of attorney
- ○ A deceased member of my family
  I understand the information about a deceased member of my family will also be used in Acxiom's fraud products to help stop fraudulent use of the deceased identity and will be shared with other marketers to suppress their marketing communications.

Figure 9.02: Opt-Out choices on Acxiom.com.

Full Names - please add all personal variations *
Michael Bazzell

Phone Numbers - please add all phone number variations
(618) 462-8253

Email Addresses - please add all email address variations
mike@computercrimeinfo.com

Mailing Addresses - please add all mailing address variations
1212 MAIN ST, ALTON, IL 62002-2829

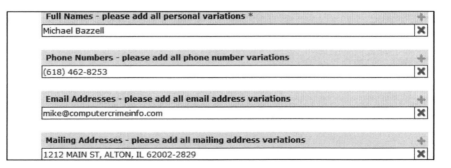

Figure 9.03: Opt-Out choices on Acxiom.com.

LexisNexis (lexisnexis.com)

LexisNexis is one of the largest data aggregation companies in existence. It is owned by Reed Elsevier, which is also the parent company of Choicepoint, Accurint, and KnowX. Chapter Ten will discuss removing your information from the vast non-public records of LexisNexis, but for now you should focus on the public records.

✓ Navigate to **lexisnexis.com/privacy/directmarketingopt-out.aspx** to access the online opt-out form. Supply your first name, last name, mailing address, anonymous email address, home phone number, and select all three options for removal.

✓ You will receive an email after the removal process has been completed. This email may include a verification link. Click it to confirm removal.

✓ Navigate to **lexis-nexis.com/clients/iip/removingInfo.htm** to read the instructions for removal from their people locator information products. Use your personal Gmail account to create two emails addressed to **lexisnexis@prod.lexisnexis.com** and **remove@prod.lexisnexis.com**. These emails should include your full name, mailing address, and anonymous telephone number in the body. This will remove your details from the P-TRAK and P-SRCH databases. Alternatively, you can mail or fax your information to the following address and fax number:

ATTN: LexisNexis Name Removal
PO Box 933
Dayton, OH 45401

Fax: 1-800-732-7672

✓ Each month, LexisNexis will re-apply the removal listings to make sure that your information continues to stay out of these databases. By default, this request will not remove your information from all fourteen people locator products provided by LexisNexis. To do this, you should add the following paragraph to the message:

Please remove the provided information from all LexisNexis People Locator products including, but not limited to, the following:

P-TRAK	USFIND
P-SRCH	X-TRAK
PSRCH2	X-SRCH
P-FIND	XSRCH2
P-CNSR	XZFIND
EZFIND	XLLFND
ALLFND	Person Report

✓ Navigate to **lexisnexis.com/risk/optstatus/default.aspx** to check the current status of web monitoring by LexisNexis. You will most likely see that your computer's internet history is being monitored. To disable this, click the link in red that is labelled "here".

Intelius (intelius.com)

Intelius has one of the largest personal information databases on the internet. Many websites that lure people into their services by offering free background checks simply forward the user to Intelius. No matter how well you have guarded your personal details such as home address, telephone numbers, work history, and family members, the chances are high that Intelius has your information. Any data that Intelius has is shared with multiple organizations and websites. Many employers use the data to inquire about potential employees. Those that visit online dating sites use the information to check on a potential date. Intelius charges a modest fee for the data they collect about you, but large volume users receive a substantial discount. Here is how to remove yourself from their system.

✓ Visiting **intelius.com** will give you a very brief sneak peek into your profile, but most information will be masked unless you pay. If you see any listing that identifies you, this means that Intelius has a complete profile of your personal data for sale. You do not need to make a purchase in order to delete the data.

✓ Navigate to **www.intelius.com/optout.php**. Within this form, upload the redacted image of your driver's license that was created in Chapter Three. Next, enter your anonymous email address. Optionally, you can enter additional information such as additional listings found under nicknames or misspelled names. Click on "Submit Opt-Out" when the form is complete.

✓ You should receive a confirmation email from Intelius once the data has been removed. Conduct another search and see if you can locate your data. If you can still see the information, wait a few days and try again. The information should be out of the system by then.

✓ It may not be necessary, but navigate to **yahoo.intelius.com/optout.php** and complete the online removal request form. This site has a removal request that applies to Yahoo's white pages listing for you, which is maintained by Intelius. It is probable that this data would be removed with the previous request, but this will make sure it is not missed.

TowerData (towerdata.com)

TowerData creates their databases based on a person's email address. They target companies that have a large database of customer email addresses. These are usually obtained from online offers and purchases from a website such as Amazon. Since you provide an email address any time you order something online, this data can easily be associated with you. TowerData creates a profile on you and your email address which includes, name, sex, age, and location. This data can currently be seen by anyone for free just by entering your email address. For less than ten cents, TowerData will disclose much more information stored about you. The next table summarizes the data attached to a profile.

Household Data	Purchase Data	Interest Data
Education	Automotive	Arts & Crafts
Net Worth	Baby	Blogging
Home Value	Beauty	Books
Home Owner	Marital Status	Business
Status	Occupation	Health
Household	Children	Travel
Income	Magazines	News
Residence Length		

TowerData offers a simple interface to remove your email address and all data associated with it. To remove your data, follow these steps:

- ✓ Navigate to **dashboard.towerdata.com/optout/**. Enter your email address and complete the captcha. Repeat for any additional email addresses.

- ✓ Alternatively, generate an email message to privacy@towerdata.com. Include each of your email addresses. You will receive an email notification at each address entered once the process has been completed. Read this email and click the verification link if presented.

Been Verified (beenverified.com)

This service has received a lot of attention after airing a series of television commercials encouraging people to locate someone. The free search conceals most of the personal information, but supplying a credit card number displays a full result. For each personal result, you will need a separate email address to remove that entry. Follow these steps for removal:

- ✓ Using your new personal email account, send an email to **privacy@beenverified.com** with a subject of "Information Removal". In the body of the message, include the following:

  Please remove all information associated with me from your site.

Your name as shown on the site
Your Age
Current address (City, State, Zip)
Previous addresses shown on the site
Listed Relatives

✓ You will receive an email confirming the receipt of the request. Click the included link and search again for the desired name to be removed. Find this exact listing among the results and click the "That's Me!" button. On the next page, enter the same email address you used to submit the removal request, and click the "Send Verification Email" button.

✓ You will receive an email notification containing a link to complete the removal; click the verification link. Shortly after the removal, you will receive a final email confirming the listing has been removed. Search the site in a few days to verify your data has been removed.

Accutellus (accutellus.com)

Accutellus is a leading provider of real-time information. The company builds profiles on people and shares them with other companies. The information collected includes the usual personal data. Accutellus goes a step further and collects personal details from promotional materials. This could include contest entries and giveaways. Removal is online and immediate.

✓ Navigate to **accutellus.com/opt_out_request.php** and complete the online form. Provide your anonymous email address and telephone number. Click "Submit request" when completed.

✓ Click the "Find People" tab and conduct a search for yourself. Supply only your name and state. You should receive no results.

Address Search (addresssearch.com)

This site provides a unique service that surprises many people. A person provides either a full name or an email address. The results will often identify a full profile including full name, email address, and residential address. Removal is immediate through an online form.

✓ Navigate to **addresssearch.com** and conduct a search on your name. If you find results, complete step 2.

✓ Navigate to **addresssearch.com/remove-info.php** and complete the online form. Supply the exact information located during the search for your details. Click "Submit" and conduct a new search to verify the information was removed.

Instant Check Mate (instantcheckmate.com)

This online database is commonly used by businesses that want to verify someone's home address and telephone number. The reports provided also include criminal records, charitable contributions, and other sensitive information. Three options are available to remove your information. Choose any one of the following.

✓ Navigate to **instantcheckmate.com/optout** and submit the online form. You will receive an email notification containing a link to verify the removal within 48 hours.

✓ You can email your request to support@instantcheckmate.com with "Opt-Out" in the Subject line. Include your full name, date of birth, and home address as it is listed on their website and they will remove your profile within 48 hours.

✓ Mail your removal request to the address listed below:

Instant Checkmate
Attn: Opt Out
4330 S Valley View Blvd, Ste 118
Las Vegas, NV 89103-4052

Core Logic (corelogic.com)

Core Logic is a consumer information company that caters to several types of companies. They provide personal credit reports, marketing information, mortgage reports, risk assessments, rental screenings, and financial analysis. They service several industries including automotive, insurance, government, retail, and legal. The opt-out process is only available through email.

✓ Create an email addressed to **custserv.res.ca@corelogic.com** with "Opt-Out" in the Subject line. Include your full name, date of birth, and home address. You should receive an email response with verification that your data has been removed.

Eliminating the public records from these databases will prevent your data from being sold to many companies and individuals. It will stop the general public from being able to access all of your details. This will not prevent your data from being shared with large organizations such as credit card companies and direct marketing agencies. For that, we need to go to the next level.

Chapter Ten

Data Brokers: Non-Public Data

In Chapter Three, you created a general opt-out request form for submission to companies. A second form, the "extended form", was mentioned which would include additional information that would qualify you to have further data removed. This data is often called non-public data. Such data is often shared with law enforcement and other government agencies. For law enforcement, this could include a local police department, a federal agency such as the FBI, or a number of offices that exist in government buildings nationwide. None of the methods in this chapter will prevent law enforcement from seeing your records. However, the techniques will help prevent your data from leaking into databases that can be bought by banks, lawyers, medical organizations, and credit agencies.

These methods are not for everyone and the removal process is much stricter. The companies that sell this data each allow people to have their information removed only if certain criteria are met. While each company offers specific wording on the requirements, the basic idea is that a person must fit into **one** of the following circumstances:

- ✓ The person is a judge, public official, or member of law enforcement

- ✓ The person is the victim of identity theft

- ✓ The person is at risk of physical harm

At first glance, you may think that you would not meet these requirements. The criterion is actually quite broad and many people can honestly declare that they fit into one of these statements. The first category is the most defined.

Judges: If you are a documented judge on a local, state, or federal level, you definitely meet the requirement. This also includes retired judges.

Public Officials: Many city, county, state, and federal employees are "public officials". There is a good chance that whatever your duties are, you have a presence in the public. Elected officials or those that provide information to the public are the easiest to declare. If your position has ever required you to speak to the press, disclose information to the public, or respond to public inquires, you are a public official. It will ultimately be up to you to determine if you meet this definition.

Law Enforcement: A large part of this book's audience is law enforcement. Whether you are a part-time or full-time officer or agent, as long as you are sworn by your local agency, county, or state, you fit in this category. This also includes retired officers and agents. The grey area is with those that are previous law enforcement but did not retire. I believe the Law Enforcement Officers Safety Act would apply here. This act establishes the meaning of a "qualified retired law enforcement officer" as it relates to the ability to carry a concealed weapon. It states that if a person was a police officer for a minimum of ten years and separated from service in good standing, the person qualifies for this definition. Therefore, if you meet this condition, you qualify for this data removal.

Identity Theft: With the number of identity theft cases on the rise every year, more of you are now technically victims of this crime. Some of these cases are much worse than others. People that have had homes and vehicles purchased illegally in their names by criminals are obviously victims of identity theft. The FTC defines identity theft as a serious crime that "occurs when your personal information is stolen and used without your knowledge to commit fraud or other crimes". Have you ever received a telephone call from your credit card company notifying you that someone is using your name and credit card number for unauthorized purchases? Have your friends told you that they received an email from your account telling them that you are stuck in another country and need money to get home? Has a disowned relative tried to open a credit line in your name to feed a drug habit? The examples are endless, but they all involve a situation where someone's "personal information is stolen and used without your knowledge to commit fraud or other crimes". Ultimately, you must determine if you fit into this category. If you are ever the victim of identity theft, report it to your local police, and obtain a copy of the report. Some data companies require proof.

Physical Harm: A person at risk of physical harm is allowed to have information removed from public access. I believe an argument could be made that any person is at risk of physical harm, but these companies do have some guidelines. Most want proof of this claim in the form of a police report identifying you as the victim of a violent crime or a copy of an order of protection issued by a court. Domestic abuse victims should have no problem meeting this requirement.

If you believe that you meet any of the criteria, you should create an extended opt-out request form. Basically, this is all of the information included on the basic form created in Chapter Three, but with a new section identifying how you meet one of the requirements. The data company may respond with a denial of your request, but this will not harm anything in your report. Many people have reported that sending a duplicate request after receiving a letter of denial resulted in a successful removal. Most likely, the person fielding requests is an entry level employee with little experience or authority in handling requests that vary from the norm.

To create the extended opt-out request form, open the basic opt-out request form that you created in Chapter Three. Remove the information that allowed for the entry of a URL of data found online. That will not be needed for these requests. In place of this section, you need to supply exactly how you fit into one of the qualifications mentioned earlier.

If you are a member of law enforcement, you could add a paragraph above your driver's license that states the following:

"I am a full-time sworn police officer in the state of _____ that is actively conducting investigations of violent subjects. This assignment has put me in immediate danger of physical harm. The attached letter from my supervisor confirms my position and assignment."

If you are the victim of domestic abuse, a sentence similar to the following could be added:

"I am a victim of domestic violence that has been reported to the police and prosecuted by the courts. I continue to fear for my safety. I have attached a copy of a police report/order of protection for verification."

If you are a parking enforcement employee for the city you live in, you could state the following:

I am a full time parking enforcement official for the city of _____. This work as a public official has created a hostile working environment and I am often targeted by the public. The attached letter from my supervisor verifies my employment and assignment."

You need to create a statement that is accurate for your situation. Be prepared to verify this claim through a police report or letter from your supervisor. Only you can determine if you are eligible for the removal of your private information. You are now ready to submit requests for removal. Figure 10.01 displays a completed form for law enforcement.

Date_____   Company_____

I request to have my name removed from your public and non-public databases. Here is the information you have asked me to include in my request:

Name: _____

Mailing Address: _____

Social Security Number *(If Required)*   _____

Date Of Birth *(If Required)*   _____

I am a full-time sworn police officer in the state of Illinois that is actively conducting investigations of violent subjects. This assignment has put me in immediate danger of physical harm. The attached letter from my supervisor confirms my position and assignment.
Thank you for your prompt handling of my request. I have also included a redacted copy of my driver's license below to prove identity.

Figure 10.01: An extended opt-out request form.

LexisNexis (lexisnexis.com)

You learned in Chapter Ten about the massive amounts of data in the hands of LexisNexis. Since LexisNexis is owned by the same company as several other data brokers, including ChoicePoint, Accurint, and KnowX, you can take the following steps to eliminate your information from all of them.

✓   Navigate to **lexisnexis.com/opt-out-public-facing-products** and complete the online form. Supply your full name and address. There will be several choices for the reason for your removal request and these options will vary by state. Select the appropriate reason and complete any additional information requested. This may include the place that you work or a report number of an identity theft. Click the "Add" button to save this record and then the "Finished" button. Figure 10.02 displays this form.

✓   On the next page, you can choose to either mail or upload your submission. For postal mail, print this page and attach the extended opt-out request form and any supporting documents. Mail these documents to the following address.

Privacy, Security and Compliance Organization
PO Box 933
Dayton, Ohio 45401

If you have a digital copy of these documents, you can upload them by clicking on the "click here" link in red. This will allow you to upload your extended opt-out request form and supporting document and eliminate the need to send these through postal mail.

Supporting Documents

LexisNexis strictly enforces their policy that demands supporting documentation for this type of removal request. For law enforcement, this would be a letter from your supervisor verifying your employment. The letter should also mention that you have an immediate threat of danger, which every law enforcement officer has. Public officials should include the details of their position and some verification of the position. This could be a copy of a workplace identification card or state certification acknowledging the position. For victims of identity theft or violent crimes, include a copy of the first page of your police report or order of protection. This will identify the police report number. You do not need to send them the detailed report about your incident.

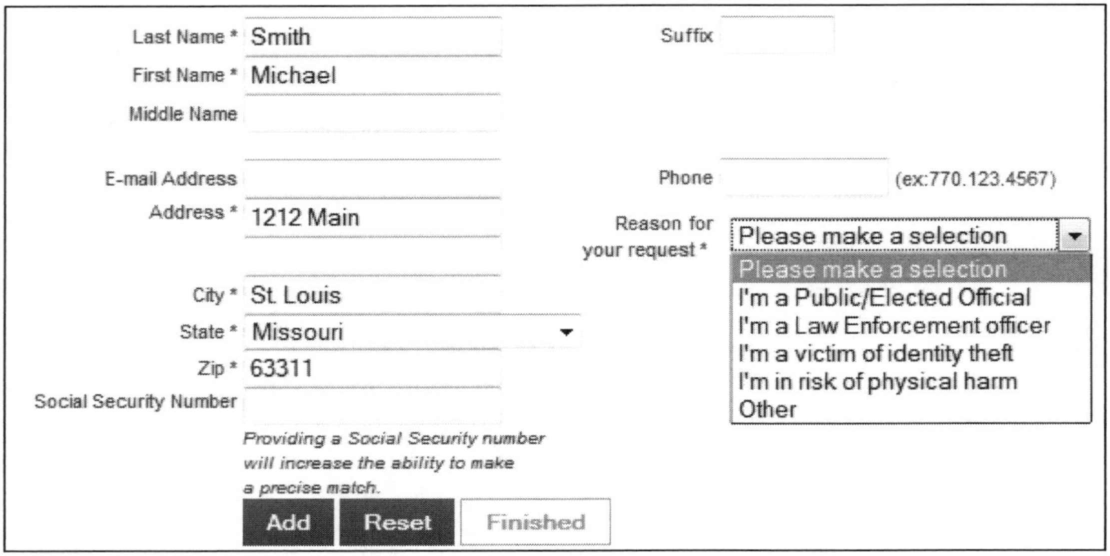

Figure 10.02: A LexisNexis opt-out form.

Westlaw (legalsolutions.thomsonreuters.com/law-products)

Westlaw is another one of the largest data broker companies and is owned by Thomson Reuters. The data is also provided to "Clear" which provides access to financial institutions, insurance companies, and healthcare entities. Similar to LexisNexis, Westlaw offers both public and non-public record searches.

- ✓ Navigate to **west.thomson.com/pdf/privacy/opt_out_form.pdf** and print the Westlaw public records opt-out form. Complete the form with your real information. You do not need to include your phone number, date of birth, or SSN. For the reason of request, provide a brief summary of your qualification for removal.

- ✓ Mail the extended opt-out request form, Westlaw public records opt-out form, and the Westlaw and Clear personal information removal request form to the following address.

Westlaw and CLEAR Public Records
ATTN: D5-S400 – Personal Information Removal Request
610 Opperman Drive
Eagan, MN 55123

InfoPay (infopay.com)

InfoPay is a public records affiliate network that provides people searches, background checks, reverse telephone lookups, and identity verification services on hundreds of websites. It consists of the following eight entities:

eVerify	EmailTracer
InfoRegistry	ReversePhoneCheck
TenantDetective	GovRecordsAccess
CreditScoreDirect	Phone Investigator

Each of these products has its own demanding opt-out process, and there is no general opt-out for all InfoPay services. The following instructions will remove your personal information from all of these services with one fax or postal request.

✓ Open a copy of your extended opt-out request form and supply the company name as "InfoPay, et al". Provide your name, date of birth, address, anonymous telephone number and anonymous email address. Provide a summary of how you qualify for the removal of records, and state that you want "all public and non-public records associated with the information provided removed from all databases including eVerify, InfoRegistry, PhoneInvestigator, ReversePhoneCheck, EmailTracer, TenantDetective, GovRecordsAccess, and CreditScoreDirect".

✓ Navigate to **www.everify.com/opt_out_form.pdf** and print this form. Provide the requested information in sections one through five. In section six, identify the reason for removal that is most appropriate for your removal request. Figure 10.03 displays the options. Note that the last option applies to anyone and does not require any documentation.

✓ If you want to send this request electronically, scan these documents and use GotFreeFax to send the completed forms to the following company and fax number:

InfoPay, et al
617-933-9946

✓ If you want to send these documents via postal mail, send both forms to the following address.

InfoPay
Data Opt Out Department
PO Box 990043
Boston, MA 02199

6. Please select the reason for your request as listed below:

☐ You are a state, local or federal law enforcement officer or public official and your position exposes you to a threat of death or serious bodily harm

☐ You are a victim of identity theft

☐ You are at risk of physical harm

☐ You have evidence the record is incorrect or expunged (please attach copy of appropriate documents along with this form)

☐ You prefer to prohibit your information from being made available through our service.

Figure 10.03: A portion of the InfoPay opt-out form.

Locate People (locatepeople.org)

Locate People is more of a person search site than a non-public data broker, but the removal process is as strict as the others in this chapter.

✓ Open a copy of your extended opt-out request form and supply the company name as Locatepoeple.org. Provide your name, date of birth, address, and anonymous telephone number and email address. Provide a summary of how you qualify for the removal of records, and state that you want "all public and non-public records associated with the information provided removed from all databases". Provide a redacted copy of your driver's license as discussed in Chapter Three. Also, include printed copies of the information that you would like removed. Figure 10.04 displays a portion of their website identifying qualifying criteria. The full opt-out requirements can be viewed at **http://locatepeople.org/index.php?xpath=privacy**. The exact requirements change often, and you should visit this site before submission.

✓ Either mail all of the forms and documents to the address below or use GotFreeFax to send all documents to the following company and fax number:

Opt Out Compliance Department
PO Box 990142
Boston, MA 02117

Locate People Fax: 888-446-1229

Figure 10.04: A portion of the Locate People privacy policy.

Smaller companies

There are several smaller companies that provide your personal information to the private sector but do not offer any type of removal process. Since they do not handle the volume that the other services mentioned here do, many people make no attempt to remove their information from these databases. Smaller data broker companies may not conduct a thorough review of the client requesting the personal data. This makes them a target for companies that may have criminal tendencies or hope to acquire data for illegitimate purposes. For this reason, I feel it is vital to request the removal of your data from their systems.

These organizations are not accustomed to opt-out requests, but I hope that this book will change that policy. I have listed the business name and form of contact for each company below. Create an extended opt-out request form for each one including your full name, address, date of birth, anonymous email, and brief summary of your situation that demands removal of your information. Send one form to each of the locations mentioned, either as a fax or an email attachment. You should receive correspondence through the email address provided which should either confirm removal or request additional information.

CBC Innovis
866-582-1514 (Fax)

EBureau
http://www.ebureau.com
/privacy-center/opt-out

First Data Security
phishing@firstdata.com

Interactive Data
info@interactivedata.com

International Research
Specialists
561-689-2256 (Fax)

Netwise Data
http://www.netwisedata.c
om/contact-us/

VeriFacts
800-381-9647 (Fax)
info@verifactsinc.com
(Email)

Chapter Eleven

Data Marketers

Data marketing companies sell personal data to businesses that want to sell a product or service. They collect information about you that assists them with matching these businesses to the most appropriate audience. These businesses include a wide range of organizations that sell everything from soda to mansions. The goal of data marketing companies is to identify people that are most likely to buy the specific product or service that a business is selling. When they do, they profit from this information and continue to build databases of your interests.

These marketing databases are less likely to be viewed by the general public than the databases discussed so far. Instead, they are bought, sold, and traded by private organizations that want to determine exactly how to entice you buy something. You probably experience the effects of this every day.

For example, if you have a vehicle made in 2007, you will start to receive extended warranty options on that type of vehicle in the mail in 2012. Your name, address, phone number, and vehicle information is in a database sold to companies that provide vehicle warranty services. The package is purposely meant to look like an official manufacture warranty, and the intent is to make you believe that you should buy this warranty in order to keep your vehicle protected. Instead, these warranties are often provided by companies that will be difficult to contact when needed.

If you are shopping on the internet and researching a specific pair of shoes, your computer stores data that identifies your shopping history. This information is passed to other websites that you visit. You may start to see shoes similar to those that you were looking at earlier begin to appear in advertisements on various pages as you browse the web. The goal of these ads is to determine what you are most likely to buy, and forward you to a website that will pay a premium for this information.

These are just two examples of the many ways that marketing companies try to keep track of what you are doing. It is common for companies such as these to have a complete profile on you that reveals more about your interests and buying habits than your closest friends and family are aware of. Similar to the earlier example of a department store knowing that a minor was pregnant before the family knew, businesses such as Amazon and Proctor & Gamble are using data to sell you more products.

If you enjoy receiving mailed advertisements, telephone calls, and emails encouraging you to buy specific products, you should skip this chapter. If you feel that this is an invasion into your privacy and are tired of being targeted for a profit, then this chapter will help eliminate this practice on you.

DMA Choice (dmachoice.org)

DMA Choice is an online tool developed by the Direct Marketing Association to help you manage your postal mail and email advertisements. DMA Choice represents about 80% of the total volume of marketing mail in the United States. This website allows you to create an account and specify what types of mailing databases you want to be included in. Further, it allows you to specify if you want to be removed from an individual company's list or all of the different company's lists. To do this, you must create a free account which requires you to provide your name, home address and a valid email account. You must then identify individual companies that have your information and request removal from their databases. Another option is to request removal by category such as catalogs, magazines, donation requests, political mailings, and credit offers. This process is time consuming and still allows companies to collect your data if you had any type of relationship in the past.

There is alternative solution. DMA Choice has two rarely used options that will remove a person's information out of the databases of all companies associated with DMA Choice. It will also remove personal information from companies that have an existing relationship with the person requesting the removal. This could include credit companies that you have had a loan with in the past or retail stores where you had previously subscribed to a mailing list. These databases are referred to as their "Deceased Do Not Contact List" and "Do Not Contact for Caregivers List". Since I do not want to encourage people to fake their own death, you should use the caregiver's list option.

- ✓ Navigate to **www.ims-dm.com/cgi/dncc.php** and complete the online form. In the "Primary Name" section, provide your name and address only. If you receive mailings under another version of your name, such as Michael or Mike, add that name as well.

- ✓ In the "Information About You" section, you must provide the name of your "caregiver". Most likely, you do not have an official caregiver, but you do not need one for this unofficial request. I recommend that you provide the name of your mother or father.

After all, they were your legal guardian while you were a child. If your parent is still living, he or she probably provides care to you in some form on occasion. If your parents are deceased, you can still put their name on this form. There is no verification process. Provide your anonymous email address where appropriate.

✓ Under the name of your "caregiver", there are five questions you must answer as your caregiver would answer. These are formalities of DMA Choice, and will not be verified. Figure 11.01 displays these questions and how I answered them as my father. Only one question needs to have an answer of "Yes" to meet the minimum qualification.

✓ You will immediately receive an email from DMA Choice acknowledging your registration. It will include a link toward the bottom that you should click to confirm the removal of your information.

✓ You can repeat this process for other family members if desired. If you are receiving unwanted advertising to a deceased relative, the website to have their information removed is **www.ims-dm.com/cgi/ddnc.php**.

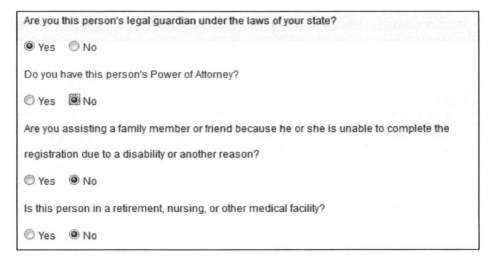

Figure 11.01: A portion of the DMA Choice "Caregivers Form".

Catalog Choice (catalogchoice.org)

If you find yourself bombarded with unwanted catalogs and advertisements in your mailbox, you are probably on many marketing lists as a valued shopper. The following instructions can be used to eliminate these mailings and remove your information from their databases. You must cancel with each individual company, but Catalog Choice makes this easy to do from one interface. If you do not receive unwanted catalogs, there is no need to complete these steps.

✓ Navigate to **catalogchoice.org** and click "Sign Up Now". Supply your initials instead of your name, a password, and your anonymous email address. Be sure to un-check the option to receive email from them.

✓ On the next page, assign a nickname to your home address. This could be "Home". Leave the "company Name" blank and add your actual home address. Click "Save new address" when finished.

✓ You will receive an email from Catalog Choice. Open this message and click on the link inside the email. This will confirm your anonymous email address as active.

✓ When you receive unwanted mailings, log into this site and select "Find Companies". Search for the company name and view the removal options. Usually, you will only need to click the "Submit Request" button at the bottom. This will send a notification to the desired company to remove you from all distributions. Since most companies remove the entry by address, your name is never required. If the company does require a name, they will see your initials that match the initials of the name that is in your profile. This will satisfy the requirements of the company removing you from their database.

✓ Occasionally log into your account and click the "Your Choices" menu option. This will display the current status of your removal requests. When a company confirms the removal of your information, this page will notify you.

I have used this successfully on several occasions. It usually works better than contacting the company directly. Figures 11.02 through 11.06 display the process of removing my information from Charter Communications after receiving over 40 mailings from them advertising new cable television choices. You do not need to submit a reason for removal; the default option is "Prefer not to answer".

Figure 11.02: The search box for Catalog Choice.

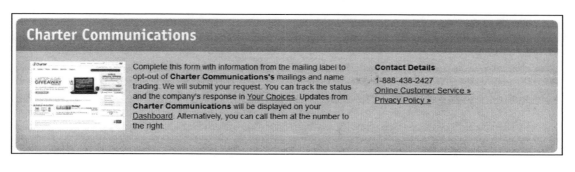

Charter Communications

Complete this form with information from the mailing label to opt-out of **Charter Communications's** mailings and name trading. We will submit your request. You can track the status and the company's response in Your Choices. Updates from **Charter Communications** will be displayed on your Dashboard. Alternatively, you can call them at the number to the right.

Contact Details
1-888-438-2427
Online Customer Service »
Privacy Policy »

Figure 11.03: Removal instructions for Charter Communications on Catalog Choice.

Name

Choose the precise spelling from the mailing label. Click the *New Name* button to add a recipient or spelling variation.

Recipient Name

Michael bazzell   ▾   New Name

Address

Choose the location where you receive this mailing. Click the *New Address* button to add a new location or address variation.

Address

Test - 1212 Main Hous ▾   New Address

Figure 11.04: The default name and address for removal on Catalog Choice. You can add multiple addresses for removal.

Catalog Info

Account or Customer Number

987698145349876

The customer number uniquely identifies you to the company, and is usually found next to the mailing label. If you do not have a Customer Number, the company may have acquired your name from a third party marketing list.

Figure 11.05: The catalog info section on Catalog Choice. Supplying the account number from the mailing will help identify the appropriate record to delete.

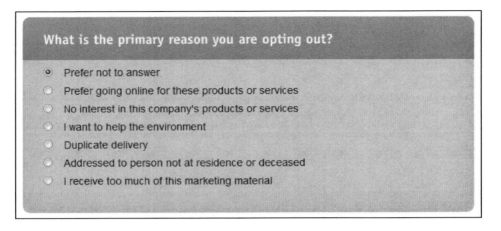

Figure 11.06: Final submission with optional opt-out reason.

Epsilon (epsilon.com)

Epsilon provides a broad range of loyalty marketing services spanning database marketing, direct mail, email marketing, web development, loyalty programs, analytics, data services, and strategic consulting, among others. It is owned by Alliance Data which has an estimated twelve billion dollars in assets and eleven thousand employees. Its clients include over 2200 global brands such as Hilton Hotels, Verizon, Kraft, and other familiar names. Epsilon collects information about you and sells it to these companies in order to assist them in deepening their relationship with customers. Fortunately, you can easily break-up with them.

Epsilon relies on DMA Choice for opt-out information on some of their databases. Completing the previous steps will remove much of your information. Your information will still be present in some direct mail advertising databases including the "Abacus Cooperative Database", the "Compiled File Database" and the "Shopper's Voice Database".

The Abacus Cooperative Database is an Epsilon database in which your name and address may be listed. Members of the Abacus Cooperative (mostly catalog and retail companies) contribute information about their customers in exchange for information about prospective customers that may be interested in their products. To remove your personal information from this database, complete the following action.

✓ Use your new personal email account and create an email message with the subject of "Removal" to **abacusoptout@epsilon.com**. Include your full name and current address in the body of the message. If you prefer, you can call them at 888-780-3869 and leave this information on a recorded message.

The Epsilon Compiled File Database is a database of consumer information, including demographics, lifestyle attributes and transactional data. This database is compiled from several public and proprietary sources (such as property deeds), self-reported responses, and transactional data. To remove your personal information from this database, complete the following action.

✓ Use your new personal email account and create an email message with the subject of "Removal" to **dataoptout1@epsilon.com**. Include your full name and current address in the body of the message. If you prefer, you can call them at 888-780-3870 and leave this information on a recorded message.

The Shopper's Voice is a membership program that allows you the opportunity to provide consumer information through voluntary surveys and other means, with an aim to improve retail services. If you have never completed any retail or online surveys, you should not be in this database. If you have, complete the following action.

✓ Use your new personal email account and create an email to **contactus@ shoppers-voice.com**. Include your full name and current address in the body of the message. There is no telephone option for this removal.

These three options will remove your information from the specified databases. You will still likely exist in the main Epsilon databases. You can choose one of the following methods for removal from their overall marketing databases.

✓ Email **optout@epsilon.com** and include the following information:

> Full name (including middle initial)
> Current address

✓ Phone 1.888.780.3869 and leave the above information.

✓ Mail the above information to the below addresses:

U.S. Consumers:	Canadian Consumers:
Epsilon	Epsilon
P.O. Box 1478	41 Metropolitan Rd.
Broomfield, CO 80038	Toronto, ON M1R 2T5
	Canada

Infogroup (infogroup.com)

Infogroup collects information on people worldwide using a variety of sources including telephone directories, public records, annual reports, government data, newspapers and publications, postal service information, mail order buyers and responders, census information, deed and assessment information, utility transaction data, and others. Its database contains information on 210 million people. The company derives yearly revenues of $380 billion by selling access to its database to companies needing new customers.

Infogroup does not offer any online opt-out request and does not accept an opt-out request form via fax. They also do not offer an option to search for personal information to identify the details needed for a removal request. If you have found your personal information located within various databases mentioned in this book, you can be sure that your information is on Inforgroup's servers as well. After numerous telephone calls and email communications with them, I have discovered that the following is the best way to remove your data from Infogroup and InfoUSA.

✓ Use your new personal email account and create an email to **contentfeedback @infogroup.com.** The subject line in the email should be "Opt Out Policy Request". In the body of the message, type the following:

> Per your Opt Out Policy at infogroup.com/home/privacy-policy.aspx, I request the removal of all consumer records located in any and all databases accessed or maintained by Infogroup and any other businesses owned by Infogroup for the following individual.
> Your Name
Your Address
Your City/State/Zip

This request is authorized based on the following statement located on the website listed above.

"Upon a visitor's request, Infogroup Inc. will initiate reasonable efforts to functionally delete the visitor and his/her personal information from its database."

✓ Wait one week. If you receive no email confirmation of the deletion of your records, call (800) 321-0869. This is a number to InfoUSA, a part of Infogroup. You will immediately receive a person that can verify that the records have been deleted.

Haines & Company (haines.com)

This company provides data in print and on compact disc to businesses looking to target a specific audience. This includes complete city directories searchable by name, address, or telephone number. They also store real estate information that can identify specific details about your house and family members. For example, they can identify a house's basement type, building size, exterior make-up, number of bedrooms, year built, and presence of a pool or fireplace. They can also filter by the age of household members, income, and length of residence. This information is ready for sale to contractors, insurance agents, and home improvement companies. They also cater to fundraising companies with intent to identify people that are most likely to donate money. Removal from these databases involves an email request.

✓ Use your new personal email account to create an email addressed to the following email addresses:

criscros@haines.com
info@haines.com
custserv@haines.com

✓ In the body of the email, type the following request:

Please remove my name and address from any and all databases maintained by Haines.
Your Name
Your Address
Your City/State/Zip
Your Telephone Number

This includes, but is not limited to, data maintained by the following organizations.

Haines & Company, Inc.
Americalist
Americalist Fundraising
HainesDirect
Haines

Coupon Packs

You are probably familiar with the coupon packs that are delivered to residential addresses. At one time, these were always addressed to "Resident" and included coupons covering a wide range of products and services for the home. While these generic packs are still delivered, companies have found that personalizing coupons to a specific audience is more valuable. Therefore, knowing your personal details and interests allows them to target you with specific offers. These companies do not share your information with the general public, but you can request the removal of your details from their databases. The following instructions remove your data from the three most popular services:

Valpak (Valpak.com)

- ✓ Navigate to **www.coxtarget.com/mailsuppression/s/DisplayMailSuppressionForm** and complete the online form. You do not need to provide any name; they submit removals by address only.

Vallasis (valassis.com)

- ✓ Navigate to **redplum.com/tools/redplum-postal-addremove.html** and complete the online form.

DirectMail (directmail.com)

- ✓ Navigate to **directmail.com/directory/mail_preference/** and complete the form on the right side of the page. Provide your complete address, but only list your initials instead of your full name. Include your anonymous email address and click "submit".

- ✓ On the next page, select the first option "I do not want to receive any special offers in the mail". Scroll to the bottom and click "Continue". On the next page click "Submit Registration".

- ✓ Check your email and confirm the link supplied in an email from DirectMail. This will verify that you have been added to their "National Do Not Mail List".

Offensive Mailings

The United States Postal Service (USPS) offers a rarely used form to prohibit specific types of mailings from being delivered to your home. It is called a prohibitory order and was created to prevent adult content from reaching an audience of children. The Prohibitory Order program provides a deterrent to continued mailings by a specific mailer advertising a product or service you consider erotically arousing or sexually provocative. Submitting this order will cause the USPS to demand the removal of your information from the database of the company that mailed the content. It is up to you to determine if content is arousing or provocative, and the power of this form should not be abused.

This method is targeted toward those with children. Police officers have used this technique to eliminate unwanted erotic mailings initiated by vengeful suspects. Families have used the form to stop adult content requested by mischievous friends of their children. Once any adult content is received at a home, it is very likely that the address will be added to several other adult content databases for future mailings. This form will also add the address to a database of addresses not wishing to receive adult advertisements.

✓ Navigate to **about.usps.com/forms/ps1500.pdf** and print the form. Complete all requested information and attach the original mailing that you find inappropriate.

✓ Deliver the form and offensive mailing to any post office.

Online Coupons

Many companies are embracing the idea of online coupons. These coupons can be printed from the internet and redeemed in stores like any other printed coupon. These appear to be very beneficial for the consumer. A person can conduct a brief search on various coupon websites for a specific product. When a coupon is located, it can be printed and applied to the sale of the product. Unfortunately, many people are not aware of what is happening behind the scenes with most online coupons.

Most of today's online coupons use special bar codes that help identify information about the life of the coupon. Each of these online coupons has a unique serial number embedded into the bar code. This can allow a company to track the date and time it was obtained, viewed and, redeemed. It can also identify the store where it was used and the original search terms typed to find it. This is all reported back to the original source of the digital coupon. Retailers are combining this data with information discovered online and off, such as your age, sex, income, shopping history, internet history, and your current location or geographic routine. This creates a profile of the customer that is more detailed than ever. This profile can also include the other products purchased during the transaction and form of payment.

If you choose to use printable coupons, you have no choice but to give up some privacy. Here are some suggestions if you want to continue receiving these deals.

✓ When prompted for personal information, supply an alternate name. These details are seldom verified by the coupon delivery system.

✓ Before and after printing online coupons, delete your temporary internet files, or "cookies". I recommend a free utility called CCleaner which is available at **piriform.com/ccleaner**.

✓ Log out of any social networks, especially Facebook, while researching and printing coupons. Companies will collect your profile data to associate you with the coupon and purchase history.

Loyalty and Reward Cards

Large stores such as Safeway and Vons offer a loyalty card, sometimes referred to as a reward card, to shoppers for instant savings on products. These stores offer "members only" sales that discount specific products for customers that have a membership card. If a customer does not have a card, the full price is charged instead of the sale price. This business model encourages a customer to favor a specific business for discounted items. Further, the business now possesses a large pool of information about customers.

Since customers are required to disclose their name, address, phone number, date of birth, gender, and email address to receive a card, stores can create an individual profile of your habits. This profile can include the items you buy, dates and times of purchases, form of payment, and location of purchase. They can also analyze the data and determine how often you buy a product, the amount you will spend on a product, and your overall value to the business. This data helps them individually target you with advertisements and track your redemption. The data can then be shared with other companies, law enforcement, private investigators, attorneys, and anyone else that will pay or use the courts to obtain the data.

I still encourage people to use these cards. In Chapter Fifteen, I will explain how these programs can be used beneficially for the purposes of disinformation. On a recent trip, I saved over $100 with my Safeway card and did not risk any privacy. I provide the following suggestions when using any type of rewards or loyalty program that relies on physical cards to redeem savings:

✓ Immediately stop using your current loyalty cards. Apply for a new card as needed at the customer service area of the store.

✓ Provide an alternate name on the application for the card. I have never heard of anyone requesting identification for verification. Provide a real mailing address, but not yours. The address should exist. I recommend supplying the address of the store that you are requesting the membership.

✓ Most loyalty cards insist on a working telephone number. This number can be used to access your account in case you lose your card. Provide your anonymous telephone number created in Chapter Three.

✓ Trade your loyalty cards with other people whenever you get the chance. Explain the privacy concerns to friends and family and encourage them to swap cards with you. I have not found success in approaching strangers with this method. It tends to generate skepticism and a complaint to the store manager.

Online Advertising

Online advertisements are practically everywhere you look on the internet. Search engines, email accounts, social networks, and media sites all use these ads to create the revenue needed to fund their free services. Many people ignore the ads and do not consider them intrusive. Unfortunately, these ads still track your internet history and collect information about you and your interests. This tracking enables companies to conduct online behavioral advertising.

Online behavioral advertising, also known as interest-based advertising, is a way of serving advertisements on the websites you visit and making them more relevant to you and your interests. Shared interests are grouped together based upon previous web browsing activity and web users are then served advertising which matches their shared interests. In this way, advertising can be made as relevant and useful as possible. Relevant ads can also be delivered based upon the website content you have just been viewing. This is known as 'retargeting'.

The browser add-ons discussed in Chapter Four will stop much of the tracking, but no software can stop it all. There are opt-out processes to prevent the most common trackers from spying on you while you are on the internet.

Network Advertising Initiative (networkadvertising.org)

The Network Advertising Initiative (NAI) is a coalition of over 80 online advertising companies that allow consumers to opt out of online behavioural advertising. It has an interactive website where you can examine your computer to identify those member companies that have placed an advertising cookie file on your computer. You can then choose to opt-out of that company's tailored marketing. The instructions below will take effect immediately. I recommend visiting the website occasionally to make sure you have the appropriate settings.

✓ Navigate to **www.networkadvertising.org/choices/**. Allow page to load and it will list numerous advertisement companies and identify the status of your participation in their advertisement campaigns. Figure 11.07 displays a small selection of the companies and a notification that an active tracking cookie has been placed on my computer.

✓ Click the "Select all" button which will highlight the "Opt-Out" checkbox on every entry. Click the "Submit" button to apply the request.

Your Online Choices (youronlinechoices.com)

This is another website that attempts to fight online behavioral advertising. It gives you control of which advertising "cookies" are allowed on your system. It will identify any tracking files present and give you the option to change the settings so that the tracking is disabled.

✓ Navigate **www.youronlinechoices.com/opt-out-interface**. Allow the website to load and scan your computer. Figure 11.08 displays the interactive menu.

✓ If you want to disable all of the behavioral tracking, click the "Off" button next to "Turn off all companies".

All NAI Member Companies (96)	NAI Members Customizing Ads For Your Browser (26)	Existing Opt Outs (0)

These 26 member companies have enabled Online Behavioral Ads for this web browser.	Company Name	Select all ☐
	24/7 Media	☐
Click the company name to find out more about a member company. To opt out from targeted ads by one or more member companies, check the box(es) in the "Select" column next to the company name(s), and then hit the "Submit your choices" button. You can also click the "Select all shown" box to pre-check all the listed companies before you hit the "Submit" button. Need help?	AddThis (including XGraph)	☐
	AdRoll	☐
	AOL Advertising	☐
	AppNexus, Inc.	☐
	Batanga Network	☐
	Break Media	☐

Figure 11.07: A portion of the Network Advertising Initiative opt-out page.

Turn off all companies	Off		Turn on all companies	On

Turn on or off individual companies

Company	On/Off	Info
Adatus	◉ On ○ Off	ⓘ
Adconion Media Group	◉ On ○ Off	ⓘ
AddThis (formerly Clearspring)	◉ On ○ Off	ⓘ

Figure 11.08: Tracking choices on youronlinechoice.com.

Datalogix (datalogix.com)

This company boasts on its website that their data includes almost every U.S. household and more than $1 trillion in consumer transactions. Much of this is digital information passed through online ordering, which you eliminated during Chapter Four. They also possess direct mail databases on most people. The following instructions will guide you in the opt-out process.

✓ Navigate to **datalogix.com/privacy** and scroll down to the section titled "Choice".

✓ The third "click here" link will expand an opt-out form that should be completed for each member of your household.

About Ads (aboutads.info/choices/)

About Ads is similar to NAI. This website will identify any files on your computer that are monitoring and tracking your online history. Choosing the "Select All Shown" option and clicking "Submit" will alter these files and enable the opt-out feature with each service. This should be completed monthly to be effective.

Publishers Clearing House (pch.com)

You have likely seen the television commercials with random people being given oversized checks at their front doors. These occasional winners are the result of millions of people sharing their personal information for marketing purposes. PCH also shares their data with "partner" companies to expose your details further. Requesting removal only requires an email message.

- ✓ Create an email to **privacychoices@pchmail.com** including your full name, address, city, state and zip code information.

- ✓ Specifically state that you "request removal of your personal information from both on-line and off-line marketing information sharing databases".

These techniques will stop a large portion of the marketing projected toward you. None of these methods will remove your information from every marketing database. There will still be occasional evidence of your details being sold to another company. Chapter Sixteen will identify methods to notify you if this happens.

Chapter Twelve

Public Records

While reading this book, you have probably found your home address, telephone number, and family member's names on the internet. Most likely, this data was collected at some point from public information. From there, it has spread to dozens of websites and marketing lists. In order to prevent your information from re-appearing on these websites, you must make some changes to your public profile.

Some of the most vital information that you should protect from public view is data that everyone has legal access to. If you think that your date of birth, divorce records, voter records, traffic offenses, and civil litigation are protected, you are wrong. This is all public data and there is nothing stopping individuals and private companies from collecting your information and selling it to anyone that wants it. This is not the end of the chapter though. Just because something is a part of the public record, it does not mean that you cannot make it difficult to find. This chapter will help you reverse some of the damage that is already out there, but your future actions are more important. Please read Chapter Sixteen thoroughly to discover how you can make yourself invisible to anyone trying to find you.

Property Tax Records

I believe that the most important data to consider in reference to privacy is your property taxes. Most likely, you own a home and you pay yearly property taxes. These may be incorporated into your house payment. Your property taxes will likely be in your or your spouse's name, or maybe both. This single record will announce your home address to the world. The numerous people search sites that were discussed in Chapter Eight rely on these records to locate people and charge a fee to disclose your location. Having an unlisted telephone number does not hide this data. There are two approaches to fixing this problem, and I recommend applying both.

Data removal

Because the tax records are public, you cannot request the information be removed from public view. However, you can request that the information is removed from the online database. Each county has a database that stores the property tax records. Most of them make this data available online through the county website. The companies that have been discussed here know how to collect all of that data and add it to their own data set. This data is more reliable in locating people than telephone directories or social networks. You cannot remove the records yourself. You will need to contact the county in a very specific way.

✓ Conduct a search on the internet for your county's property tax database. If you live in Cook County, Illinois, your search may look something like "Cook County IL property tax search". For most counties, this will display some type of database that can be searched by name, address, or parcel number. Search your own information and make note of the parcel number and a telephone number for the Clerk's office.

✓ Telephone your County Clerk's office and politely make the following request:

"I have noticed that my personal information and address are visible on your property tax website. I realize my property tax records are public records and must be made available to anyone that wants to personally view them, but I would like to have the online records removed. I have recently discovered several websites that have extracted the information from your database and made it available for the purpose of locating people."

✓ Continue the conversation and include any other reason to enforce the removal request. This can be any of the reasons identified in Chapter Ten that may make you more vulnerable to danger. Below are four examples.

"I am a (choose one) police officer / public official / community leader and possess a higher risk of danger from the community."

"I have been the victim of identity theft and I am removing my personal information from data mining companies in order to prevent further criminal activity"

"I have been a victim of a violent crime and fear for my safety. The ability to locate me based on your online records has increased the danger of bodily harm"

"I have been the victim of threats and harassment. The ability to locate me by searching your online database places me in immediate danger of bodily harm."

Choose your response wisely. You may be asked to provide proof of your claim. Subjects that attend my training sessions have notified me that proof of their statements were never requested. Some attendees have stated that they received great resistance in these telephone calls and were occasionally told that the request was impossible. If this happens, call again and request the Information Technology (IT) division. Repeat the above process to them. Most likely, a computer professional will be the person that will ultimately be responsible for removing the information. Attendees have confirmed that this second call was successful.

Removing your information from this online database is a huge victory. However, this does not hide your address from the public completely. It also does not remove your information from companies that have already obtained the data. The previous chapters should help with that. It will prevent data mining companies from getting easy access to it, but someone can still find you with a personal visit to the County Clerk's office. Most likely, a helpful employee would even conduct the search for them and offer to write down or copy the information. My recommendation is to never have your property taxes in your name.

Ownership Change

If you plan on living in your current home for the next several years, you may want to consider legally changing the owner of your residence to a living trust. This will also change your property taxes to the name of the trust. Before you do this, you must establish a living trust for yourself and your spouse. The full details of establishing a living trust are far beyond the scope of this book. There are many great books that will help you accomplish this, and many people complete the process without the guidance of an attorney. Here are a few of the benefits.

- ✓ You can place any assets in a living trust including real estate, investment accounts, and personal property in your home.

- ✓ Having all of your assets in a living trust can keep your assets out of probate, which provides a great layer of privacy.

- ✓ It will give you complete control of what happens to your assets when you die without making the details public.

- ✓ The trust can be amended at any time or completely revoked.

- ✓ You can name your trust anything you want. It does not need to include your name, and I do not recommend identifying yourself or your family in the name of the trust. It could even be "Hiding from the Internet Living Trust".

After you establish a living trust, you can contact the County Recorder in your county to change the ownership of your property. In my county, the fee was $41.

New Ownership

If you are planning on purchasing a new home or making any permanent move, this is a huge opportunity to make it practically impossible to be located. This method is only for those of you that are truly committed to being invisible from the public. The general idea of this process is credited to J.J. Luna, the author of the book *How to be Invisible*. This book is considered by many to be the definitive guide to removing yourself from public view. A new edition was released in 2012. The basic premise of this specific method is the following:

✓ Purchase an official LLC from a registered agent in New Mexico. These are never publicly associated with your real name, but you own the business. These are very affordable.

✓ Purchase your new home using the LLC as the owner. The LLC can also purchase vehicles and other property.

✓ Never associate your name with the house you live in. Personal mail should be delivered to a PO Box. Utilities should be in the name of the LLC.

If you are at all intrigued by these possibilities, purchase Luna's book immediately. The methods are completely legal. If you are in any way targeted by the public, such as police officers or victims of harassment, this will guarantee that you will have a home to be safe in.

Voter Registration Records

If you are a registered voter, your home address is visible to the public. Most likely, there is a database on your county's website that will list every registered voter's home details for the entire county. Figure 12.01 a redacted portion of this report. It identifies a person's full name, home address, dates voted, and political affiliation. Data mining companies know about these and use them to collect information about you. Removing this information is vital to protecting your privacy.

✓ Navigate to **blackbookonline.info/USA-Voter-Records.aspx** and select your state. On the next page, select your county. This will forward you to the online voter database for the county you live in. Some counties do not have online access yet.

✓ Search for your name in the database. If you locate your records, it will probably identify both your residence address and a unique number associated with your voter record. Make note of this number. It will also likely display each date that you have voted in either local or national elections.

✓ Contact your County Clerk's office and request to add your voter registrations information to the "Address Confidentiality Option". This can be done at the same time you request the removal of your property tax information from the online database. This option was originally designed to help participants keep their home address secret. Most people that take advantage of this program are victims of violent crime, harassment, or identity theft. If this request is denied, request an address change and provide your post office box information.

Precinct-25

NAME	HOME MAILING ADDRESS	DATE LAST VOTED
GINGERICH, A█	15█████ ST BETHALTO 62010	0409D
GINGERICH, H█	15█████ ST BETHALTO 62010	
GINGERICH, M█	15█████ ST BETHALTO 62010	0312R 0411 1110
GOLDEN, THE█	13█████ BETHALTO 62010	
GONZALEZ, G█	44█████ APT 5 BETHALTO 62010	

Figure 12.01: A voter registration report from a county website.

Military Recruiting Databases

Section 9528 of the No Child Left Behind Act of 2001 requires all school districts to release student names, addresses, and telephone numbers to all military recruiters. If you do not want military recruiters to add your child to their recruiting database, you can demand that the school not release the information. This removal option is a part of the Family Educational Rights and Privacy Act (FERPA), but is rarely offered.

✓ Navigate to **leadps.org/images/content/479/Military_OPT-Out.pdf** and print the form. This form only requires the school name, student name, student signature, and parent signature. Figure 12.02 displays a portion of this form.

✓ Deliver this form to any schools that your child attends.

> I, _____ , hereby exercise my federal right, granted to me by the Congress of the United States under Section 9528 of the *Elementary and Secondary Education Act of 1965*, as amended by the *No Child Left Behind Act of 2001*, (and any other applicable state, federal or local law or any school policy), and hereby request that the name, address, and telephone listing of
> _____ , a current student at _____ High School, not be released to military recruiters without prior written parental consent. I do, however, consent to the disclosure of such information to institutions of higher education other than military schools.

Figure 12.02: The removal options of a FERPA form.

Aristotle (Aristotle.com)

This website relies on public records to assist in political campaigns. This includes voter records and county data. If you located your personal information on any county website, Aristotle has your data for sale. A removal request is accomplished through email.

- ✓ Use your new personal email account and create a message to **remove@aristotle.com**. In the body of the email, state that you request "Any and all information associated with the following person removed from all online and offline databases maintained by Aristotle". Include your full name and home address.

Date of Birth

Many companies request your date of birth from you to verify that it is indeed you that they are talking to. This information, as well as a social security number or mother's maiden name, are poor methods of verification. This data is readily available to the public. The government often provides your date of birth through public records such as birth certificates, voter records, marriage records, license details, and court records. Many of the companies discussed in Chapter Nine and Chapter Ten are responsible for the availability of this information. Removing yourself from their databases is a great start. The following opt-out requests will eliminate specific public records archived about you.

DOB Search (dobsearch.com)

This website has a focus on obtaining a person's date of birth, but also provides more content

including address, family members, telephone numbers, and business affiliations. The removal process is through their website.

- ✓ Navigate to **dobsearch.com** and conduct a search of your own information. The result will list links to possible profiles of you. This will often display your age and family member's names. You must pay $3.99 for the full report, but that is not necessary.

- ✓ Select your profile(s) and click the link at the bottom labeled "Manage My Listings". Type "I AGREE" in the acceptance box and click "Continue". Select your entries and click "Continue". On the next page, enter the anonymous email and anonymous phone number you created in Chapter Three and select how you want to receive the confirmation code. Click "Submit" when finished.

- ✓ Enter the supplied confirmation code and click "Submit" to complete the block request.

Archives (archives.com)

This website has an emphasis on genealogy, but also caters to those conducting background checks and looking for public records. I found many personal details about me including my birth date and location, parents and other relatives, and home address. They offer an online removal request that is valid for five years.

- ✓ Navigate to **archives.com** and conduct a search on your name. The site will identify the types of records located, but will require an account to see the records. You do not need to create an account.

- ✓ Navigate to **archives.com/?_act=Optout** and complete the online form. Include your name as it appeared in your search. In the additional information box, include details of your request such as "Please remove all records associated with me" or further information about safety concerns. Click "Submit". Figure 12.03 displays a portion of the removal request.

- ✓ You will receive an email confirmation when the request has been processed.

Please tell us who you are	
☑ *Same as above*	
Your First Name: *	Michael
Your Last Name: *	Bazzell
Your Email Address: *	987sdf@notsharingmy.info — *This is where your confirmation email will be sent. If we have trouble locating your personal record or have any questions, this is how we'll contact you.*
Confirm Your Email: *	987sdf@notsharingmy.info
Additional Information: *	Please remove all records associated with me

Figure 12.03: A removal request on archives.com.

Ancestry (ancestry.com)

This is the most popular online genealogy website. The majority of the millions of records contain details of people that have been deceased for a long time. However, there are many current records of living people. The personal profiles in the database are created by a combination of public records and content provided by users of the website. If you have a relative that is interested in your family history, there is probably a profile of you on the website. This often includes your date of birth, marriage record, and home address. Request for removal is through email communication. This removal process will also delete personal information from familytreemaker.com, genealogy.com, rootsweb.com and others.

✓ Navigate to **ancestry.com** and click "Search all records". Search for your first and last name and provide the year of your birth. This will identify any records associated with you. The details of the records will be masked unless you purchase an account, which is not required. Figure 12.04 displays two search results from public data.

✓ Selecting one of these results will display the details that the actual record contains. These details are only visible to registered users. Figure 12.05 identifies the type of information available about me to registered users of Ancestry.

✓ Use your new personal email account to email **support@ancestry.com.** In the subject of the email, type "request for information removal". Include in the email your full name and date of birth. If you know the exact URL address to the page in which the information appears, specify it and identify the portion of the page you would like to have removed. You may be asked to provide a copy of government issued identification.

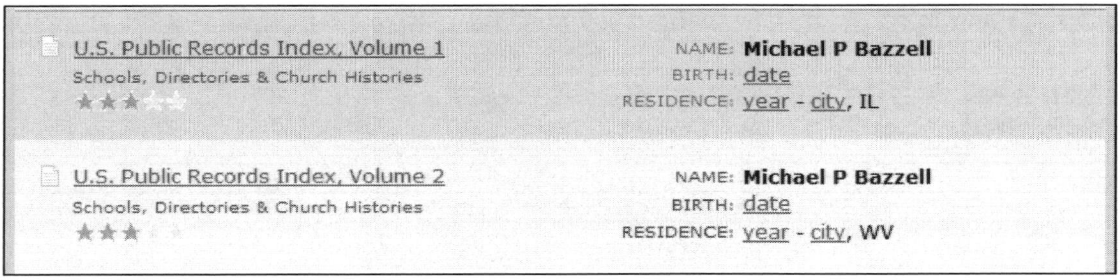

U.S. Public Records Index, Volume 1	NAME: **Michael P Bazzell**
Schools, Directories & Church Histories	BIRTH: date
★ ★ ★ ★ ★	RESIDENCE: year - city, IL
U.S. Public Records Index, Volume 2	NAME: **Michael P Bazzell**
Schools, Directories & Church Histories	BIRTH: date
★ ★ ★	RESIDENCE: year - city, WV

Figure 12.04: A search result on Ancestry.

Michael P Bazzell's
actual record contains:

- **Full name**
- **Address**
- **Phone number**
- **Birth date**
- **Residence state**
- **Residence city**
- Plus, more interesting facts to help you build your family tree.

Figure 12.05: A teaser from Ancestry.

Court Records

Civil and criminal court records are public information. Anyone can visit their county court and search local court cases on county owned computers. Most courts have uploaded this live database to the internet. A quick search on my county's court database identified profiles by subject name which included civil cases, traffic offenses, misdemeanors, and felonies. There is very little that you can do about information in your profile. You should visit the following website and select your state of residence.

blackbookonline.info/USA-County-Court-Records.aspx

Select your county and visit the county's online court database. Search your name and verify any cases that you are involved in. If you have only one offense, you can contact the state's attorney's office for your county and request an expungement form. If the expungement is approved, the details of the event will be removed from all court databases. This will not remove the data from any private websites that possess a copy of the archive. Below is a list of websites that provide court records for a small fee. If you want to be sure that your expunged case is removed from these websites, visit the link for contact information. Contact each site and inform them that their database discloses details of an expunged case. You should receive no resistance in removing the data.

BCS Backgrounds	https://usabackground.com
Complete Backgrounds	completebackgroundchecks360.com/privacy.html
Court Records	http://www.courtrecords.org/2011/privacy.php
Court Registry	courtregistry.org/index.php?xpath=privacy
Court Click	courtclick.com/terms.php
Criminal Pages	criminalpages.com/optout/
Criminal-Records	criminal-records.org/privacy.php
Data Detective	datadetective.com/privacy.php
Detective Unlimited	detectiveunlimited.com/privacy-policy.html
Public Backgrounds	publicbackgroundchecks.com/privacypolicy.aspx

Chapter Thirteen

Telephone Directories

If you have made it through the techniques mentioned in previous chapters, this section will be a breeze. Removing your telephone numbers from these databases is usually an automated online process that provides immediate results. Most telephone databases also include a home address associated with each telephone number. This makes it very important to remove these listings if you want to keep your home address private from the general public. These steps will also stop many of your unwanted calls.

Do Not Call Registry (donotcall.gov)

This is the most common opt-out request conducted by people. It adds your telephone number to a database of numbers that are passed on to telemarketing companies from the government. The companies are forced to remove these numbers from their automated systems used for telemarketing. This should stop unwanted sales calls and add a tiny layer of privacy for you. You can register landlines and cellular numbers, and it is recommended that you register all numbers that you own.

- ✓ Navigate to the site listed above and click the "Register a Phone Number" button. Identify up to three telephone numbers that you want removed from telemarketers' databases. Provide your anonymous email address and click "Submit". Verify the information and again click "Submit".

- ✓ Check your inbox. You will receive a separate message for each number that you registered. Click on the link in each message to confirm the removal request. You will be forwarded to confirmation that the number was entered into the registry. Figure 13.01 displays a portion of this online form.

REGISTER YOUR HOME OR MOBILE PHONE NUMBER

Follow the registration steps below. Click here for detailed registration instructions.

1. Enter up to three phone numbers and your email address. Click Submit.
2. Check for errors. Click Register.
3. Check your email for a message from Register@donotcall.gov. Open the email and click on the link to complete your registration.

If you share any of these telephone numbers with others, please remember that you are registering for everyone who uses these lines.

NATIONAL DO NOT CALL REGISTRY

STEP ONE

Phone Number:	3145551212
	3145551213
	3145551216
Email Address:	2kjhg34@notsharingmy.info
Confirm Email Address:	2kjhg34@notsharingmy.info

Figure 13.01: The National Do Not Call Registry entry page.

Political Calls

The Do Not Call Registry does not apply to politicians and the robo-call systems that they use. There is no law that prohibits these calls or allows you to demand to be removed from their systems. However, there is a non-profit organization that is trying to fill this void.

Stop Political Calls (stoppoliticalcalls.org)

This website allows you to create an account and request that your telephone number be removed from political call databases. The free service will then send your contact information to all political parties, candidates, political action committees, and any other organization that makes political robo-calls and ensure that they are told that you no longer want robo-calls from them. There is currently no enforcement of this removal, but most politicians will remove your number in fear of losing a vote.

✓ Navigate to **stoppoliticalcalls.org** and click "Skip to the website". In the middle of the page, click the highlighted link "Register for free now". Carefully complete the online form with specific information. Use only your first and last initials as your name, pick a security question that does not divulge any personal information about you, and provide your real telephone number that you want removed from the databases. Provide your anonymous email address as the contact. Do not provide any mailing address.

You will need to renew this free subscription every year. Only supply the minimal amount of information required and do not disclose any personal details.

Landline Telephone Numbers

Telephone number directories are generally split into two categories, landline and cellular. The way that landline data is acquired is much different than cellular data. Much of the landline data is obtained from the companies that create phonebooks and city directories. This data originates with the telephone companies that provide the service. If you have a landline telephone at your house in your name, this information is available to the public. If your number is unlisted, that does not mean that it is not in public databases. In fact, most people with unlisted numbers are listed in the online directories mentioned in this chapter. This is because public information such as voter records and tax data leak telephone numbers into public databases. If your number is not listed as private, you should request this option with your telephone service provider.

During this contact with the telephone company, I recommend that you update your contact information with them. Once you have established service with the telephone company, there is no further need for them to verify your details and check your credit. You can now basically change your information to whatever you want. Obviously, the address of service must stay the same. However, you can change your billing address to your post office box address. This will eliminate your home address from a database that is shared for marketing purposes. Your bill will now be sent to the post office box.

Next, consider changing the name on the account. This cannot be a complete change, but changing a portion of the name will make your listing more difficult to find. For women, the easiest change would be your last name. Calling the telephone company and notifying them of a last name change is common. There is no verification process. If you are married, you may want to change it to your maiden name. If you are not, tell them you recently were married and give them your mother's maiden name. For men, consider a change of the spelling. I have found success with the following conversation.

"Hello, my name is Michael Bazzell, and I have service through your company. This really is not that big of a deal, but your contact information for me has my name spelled completely wrong, and I would like to finally correct your records. You have my first name as "Mike", but it is actually "Michael" spelled M I C H E L. My last name is spelled B A S I L. Could you correct the record?"

These corrections are made immediately and never verified. Now, my listing has my first and last name spelled wrong. Anyone researching my location will have difficulty finding this listing. Companies will probably get a hold of this data and continue to make new databases. This will not have a big impact on you since your last name is spelled differently or changed completely. You should now focus on removing the correct data from the internet.

White Pages (whitepages.com)

White Pages possesses one of the largest national databases of landline telephone numbers. More importantly, they offer free access to their data to other online directories. They even share the data through an application programming interface (API) that makes collecting this data very easy. Fortunately, the removal process is simple.

✓ Navigate to **whitepages.com** and click on the "Reverse Phone" tab. Search for your listing by entering your telephone number. You can also search by name or address. If your listing is present, click on your name to open the profile.

✓ Click the "Edit" button to create an account on White Pages with your real name and anonymous email address. You can bypass the "Login with Facebook" option by clicking the link at the bottom. Identify any sensitive information and click the "Edit" button. This will allow you to delete any information desired. After the listing looks appropriate for your level of privacy, click the "Submit" button. The data will be removed immediately. Figure 13.02 displays part of this page.

✓ Subsidiary websites of White Pages, such as **411.com** and **phonenumber.com** will eventually be updated with the lack of the removed content.

Figure 13.02: A White Pages removal request.

Yellow Pages (yellowpages.com)

Yellow Pages is owned by AT&T and is a partner of AnyWho. They use Intelius as a provider of data, but maintain their own database of listings. The removal option is online and immediate.

✓ Navigate to **anywho.com/reverse-lookup** and type your telephone number. This will forward you to the Yellow Pages side of the site and will identify any profiles that include that number. Click on the first profile with your name on it to view the profile. Directly below the name, address, and telephone number, you should see a small blue link labeled "Remove Listing". Figure 13.03 displays this link.

✓ Click the link and verify the information in the online removal submission form. For

"Removal Reason", select "General Privacy Concerns" and click "Remove Me". You do not need to provide an email address. The listing should be removed within 24 hours. Repeat this process for all profiles associated with the telephone number.

Freda J Bazzell   Add to Address Book | Print

757 Purvis Dr, Wood River, IL 62095
618-259-7625

Are you Freda J Bazzell? » Remove Listing   Information provided solely by Intelius

Figure 13.03: A Yellow Pages profile listing.

Addresses (addresses.com)

Addresses also uses an Intelius database for reverse phone number searches and provide their own unique online opt-out request form. The process is identical to the process for Yahoo.

- ✓ Navigate to **addresses.com** and conduct a search for your telephone number. The result should appear as a profile for each person living at that address. Make note of the exact name identified with the number.

- ✓ Navigate to **addresses.com/optout.php** and complete the online form. For "Removal Reason", select "General Privacy Concerns" and supply your name and address as it appeared on the original search of your telephone number. You do not need to provide an email address. Click "Remove Me" when finished and search again in a few hours. The listing should be removed. Repeat this process for all profiles found.

Infospace (infospace.com)

Infospace is yet another website using Intelius for search results. The following process should look familiar by now.

- ✓ Navigate to **infospace.com** and conduct a search for your telephone number. Make note of the exact name identified with the number.

- ✓ Navigate to **infospace.intelius.com/optout.php** and complete the online form. For "Removal Reason", select "General Privacy Concerns" and supply your name and address as it appeared on the original search of your telephone number. You do not need to provide an email address. Click "Remove Me" when finished and search again in a few hours. The listing should be removed.

Super Pages (superpages.com)

Like many telephone directory websites, Super Pages queries a database associated with White Pages. Removing a profile from White Pages does not necessarily remove a listing from Super Pages. Therefore, you need to request removal from this specific database.

    ✓ Navigate to **superpages.com** and click "Find People". Conduct a search of your name or telephone number. This will display any profile that is associated with the information. Click each name to view profile.

    ✓ Directly below the listing is a blue link labeled "Remove Listing. Click this link to open the removal request. Figure 13.04 displays this listing option.

    ✓ Click the link and verify the information in the online removal submission form. For "Removal Reason", select "General Privacy Concerns" and click "Remove Me". You do not need to provide an email address. The listing should be removed within 24 hours. Repeat this process for all profiles associated with the telephone number.

    ✓ Subsidiary websites of Super Pages, such as **switchboard.com** will eventually be updated with the lack of the removed content.

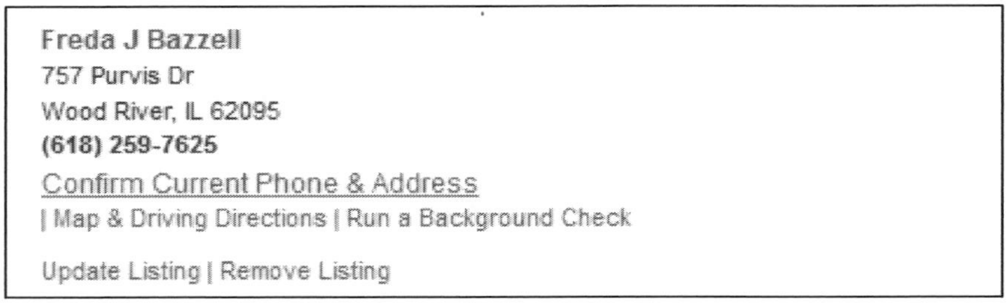

> Freda J Bazzell
> 757 Purvis Dr
> Wood River, IL 62095
> **(618) 259-7625**
> Confirm Current Phone & Address
> | Map & Driving Directions | Run a Background Check
>
> Update Listing | Remove Listing

Figure 13.04: A Super Pages removal option.

411 Info (411.info)

This site is different than 411.com and possesses a unique database independently of the other listings here. The removal process has a new twist as well.

    ✓ Navigate to **wpremove.411.info** and enter your telephone number. This will load a new page with a verification form.

    ✓ Verify that your name and address are associated with the telephone number. If no listing was found, there is no action to take. Dial the toll free number listed on this page from the landline number that you want removed from the database. If you call from a different number than the number to be removed, it will not work. You will hear a message announcing a four digit pin number. Enter this number in the online form and click "Submit". Figure 13.05 displays this screen.

Search Bug (searchbug.com)

In its prime, Search Bug was the preferred site of law enforcement for reverse telephone searches. The site has not kept up with newer services but still maintains a lot of information. In 2014, Searchbug began demanding a $20 fee for information removal. The following instructions will explain the official process plus an unsupported option to request a fee waiver.

✓ Navigate to **searchbug.com/tools/reverse-phone-lookup.aspx** and search for your number. If you see a successful result in the "Free Records" section, click on the result and then the "Remove" button for immediate removal. The free results are usually only available for business listings.

✓ If you see a successful result in the "Premium Records" section, click on "Premium Records - free preview" tab and print the page(s) with your listing(s).

✓ Circle or highlight your listing(s) to be removed and create a letter requesting to "block your listing" from appearing on Searchbug. Include your name, complete current address listed, and signature.

✓ Include this printed documentation and a check for $20 payable to Searchbug.

✓ Send your removal request to:

> SearchBug, Inc. c/o Removal
> 364 2nd St, Suite 4
> Encinitas, CA 92024

✓ Optionally, if you meet any of the qualifications mentioned below, include the following text to request a waiver of the $20 fee.

> "Due to (Choose one: numerous privacy concerns, threats of bodily harm or death, my status as a domestic violence victim, a documented severe identity theft, or my position as a police officer, judge, etc.), I request a waiver of the $20 fee for personal information removal from your website. I thank you in advance for your assistance with my physical safety."

This is not guaranteed to work, but most companies would rather delete your records than risk a liability lawsuit if something happens to you.

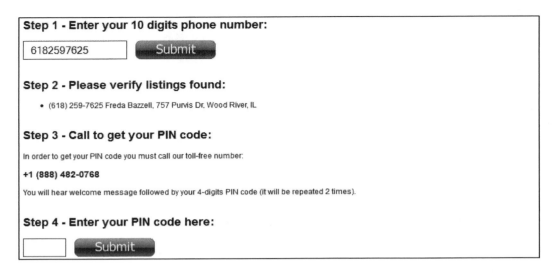

Figure 13.05: A removal request on 411.info.

Reverse Phone Lookup (reversephonelookup.com)

This website appears to possess an independent database of landline telephone numbers similar to White Pages. The following technique will remove your number.

- ✓ Navigate to **reversephonelookup.com** and search your telephone number. If you receive a result, continue to the next step.

- ✓ Navigate to **reversephonelookup.com/remove.php** and complete the form. Provide your telephone number, initials, anonymous email, and generic removal request. Your listing will be deleted during the next scheduled database update.

Phone Detective (phonedetective.com)

This website offers reverse telephone number searches of all types of telephones. An online opt-out request form provides immediate removal.

- ✓ Navigate to **phonedetective.com** and search your telephone number. If you receive a result, continue to the next step.

- ✓ Navigate to **phonedetective.com/PD.aspx?_act=OptOut** and complete the form. Provide your telephone number, initials only, and anonymous email address. Figure 13.06 displays a properly completed request.

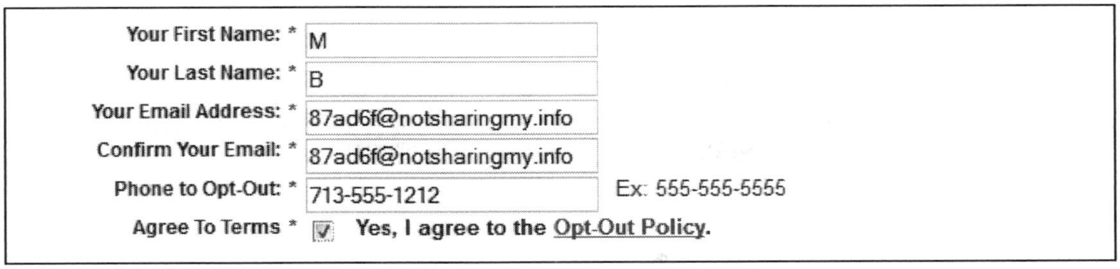
Your First Name: * M
Your Last Name: * B
Your Email Address: * 87ad6f@notsharingmy.info
Confirm Your Email: * 87ad6f@notsharingmy.info
Phone to Opt-Out: * 713-555-1212 Ex: 555-555-5555
Agree To Terms * ☑ Yes, I agree to the Opt-Out Policy.

Figure 13.06: A Phone Detective opt-out submission.

10 Digits (10digits.us)

This service's name indicates that it is a telephone lookup website. While it does offer telephone search by name or number, its capabilities also extend into address records. The self-removal process is easy.

✓ Navigate to **10digits.us** and search your name, address, or telephone number. View any results and note the address (URL) of the profile that you want removed.

✓ Navigate to **10digits.us/remove** and complete the online form. You will need to identify the exact address of the page(s) that you want removed and upload a digital copy of your redacted driver's license that you created earlier. You should receive a notification of removal within two days.

Cellular Telephone Numbers

There are fewer cellular number directories than landline directories. There is no official white pages style of phonebook for cellular numbers. That does not mean that the numbers are private. Many companies are attempting to create databases of cellular numbers and make them available to the masses. There are several methods they use to collect your number.

All of these databases rely on someone supplying a cellular number to them. Usually, this is you. When you use your cellular number as a contact for anything official, you take the chance of this number becoming public information. For example, when you sign up to win the new car at the mall and supply your name, number, and address, that information gets added to a large database. When you locate and print online coupons, you are often required to provide your personal information including a telephone number. This content also gets added to various databases. The advancements in technology allow for immediate identification of a telephone number to determine if it is a landline or cellular number. This identification can also be added to the database. Chapter Sixteen will discuss how you should protect this information in the future. Next are the methods for removing your cellular number from databases.

Reverse Genie (reversegenie.com)

Reverse Genie is one of the best websites for a reverse telephone number search. Because of this, it is one of the first that I recommend for removing your personal information. Since they do not offer an online submission for removal, you must submit a request by mail or fax. I prefer the fax method as it is free and receives a faster response. The complete privacy policy for this site can be found at **www.reversegenie.com/data_optout.php**.

✓ Navigate to **reversegenie.com** and enter your telephone number to search for your number's profile, if it exists. Copy this address (URL) to place it on your request. The URL of the result will look something like the address below. Figure 13.07 displays one of several results associated with a telephone number. The results often display full contact information as well as a map.

    http://www.reversegenie.com/reverse_phone/618-463-3505

✓ Edit your Custom Opt-Out Request Form discussed in Chapter Three. Add the URL of your profile to your request form. The company name should be Reverse Genie.

✓ Using GotFreeFax, send the completed from to the fax number 888-446-1229.

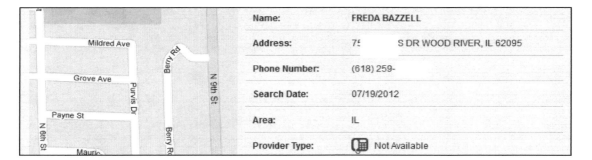

Figure 13.07: A redacted Reverse Genie search result

Free Phone Tracer (freephonetracer.com)

This is one of the sites that had my information associated with my cellular number. I will never know how they obtained my information, but I now know that they no longer have it.

✓ Navigate to **freephonetracer.com** and conduct a search of your cellular number. Take note of the exact information that is associated with the number

✓ Navigate to **freephonetracer.com/FCPT.aspx?_act=Optout** and complete the online form. Provide the exact information that you observed during your search and your anonymous email address. For the reason, type "General Privacy Concerns". Click "Opt Out" when complete. Figure 13.08 displays a completed sample form.

✓ Return to **freephonetracer.com** and conduct a search. The information should purge immediately.

Your First Name: *	Bob
Your Last Name: *	Wilson
Your Email Address: *	kj2345@notsharingmy.info
Confirm Your Email: *	kj2345@notsharingmy.info
Phone to Opt-Out: *	713-555-1212 Ex: 555-555-5555
Reason For Opt-Out: *	General Privacy Concerns

Figure 13.08: A Free Phone Tracer opt-out form.

Caller ID Databases

You probably know that when you call a landline telephone number from your home landline service, you pass along the caller ID information about your account. If your home phone is registered in your name, your name will appear on the caller ID screen of the receiving telephone. Many people do not realize that the name associated with your cellular telephone is also provided to the receiver's caller ID. Most cellular companies now announce your name and number when you call landline telephones. You cannot stop this data from being transmitted, and this practice is acceptable to the telephone companies because you are generating the contact by placing the call. Only a few years ago, this would have been fairly safe. Today, anyone can look up your cellular number.

There are an abundance of reverse caller ID service providers that will allow anyone to identify the owner of a number for less than a penny. One service that offers a free trial of this type of query is Service Objects. Navigate to the following website and search your cellular or landline number.

www.serviceobjects.com/developers/lookups/geophone-plus

You will likely see your name and cellular service provider displayed publicly. Attempting the same search at **privacystar.com** will also likely present your name as associated with your cellular number. There is no point in contacting the numerous reverse caller ID providers and requesting removal. While some have this option, most do not. Additionally, your data will be repopulated soon by your service provider or another third party company. Instead, you should consider modifying the subscriber information on your account. The following true scenario should help guide you through your own process.

I conducted a search for a relative's number through seven unique reverse caller ID services. All of them accurately identified her name as associated with her number. With permission, I logged into her online billing account and viewed her details. She was one of five members of a family plan with AT&T. Not only was AT&T providing the information of the subscriber, but also each individual name associated with each number on the family plan. I changed this relative's name to "A. Unknown". Within seven days, I conducted another query on her cellular number. The caller ID information associated with it was updated to "A Unknown".

You can likely log into your own online portal for your cellular account. If you are on a family plan, attempt to change the name as it appears for your individual number. If you are not within a family plan and have only one number on the account, attempt to change the name associated with the bill. Some services allow this activity through their website. If yours does not, consider calling them and specifically ask to change the information associated with your caller ID.

Other Online Directories

New websites promising accurate reverse telephone number information appear routinely. Some of these stick around and achieve slight growth, but most disappear or become unused. Those that are promising tend to become acquired by a larger data company. You should routinely conduct a search of your telephone number on Google and Bing to view the results. If you find too many spam results, try placing quotes around the number. If you find a website that has posted your personal information, start snooping around and try to find a link titled "Privacy" or "Terms of Service". These links often identify the procedure for removing your information. If you cannot find such a process, there is one last thing to try.

Most data mining websites, including telephone directories, have established some type of policy that prohibits children from posting their information. If this information is identified by the company, a manual removal is conducted immediately. As an example, assume that you found your telephone number and address on the website cellrevealer.com. This site offers mediocre reverse cellular telephone number lookups. They do not have any sort of removal option and provide no opt-out instructions. However, at the end of their privacy policy is the following content.

"We are in compliance with the requirements of COPPA (Children's Online Privacy Protection Act), we do not collect any information from anyone under 13 years of age. Our website, products and services are all directed to people who are at least 13 years old or older."

COPPA is an act passed by congress in 1998 which can be found in its entirety online. It was created to place parents in control over what information is collected from their young children online. The Rule was designed to protect children under age 13 while accounting for the dynamic nature of the Internet. The Rule applies to operators of commercial websites and online services directed to children under 13 that collect, use, or disclose personal information from children, and it applies to operators of general audience websites or online services with actual knowledge that they are collecting, using, or disclosing personal information from children under 13. Basically, it makes it illegal for a website to knowingly display any personal information about children under the age of 13. This is one reason you see many social networks enforce an age limit.

You can use this to your advantage. If you have a child under the age of 13 in your home, this may be a way to force websites to remove your information. Let me explain by providing two different scenarios.

Scenario # 1: Your child is eight years of age and lives in your residence. You conducted a search of your cellular telephone number on cellrevealer.com which identified your name and address. On occasion, your child uses this telephone number to communicate with friends and family. Therefore, it is fair to say that cellrevealer.com currently displays information that identifies a cellular telephone number used by a child under the age of thirteen and associates the number with the child's home address.

Scenario # 2: You have no children, but you have a niece that is ten years of age that occasionally visits your house. When she is there, she often uses your landline telephone to stay in touch with her parents. You located your landline telephone number listed on numberguru.com which identified your home address. Therefore, it is fair to say that numberguru.com currently displays information that identifies a landline telephone number used by a child under the age of 13 and associates the number with the child's current location.

Sending the following email to any contact email address on the website should generate immediate action.

"It has come to my attention that your website displays information that identifies a cellular telephone number used by a child under the age of 13 and associates the number with the child's home address. This is a violation of the Children's Online Privacy Protection Act (COPPA). I request that the following information be removed from your database immediately."

This probably sounds sneaky and misleading and it is. Only you can decide if protecting your privacy is worth any ethical dilemmas. In my conscious, it is more unethical to collect personal information from people and broadcast it to the world for a profit than to use legal loopholes to have your own information removed. This tactic could be applied to other websites that disclose information such as home addresses, social network data, personal interests, and friends or associates. In my experience, few companies will decline a request such as this. They are more afraid of being sued than eliminating a single entry.

Chapter Fourteen

Everything Else

By the time that you read these words, much will have changed in the world of digital privacy. I began documenting methods for information removal in 2011. It was much more manageable then and changes rarely occurred. Today, new data collection websites seem to appear daily and the existing sites change their removal process often. No written work like this can remain timeless in our digital age. This chapter is designed to aid you with any future issues that you discover which jeopardizes your right to privacy.

Privacy Policies

You will likely encounter new personal information websites that are not listed in this book. During your Pre-Assessment in Chapter One, you may find unique online information about yourself that you want removed. When an opt-out process is not obvious on the website, always look for a privacy policy page. These are often linked from the very bottom of the home page and the link is commonly in small print. Figure 14.01 displays the home page of pipl.com. The privacy page link can be seen in the lower left corner.

The privacy pages often contain very detailed text about how the company receives and shares the personal information that it collects. It will usually discuss how it uses cookies on your computer to collect further details and what your options are for disabling this technology. Many of the techniques that I have shared in this book come directly from privacy pages of the businesses discussed. Look for specific instructions to opt-out or remove your information through these pages.

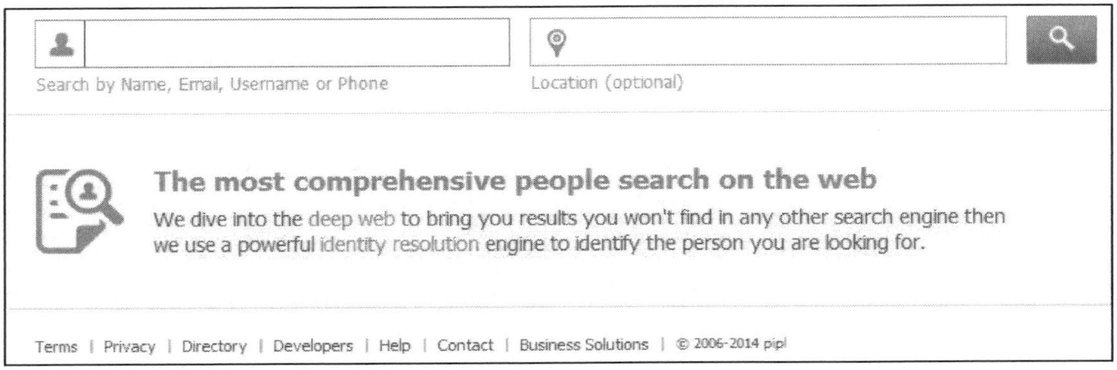

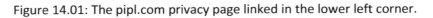

Figure 14.01: The pipl.com privacy page linked in the lower left corner.

Some websites possess a privacy policy page but do not link to it from their home page. This fulfills the requirement to offer an opt-out process, but makes it difficult to locate the page with instructions. A specific query on Google or any other search engine should assist you. When I was researching everify.com, I immediately noticed that there was not an obvious opt-out process or privacy page. I eventually learned that these details were stored within a small "Legal" link between several other unrelated links. Instead of clicking through a lot of irrelevant content, I conducted the following search on Google.

Site:everify.com "Opt-out"

In this example, "site:everify.com" instructs Google to only search one specific domain. It will ignore any other websites and bring all results relevant to your search. The "Opt-out" within quotation marks informs Google to only display results that have that exact phrase within the page or document. Figure 14.02 displays the first search result. It is a PDF document that is exactly what you would need to complete their removal process. Still using everify.com as an example, the following searches may be helpful. Replace everify.com with the website name from which you are trying to remove your information.

Site:everify.com "privacy page"   Site:everify.com "opt out"
Site:everify.com "privacy policy"   Site:everify.com "removal"
Site:everify.com "privacy"   Site:everify.com "legal"

Figure 14.02: A Google search result for an information removal page.

Email Messages

Some services will not offer an online form or document for personal information removal. They may force you to contact them directly with your request. For many companies, this fulfills their obligation to offer a removal option. The direct contact deters many people from proceeding with the process. An email message will often achieve the desired result.

Identifying the appropriate email address to send requests can range from obvious to difficult. Many privacy policy pages include a generic account for opt-out requests such as privacy@ebureau.com. This is likely an account that is monitored by many different people. Some services do not publicly list the most appropriate address, so you will need to take a couple of additional steps in order to locate a helpful address.

Email Assumptions

Most companies have a standard format for all or their email addresses. This will often include a combination of a last name and first name at the business domain, such as john.smith@ebureau .com. These companies usually also have a standard account that is set up to receive requests for removal of information, such as privacy@ebureau.com. Any time you find a company that does not include an obvious removal process for your personal data, consider sending an email to several possible accounts. In the case of ebureau.com, you could send a removal request to the following accounts.

remove@eburau.com	opt-out@eburau.com	info@eburau.com
removal@eburau.com	privacy@eburau.com	questions@eburau.com
optout@eburau.com	legal@eburau.com	contact@eburau.com

Some of these email addresses will likely not exist and you will receive a message delivery error. Often, you will be fortunate in delivering at least one message to someone that can help. If you want to be more precise about this tactic, you could test the email addresses first.

Email Verification (mailtester.com)

Mail Tester is a free service that will allow you to immediately test an email address to determine if it is valid. The response will confirm that an email server exists, that it is functioning, and that the designated email address is real. Figure 14.03 displays a result for remove@ebureau.com, which is not valid. Figure 14.04 displays a result for privacy@ebureau.com which is valid.

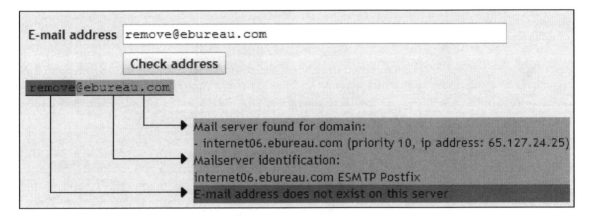

Figure 14.03: An invalid mailtester.com email verification.

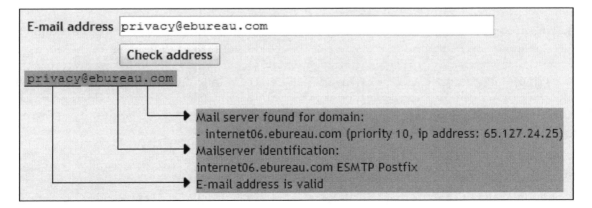

Figure 14.04: A valid mailtester.com email verification.

LinkedIn (linkedin.com)

If you have submitted email messages to the standard accounts such as remove and privacy, and did not get any results, you may consider contacting key employees directly. The best way to identify the appropriate contacts is through LinkedIn.

As a fictitious example, assume that you have completed the information removal process at EBureau, but your information was never removed. You now want to reach out to a real human for assistance. The following steps will likely receive a response from an employee.

✓ Conduct a search for "EBureau" on LinkedIn. Figure 14.05 displays the result including the profiles of 116 employees. Many of these will not display the name of the person, and will only display "LinkedIn Member". Many will display the name of the employee as seen in Figure 14.06

✓ Attempt to identify an employee that possesses an important role at the company. Figure 14.05 displays the profile of a senior vice president of EBureau. Unfortunately, the name is redacted, but you can still identify it with some internet investigation.

✓ Open the profile and right-click on the photo. Choose the option to copy the image location, which is sometimes referred to as the image URL.

✓ Connect to images.google.com and click on the small camera icon within the search field. This will display a new window. Paste the URL or address of the LinkedIn image and click "Search by image". Figure 14.07 displays one of the results when searching the image of the unknown employee visible in Figure 14.08. It identifies another identical image which identifies him as Mic O'Brien.

✓ Alternatively, search Google for the terms "Vice President EBureau" and document any employee names discovered.

✓ Determine the email format of employee addresses at the company. Search for "@ebureau.com" with the quotation marks to identify any email addresses publicly visible. Figure 14.09 identifies a website announcing an EBureau event that includes contact information. These details announce that Anna Haire's email address is annahaire@ebureau.com. We can now assume that the email format is first name + last name @ebureau.com.

✓ Combine the employee names that you discovered with the domain of @bureau.com and test them with mailtester.com. Figure 14.10 displays a result confirming micobrien@ebureau.com is valid. You now have the email address of a senior vice president at the company.

✓ Repeat this process for numerous employees and send each a polite request for action in regards to your removal request.

Figure 14.05: A LinkedIn search result without the name of the employee.

Figure 14.06: A LinkedIn search result with the name of the employee.

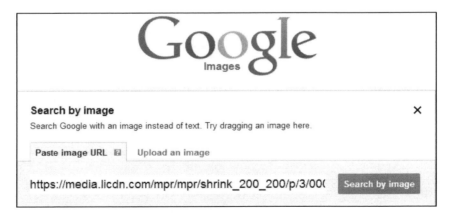

Figure 14.07: The Google Images reverse search option.

Mic O'Brien, Senior Vice President Analytics

Mic joined eBureau in August 2005 to build and manage the sales support and client services teams for eBureau. Today, he serves as the Senior Vice President of Analytics where he leads all custom modeling projects as well as the statistical analysis and reporting for eBureau's customers.

Figure 14.08: A search result that identifies the name of a target employee.

MEDIA/ANALYST: To arrange a media or analyst briefing with Mr. Dowhan please contact:

Anna Haire
Marketing Manager
320-534-5148
annahaire@ebureau.com

Figure 14.09: A search result identifying the format of employee email addresses.

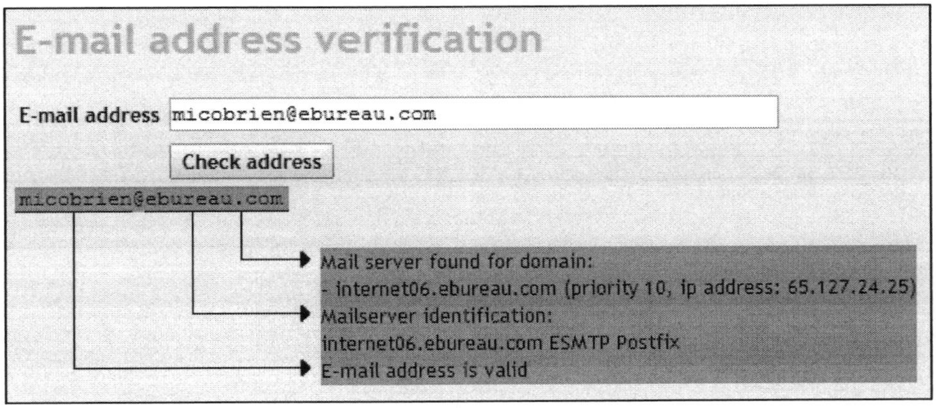

E-mail address verification

E-mail address micobrien@ebureau.com

Check address

micobrien@ebureau.com

Mail server found for domain:
- internet06.ebureau.com (priority 10, ip address: 65.127.24.25)
Mailserver identification:
internet06.ebureau.com ESMTP Postfix
E-mail address is valid

Figure 14.10: A Mail Tester result confirming a valid employee email address.

Fax Requests

Many businesses will publish a facsimile (fax) number on their public websites. While these numbers may not be the appropriate reception for removal requests, the message will be received by an employee who may forward it to the person responsible for the information. Conduct the following steps in order to identify the fax numbers of a business.

Perform a Google search for the name of the company and the word fax, both within separate quotation marks. Figure 14.11 displays an example and the results. This identifies a valid fax number of 320-534-5020 for that business.

Figure 14.11: A Google search for valid fax numbers.

Telephone

If all else fails to get you the results you desire, consider making a telephone call. This has been the least effective method in my experience. However, I have on occasion spoken to very helpful employees which acted right away and removed my information. Since most people do not choose this method, employees are fairly surprised to get a call for a removal request. Search through the target business' websites and conduct searches for the company name and the word "phone".

Additional Privacy Information

I learn new information about our privacy, and lack of, every day while I conduct research for my own purposes. One of the best resources for extremely current content is the Privacy page on Reddit. I encourage you to visit and bookmark the following website for the most vital information about the state of privacy in all of our lives.

reddit.com/r/Privacy

Figure 14.12 displays the top stories as I write this paragraph. The links take you to articles about Google allowing European's to remove sensitive online information, a conversation about reporting privacy violations, and a discussion of Android applications for security. This page literally changes every hour.

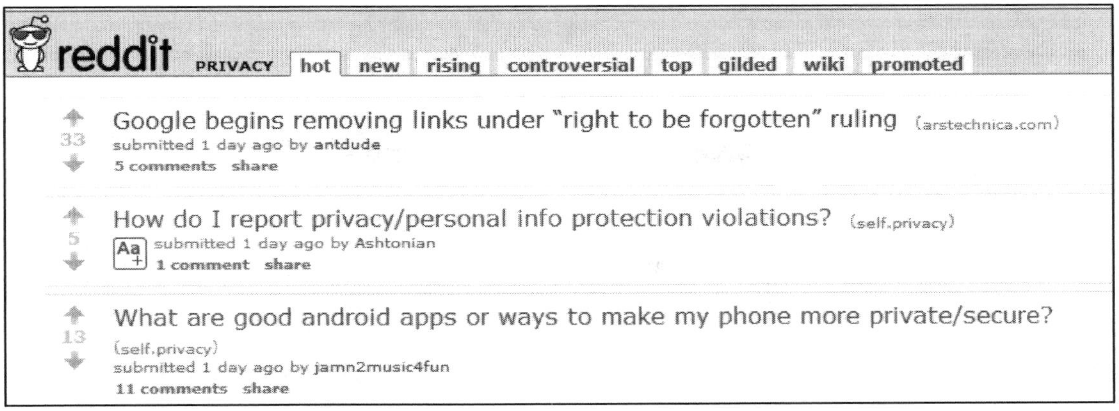

Figure 14.12: A Reddit page about privacy.

Privacy Rights (privacyrights.org)

You can always find a current list of Opt-Out instructions for most data vendors at the following website.

www.privacyrights.org/online-information-brokers-list

While this book maintains a focus for removal from the most prevalent data collection companies, you may find your information on a smaller and unlisted website. Privacy Rights will likely list the removal options and a direct link to a page to assist with the process.

Chapter Fifteen

Disinformation

The first edition of this book made a brief mention of what many people refer to as misinformation. Technically, misinformation is when a person unintentionally provides inaccurate information which causes inappropriate content to be released or replicated. Most people are really talking about disinformation. This is when a person intentionally provides false or misleading information with an attempt to create inaccurate data. Disinformation is exactly what we want to do more of.

So far, this book has explained the many ways to remove your information from the internet. However, it is important to understand that it is not always possible to erase every piece of data about you. Disinformation will make that small amount of permanent data seem useless inside a stream of completely inaccurate content. I have devoted an entire chapter to disinformation techniques that I believe should be applied in some situations. This step is optional, and not suitable for everyone.

If you have been extremely successful with eliminating your online information, you may not need disinformation. However, if you have found a few services that refuse to remove your data, any websites that will not respond to your requests, or simply want to harden your overall security, disinformation may be the perfect solution. Providing inaccurate details while completing the removal processes discussed earlier will also increase your effectiveness substantially.

Before proceeding, consider whether this action is right for you. Completing these tasks will add more information about you to the internet. Since the information supplied is false, there is little privacy concern. However, this will lead to much more content available about your name. Many people like this because it creates a difficult scenario when someone tries to locate them. Some people do not like this tactic because it makes their name more visible throughout the internet.

Only you can determine if this action is appropriate. Understand that it may be difficult or impossible to remove the false information that you provide.

You have learned how public records, data brokers, advertising companies, and various businesses build complete profiles on you and your family. My main concern with these reports is the inclusion of my home address. Most people's home address can be found on 40 different websites within a minute. This is not only an invasion of privacy, but a danger to many people.

My goal with hiding from the internet was always to have a home that no one could associate with me. I wanted a safe location that I could feel comfortable in without looking over my shoulder. Police officers and other people targeted because of their profession will understand. After accomplishing this, I experienced an interesting moment.

In 2012, I received a piece of mail to my residence addressed to "New Resident". It was an automated welcome packet from several local businesses containing coupons for home related purchases. Basically, I had fallen so far off of the radar that data mining companies had assumed that someone else must have moved into my house. This was a rewarding feeling, but it quickly concerned me. If I was no longer likely to be living at my house, where did the data companies think I was living? I thought that too little information available about me could be causing more harm than good. This is when I became fascinated with disinformation.

A friend of mine is a private investigator. I had him lookup my information through a popular data broker that he had premium access with. There were no entries associated with me for the past few years. This indicates to an investigator that I was dead, homeless, or hiding. The only recent activity was my PO Box. I retained a copy of this report and used it as a comparison for future analysis.

The first call I made was to my internet service provider for my home. This was a major cable company and I started the conversation by requesting a discount on my service. I was advised that if I extended my contract two years, I could negotiate a lower price. One of my arguments was that this was a second home and that I was hardly there. We agreed on a price, but I had two conditions. The first was that I wanted the bill and all associated records to be addressed to my full time residence. Second, I insisted that they only send me an electronic bill via email. This eliminated any need to have access to any physical mail coming from this company.

For my "full time residence", I supplied an address that did not exist in a neighboring town. I went to Google Maps, identified a random nearby street, and found the last address available. I then added two digits to that address and attempted a search for it. Google identified it as a possible address, but it could not pinpoint exactly where the house was. I wanted to provide an address that would seem realistic, but not jeopardize anyone else. I never use any information that is unique and real to another individual. Another option would have been to identify a new neighborhood being built, locate the highest number for an address on the street, and add a few digits. If you are met with any resistance, you could say that it was a brand new house.

Within 30 days, I had my friend request another report on me. This time, it indicated that I had recently moved to an address that matched the disinformation that I provided to the cable company. I considered this a success and continued with my disinformation campaign.

The remaining content of this chapter will identify possibilities that you may consider for your own disinformation attempts. They are divided into three specific groups. The options are endless, and I encourage you to email me any great ideas that you have.

- ✓ **Name Disinformation**: This will focus on providing many different names to be associated with your real address and real telephone number to make it difficult to identify the true owner of each. This is beneficial for hiding your real name from people or companies searching for information about your address or number.

- ✓ **Address Disinformation**: This will focus on associating various addresses with your real name to make it difficult for people or companies to determine which address is your real home.

- ✓ **Telephone Disinformation**: This will associate various telephone numbers with your real name to make it difficult for a person or business to identify a valid number to contact you.

Name Disinformation

In the perfect scenario of hiding from the internet, every reader will be moving soon, can purchase the home in cash, possesses an invisible New Mexico LLC for the title, and will never associate the new address with a real name. In order to be realistic, I will assume this is not the case for you. Name disinformation will create an appearance that numerous people live at your residence. This could increase the delivery of mail and advertisements to your house. However, none of it will jeopardize your privacy. In fact, it will increase your privacy quickly. At the end of this section, I will display actual results from these techniques.

Bills

Earlier, I explained how to use disinformation to have a landline telephone listing modified to inaccurate information. This technique works well on practically any service provided to a home or business. Contact the service provider, possibly your cellular telephone provider, and request a change to your billing information. Advise the representative that the account is listed under your middle name and that you are uncomfortable with that and desire it to be associated with you first name. Provide any first name that you like. Within weeks, third party companies will receive the updated information which will eventually override the real information on file. I prefer to choose a different first name for every bill.

Magazines

If you have a subscription to any magazines in your real name, you should stop that practice immediately. This data is openly shared with many companies and will quickly identify your name and home address online. Contact the magazine company and tell them that you were recently married and want the magazines delivered in your married name. Provide any last name that you desire, as long as it has no personal association with you. This works for men as well. Since same sex marriage has been so controversial lately, no magazine company is likely to challenge a man on changing his last name to his partner's.

If you do not have any magazines delivered to your home, it may be time to start. Identify a couple of popular magazines that you are interested in a subscription. Conduct a search for that magazine plus "free subscription". You may be surprised at the abundance of magazines that will give anyone a free subscription. This will often involve the need to complete a short survey. The survey can also be used as a disinformation opportunity.

The most vital part of this exercise is that you do not provide anything close to your real name. Additionally, provide a different name for each subscription. I like to relate each name to the magazine that is being requested. The following could be a guide.

Men's Health: John Sporting
Money Magazine: Tim Cashman
Wired: Alex Techie
Food Magazine: James Cook

I also encourage you not to go overboard. Please only obtain subscriptions that you will read or pass on to someone that will enjoy them. There is no need to waste the product and immediately throw them in the trash. You will also eventually get frustrated if you have several issues arriving every week filling your mailbox.

Newspapers

Similar to magazines, I encourage you to identify a single newspaper that you would enjoy receiving. Newspaper subscriber databases are unique and cater to a specific market. This subscription information will leak out slowly to third party companies. I do not recommend multiple newspaper subscriptions unless this is appropriate for your daily reading abilities.

I enjoy reading the Wall Street Journal every day. A search online for "Wall Street Journal 39 week" will identify dozens of websites that will allow you a 39 week free trial of the paper.

Complete the request and provide a unique name. I have found Mary S. Market to be appropriate. You will begin receiving your daily print and digital editions within one week.

Trade Mailings

Trade magazines and mailings are designed to target a specific industry or trade. These are usually free by default and generate revenue from the advertising within the publication. Visiting freetrademagazines.com will display numerous options to consider. I encourage you to be cautious with this method. Many people will load up on magazines of interest and use a false name. While this is acceptable, it does create an association with your home address to your real interests. For example, if you subscribe to seven different web design magazines, and you are a web design artist, this could lead to an accurate profile about the people that live at your home. I would only choose this option if you do not take advantage of a magazine or newspaper subscription.

House Repair

The time will come when you will need some professional work completed at your home. This will often happen the moment that you stop associating your real name with your home address. Use this as a disinformation opportunity.

A friend recently discovered that he needed a new roof. Calling a stranger on Craigslist and paying cash would have been acceptable for privacy concerns. However, he understandably wanted to hire a professional company and possess a valid warranty on the new roof. He had recently conducted a complete cleaning of his personal information on the internet, and was concerned that this could jeopardize his privacy.

I recommended that he identify the company that he wished to hire and ask them to provide a quote. He gave them his real address for the roof job, but provided the name of a fake contracting company that was similar to the name of his invisible LLC. If your LLC was named Particle Ventures LLC, you could provide Ventures Contracting. This allowed him to keep his real name away from the process and attach yet another type of disinformation to the address. Upon completion of the work, my friend possessed a written warranty attached to the address and not to a person. This would suffice for replacement if problems with the roof appeared. If you do not possess an invisible LLC, you could use the name of your living trust. Instead of providing the full name of the trust, leave off the description at the end. If your trust was titled The Big Adventure Revocable Living Trust, you could use The Big Adventure Contracting Company.

Remember, we are not using any of these methods to commit fraud. We are only protecting our privacy and will pay any accounts in full. For most work like this, paying either cash or with a check is acceptable. It is not likely that the name on the check will be attached to the data from the work, but it is possible. If you have an LLC or a trust, consider opening a free checking account in the name of it. This will not only add a layer of anonymity, but it will also enforce the appearance of legitimacy.

Name Disinformation Results

A friend allowed me to conduct various forms of disinformation on his home address. Before I took any action, I performed a basic search on Spokeo for his address. It provided one result, which positively identified his name, address, telephone number, email address, and family member's names. Figure 15.01 displays a redacted view of this result. At the completion of my disinformation campaign, I allowed 60 days to pass. Figure 15.02 displays the result that identifies 80 unique people that live at his address. Much of this is due to the methods that will be discussed in the following sections.

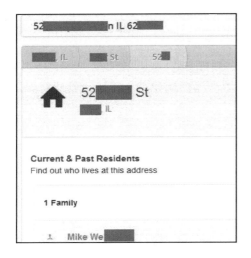

Figure 15.01: A Spokeo search result before applying disinformation.

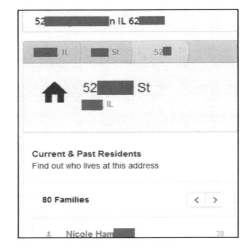

Figure 15.02: A Spokeo search result after applying disinformation.

Address Disinformation

This is the most vital type of disinformation if you are trying to disassociate your real name from your real address. The goal with these methods is to create an illusion that you currently live somewhere that you do not. This will make accurate name searches difficult. Before proceeding, you should have an idea of which addresses you will be providing.

Choosing an Address

This section will explain how to create at least three valid addresses that you will intentionally associate with your real name. The purpose is to show recent activity if someone was to search for you within a people search service. These services always display the most current information first. Therefore, you may want to complete as much of the removal process that is discussed later as possible before providing this disinformation. Additionally, you would only want to do this after you have stopped associating your real name with your real address.

It is very important not to use another individual's home address. While it may not be illegal, it is not ethical and not fair to the other person. If you are hiding from an abusive ex, you do not want to put someone else in danger when he or she decides to break into a house believing it is yours. If you are a police officer trying to protect your family from criminals seeking revenge, you should not send them to some stranger's house and let those residents deal with it. We will only choose locations that do not pose a threat to anyone.

The first address may be a place that does not exist. This is my favorite technique. Many companies possess verification software that will identify invalid addresses. These programs can often be fooled by selecting addresses in new neighborhoods. The following instructions will easily identify a new address for you.

- ✓ Conduct a Google search for "new construction city, state". Replace "city, state" with a location at least a few towns away from you. I also recommend clicking "Search Tools", "Any Time", and selecting "Past Year". This will display recent results. Figure 15.03 displays the first result during my search.

- ✓ Choose a search result that connects to a real estate website that displays new homes for sale. Figure 15.04 displays the previous search result that identifies two new homes with addresses very close to each other. The newly planted grass, identical houses, and same list price in each listing are also an indicator of a brand new neighborhood.

- ✓ Conduct a search on Zillow.com for the highest number visible on the chosen street. In Figure 15.04, the search would be 1007 Park Charles Blvd. You should see a house attached to this address. Increase the address by ten or twenty digits. In this scenario, I searched 1017 Park Charles Blvd. Zillow informed me that there was no house at this address.

- ✓ Search this new address on Google maps and confirm the house does not exist. Switch to the satellite view and confirm that there would not likely be enough land to add the number of houses necessary to create this address.

- ✓ Document this new address and use it for disinformation.

Occasionally, advanced verification software will identify a fake address as invalid. You may need to provide a real address that is listed as residential but does not belong to an individual family. You may want to choose the address of an emergency shelter. The residents in these are constantly changing, and most of them have 24 hour staff and security. Since many people must consider these a temporary residence, the addresses often defeat the most advanced verification services. Choosing a city and searching it online including the terms "shelter", "men's home", "women's home", and "homeless" will usually provide options. I use this as a last option.

Figure 15.03: A Google search for new homes.

Figure 15.04: A search result of new homes for sale.

Public library addresses are almost always identified as commercial, but the addresses will pass standard validation. For most disinformation purposes, the address of any public building, including a library, will suffice. Now that you have some ideas for your new address, the next techniques will help you populate online records with this information.

Internet Surveys

There will never be a shortage of internet surveys. These are websites that ask you to answer numerous personal questions and offer small rewards in return. Most of them never fulfill their promise to send you money, tech devices, or Amazon gift certificates. They all collect your information, create large databases of personal details, and sell that data to marketing companies. The content associated to you often makes its way to the public visible internet.

These surveys are time consuming but effective. The content that you provide will quickly be disseminated to various public sources. Be sure to always provide your real name, but never provide your real address, personal email account, or any real information about you within the survey responses. You do not want to create an accurate profile of your interests and family situation.

Many readers will want nothing to do with this section. I completely understand this stance, especially when seeing the level of intrusive questioning that is involved. I only recommend this approach when you have been unsuccessful at removing your personal details from the internet such as the city and state you live in, your age, and family members' information.

In order to explain the appropriate way to provide disinformation through online surveys, I will demonstrate using swagbucks.com. The following instructions will walk you through the process.

- ✓ Navigate to swagbucks.com and create a new account. Provide a 33 Mail address created earlier and a password used only for that website. I recommend using a specific 33 Mail account such as swagbucks@nsa.33mail.com. Be sure to use a 33 Mail account that will forward to you. You will need to verify this email address by clicking the option within an email sent to your 33 Mail account.

- ✓ You will be given the option to "Complete Your Profile" in a popup window after email verification. Choose this option and provide you real name. This website will walk you through providing your gender, date of birth, zip code, and other personal details. Provide inaccurate responses to all of these. Within weeks, this false information will start to appear within public people search sites.

- ✓ Complete a few surveys always providing inaccurate answers. You will be prompted to complete a "Profiler" which will ask many invasive questions related to income, race, employment, education, health issues, and sexual orientation. Always provide inaccurate data. Three to five surveys should be enough to pass your name, false age, and incorrect location details to third party companies.

TV Offers

A less invasive way of populating bad information about you on the internet is responding to television offers during infomercials. You have likely seen various offers for information about devices such as medical alerts, home security systems, and reverse mortgages on both daytime and late night television. They all offer to send you an informational packet describing how they can help any situation that you are in. These are always a profitable business anticipating huge financial returns when they engage you for their services. Instead, we will use this as a way to mask our true home address.

I recently watched a commercial for a slow motorized device created to help the elderly and those with disabilities. It was a combination of a wheelchair and a moped that could move anyone around the street, grocery store, or mall. You are probably familiar with these "scooters". I called the number and requested information. I used my real name and an address in a new subdivision that did not exist. I do not like to use real addresses because someone will need to deal with the junk mail that is received. This way, the mailings are simply returned to the business. I purposely provided a street name that I located called "Mobility Way".

Within 90 days, while conducting a routine query of my name of people search websites, I located an entry for me on "Mobility Way". I now know with certainty that this company shares personal information. If someone is trying to locate me, he or she will have one more address to research and be disappointed.

Online Offers

There is no need to wait in front of a television all night with the hopes of catching a great disinformation opportunity. The internet has thousands waiting for you at all times. Searching for any of the following topics will likely present numerous websites eager to send you a free information packet. Providing your new "fake" address will get you listed in several marketing databases quickly with this false information.

Home Scooter
Time Share
Home Alarm
Lawn Treatment Service
Home Food Delivery

Please do not ever provide any real information about yourself, besides your name, to any of these services. Never provide a credit card number or any other type of payment information.

You should only use this technique to create the illusion that you live somewhere other than your real home. Additionally, if you have a common name, such as John Smith, address disinformation is not likely necessary.

Be aware that paper mailings will likely be delivered from and returned to the businesses that you contact. This is very wasteful for both the business and the planet. I encourage you to only perform the actions necessary to obtain your address disinformation goal. I do not encourage you to unnecessarily contact hundreds of companies. It only takes a few large companies to make an impact on your overall address identity.

Social Networks

I usually do not promote the creation of personal social network profiles. However, they can be very useful in some cases. I once consulted a young woman that was the victim of severe harassment by a man who was a former high school classmate of hers. His unwelcome approaches caused her to move and purchase a different vehicle. She was doing well at staying off of his radar, but still knew he was looking for her. She created a Facebook page, added a couple of photos of her pet, and publicly displayed her location as a town over an hour away. While monitoring the Twitter account of her stalker, she observed him "check into" a bar in that very town, likely looking for her. While this does not solve the issue long-term, it provided enough uncertainty to confuse the stalker and waste his time.

Creating several social network profiles and including publicly visible location data can be beneficial. You can either make them very confusing by placing different locations on each profile, or place the same city on all of them to create a convincing situation. If this type of disinformation is appropriate for you, it can be taken further with the following technique.

GPS Spoofing

Most social networks allow you to share your current location at all times with the world publicly. The readers of this book will likely think that this is ridiculous. While I agree, we can also use it to our advantage. Manipulating the location information stored within social network posts can be very easy or fairly difficult. I will explain two different options to consider based on your level of technical skill.

Please Don't Stalk Me (pleasedontstalkme.com)

The easiest way to spoof your location on Twitter is to use the service Please Don't Stalk Me. This website will perform all of the necessary actions in order to provide a false location during your "Tweets". The following instructions will explain the process.

✓ Either create a new Twitter account or log into your current Twitter account from which you want to post messages. Confirm that you have location sharing enabled by going to Settings > Security and privacy > Tweet Location. You want to check the box that allows you to add location information to your Twitter posts.

✓ Navigate to pleasedontstalkme.com and allow it to connect to your Twitter profile through the "Sign in with Twitter" button.

✓ Enter the address or general location from which you want to appear to be posting your message. Click the "Tweet" button to post the message. Figure 15.05 displays my post from Times Square in New York City.

✓ Navigate to your Twitter profile to view the post and associated location information. Figure 15.06 displays the message created in the last step. The upper right marker and location confirm that the message was posted from New York City while I was really sitting in Chicago.

✓ If you want to test the accuracy of your false GPS information, load your profile on the website tweetpaths.com by entering your Twitter user name. Figure 15.07 displays my profile after making two additional posts from nearby areas. This creates the appearance that I am really in New York City.

Providing false location information to your Twitter posts can be extremely effective for disinformation purposes. While I usually encourage people to stay away from social networks, this can be helpful. If you are trying to convince an abusive ex that you now live in a new area, frequent posts with false location data from that area can be very convincing. If you want your family and friends to believe that you are vacationing overseas, this technique should fool them and allow you some peace and quiet in your own home.

Please use caution not to divulge any accurate personal details. Always remember that the content that you post to the Twitter servers will likely be present forever and can never be completely removed.

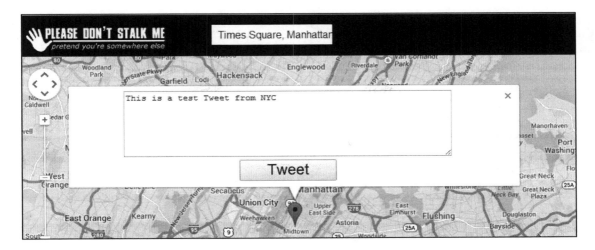

Figure 15.05: A Twitter post with false location data on pleasedontstalkme.com.

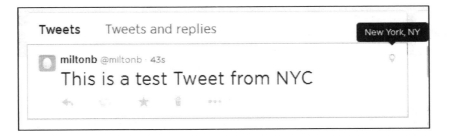

Figure 15.06: The Twitter post created with pleasedontstalkme.com

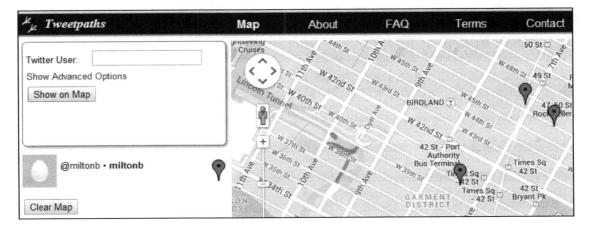

Figure 15.07: Confirmation of false location data on tweetpaths.com.

Web Browser GPS Data

The previous technique is great if you only need to fool someone through Twitter. It does not work for other services. We can emulate a GPS location within our web browser and allow the browser to share this with any website. This will cause social networks to broadcast our current location, which we can control with misleading information. This can quickly confuse anyone that is stalking or harassing you. The following instructions will walk you through the entire process of providing false location data to a Twitter profile and posts.

- ✓ Download and install the Chrome web browser. This free browser works on all operating systems and will often provide a faster internet browsing experience. Navigate to google.com/chrome and follow the directions.

- ✓ Launch Chrome, click the menu in the upper right corner, highlight "Tools" and select "Developer Tools". This will launch a new window at the bottom of your screen. Strike the "ESC" key on your keyboard which will launch the necessary console. Click the word "Sensors" on the left menu of this window. Select the "Emulate geolocation coordinates" checkbox and enter any GPS location that you desire. Figure 15.08 displays my result that will tell the world that I am in Hawaii.

- ✓ Close the developer tools console by clicking the "X" in the upper right corner of the tools box at the bottom of your screen. You should now only see the web browser page.

- ✓ Navigate to Bing Maps (bing.com/maps) and click the icon next to "Click to center the map on your current location". Your browser will likely ask you if you want to share your location. Accept this request and the map should identify that you are at the location that you provided. Figure 15.09 displays this option and my result. This is confirmation that the technique is working.

- ✓ Connect to any network that you want to use to broadcast a false location. You should connect to the mobile versions of the services you want to fool. Instead of facebook.com, you should connect to m.facebook.com. Adding "m." or "mobile." In front of most websites will take you to the mobile version which will ask for location information.

Be aware that this technique does not hide or change your IP address. Websites that you visit will still know this information and may be able to determine your approximate real location. This should only be used for purposely posting false location data through social networks. Always test this procedure with a non-sensitive account to validate the result.

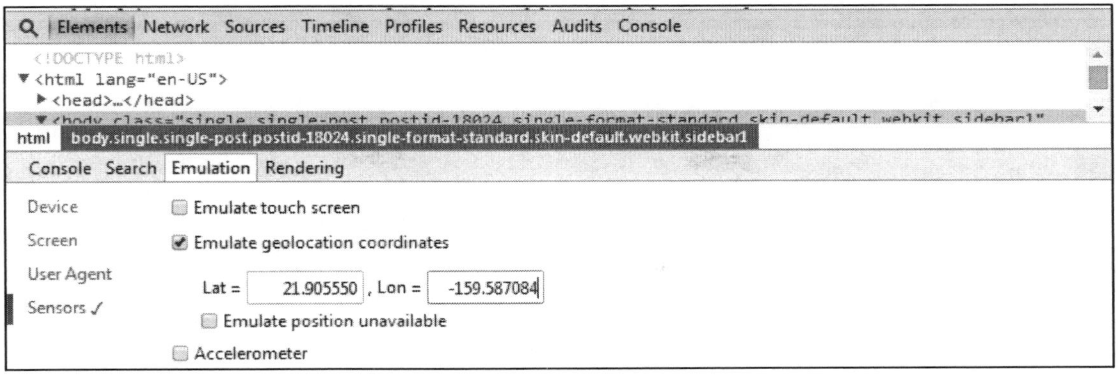

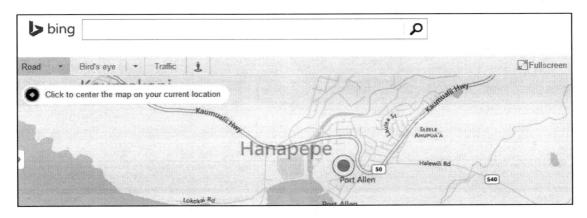

Figure 15.08: The Developer Tools menu in Chrome that allows you to emulate GPS location.

Figure 15.09: Confirmation on Bing Maps that the location spoofing is functioning.

Address Disinformation Results

I consulted a government employee that was being harassed by a federal prisoner that he had arrested. The prisoner threatened to find his family and kill them in their sleep when he was released from prison. With permission, I began a disinformation campaign for him. He had a unique name and lived in Chicago. Before the process, searching his name in Spokeo identified two locations. One was his home and the other was his workplace. Figure 15.10 displays a similar result with redacted and modified information. After removing these entries, which was discussed earlier, I helped populate false information through the techniques discussed here. Figure 15.11 shows the current result when searching his name. Over 20 possible addresses are displayed, and none of them relate to his actual home.

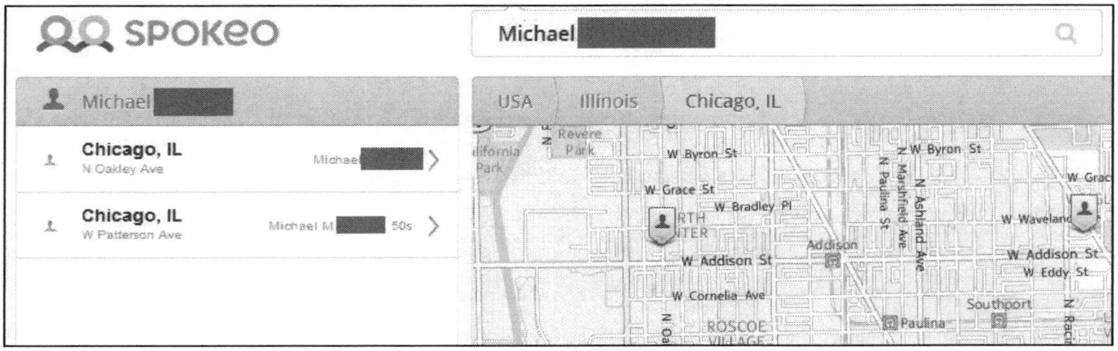

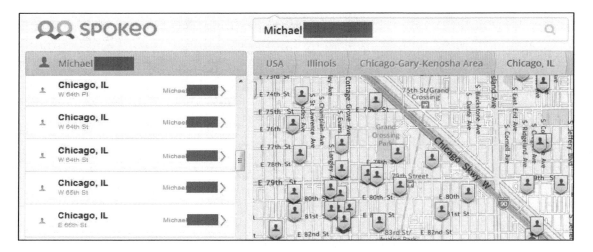

Figure 15.10: A Spokeo name search before disinformation techniques were applied.

Figure 15.11: A Spokeo name search after disinformation techniques were applied.

Telephone Disinformation

Receiving unwanted telephone calls from telemarketers can be annoying. Calls from them to random numbers are unavoidable. However, targeted calls specific to you can be extra frustrating. You have already learned how to eliminate public record of your telephone number. You may now want to populate disinformation to prevent a person or business from discovering your true home or cellular telephone number.

Identifying New Numbers

Before you can provide the false telephone number information with hopes of it being attached to your name within public databases, you must select some appropriate numbers. Most importantly, you never want to provide a false number that belongs to another individual. That is not only rude, but it can also jeopardize that person's right to privacy from unwanted callers. Instead, focus on telephone numbers that either do not exist or belong to services that are never answered by an individual.

Busy Numbers

My favorite telephone numbers for disinformation are numbers that are always busy and cannot be answered. These were once abundant, but many of them have now been assigned to customers. There are still two large groups of telephone numbers that will always be busy when dialed. The following sets of numbers should work well.

909-661-0001 through 909-661-0090
619-364-0003 through 619-364-0090

The 909 area code serves the Los Angeles area of California and the 619 area code serves the San Diego area. These were early line numbers when service began in this area and the numbers should not be assigned to any customers. Since these are not toll free numbers, they should not be flagged as non-residential. Because numbers are ported so often, possessing a number in another area code should not raise any suspicion. When you give someone a number that is always busy, it does not create the appearance of a fake number. These can appear to be real.

Disconnected Numbers

There are plenty of unused numbers that announce "disconnected" when dialed. Most of these are temporary and will be assigned to a customer at some point. The following range of numbers all announce a "non-working number" when dialed. The area code serves Pennsylvania. Giving one of these numbers to a person or business can enforce a desire to not be contacted.

717-980-0000 through 717-980-9999

Always test the numbers that you choose before using. The following table displays a useful chart of the "busy" numbers with an area next to each to document the numbers used and specific application of each. You could use this to keep track of your disinformation.

909-661-0001	_____	909-661-0031	_____	909-661-0061	_____
909-661-0002	_____	909-661-0032	_____	909-661-0062	_____
909-661-0003	_____	909-661-0033	_____	909-661-0063	_____
909-661-0004	_____	909-661-0034	_____	909-661-0064	_____
909-661-0005	_____	909-661-0035	_____	909-661-0065	_____
909-661-0006	_____	909-661-0036	_____	909-661-0066	_____
909-661-0007	_____	909-661-0037	_____	909-661-0067	_____
909-661-0008	_____	909-661-0038	_____	909-661-0068	_____
909-661-0009	_____	909-661-0039	_____	909-661-0069	_____
909-661-0010	_____	909-661-0040	_____	909-661-0070	_____
909-661-0011	_____	909-661-0041	_____	909-661-0071	_____
909-661-0012	_____	909-661-0042	_____	909-661-0072	_____
909-661-0013	_____	909-661-0043	_____	909-661-0073	_____
909-661-0014	_____	909-661-0044	_____	909-661-0074	_____
909-661-0015	_____	909-661-0045	_____	909-661-0075	_____
909-661-0016	_____	909-661-0046	_____	909-661-0076	_____
909-661-0017	_____	909-661-0047	_____	909-661-0077	_____
909-661-0018	_____	909-661-0048	_____	909-661-0078	_____
909-661-0019	_____	909-661-0049	_____	909-661-0079	_____
909-661-0020	_____	909-661-0050	_____	909-661-0080	_____
909-661-0021	_____	909-661-0051	_____	909-661-0081	_____
909-661-0022	_____	909-661-0052	_____	909-661-0082	_____
909-661-0023	_____	909-661-0053	_____	909-661-0083	_____
909-661-0024	_____	909-661-0054	_____	909-661-0084	_____
909-661-0025	_____	909-661-0055	_____	909-661-0085	_____
909-661-0026	_____	909-661-0056	_____	909-661-0086	_____
909-661-0027	_____	909-661-0057	_____	909-661-0087	_____
909-661-0028	_____	909-661-0058	_____	909-661-0088	_____
909-661-0029	_____	909-661-0059	_____	909-661-0089	_____
909-661-0030	_____	909-661-0060	_____	909-661-0090	_____

Store Giveaways

One of the quickest ways to associate a false telephone number with your real name is to enter various contests. You have probably seen a brand new vehicle parked inside your local shopping mall. A box next to it likely contained blank pieces of paper asking for your name, address, and telephone number with promises that someone would win the vehicle. Have you ever known anyone that won a vehicle this way? I do not. Instead, these gimmicks are often used to obtain a great list of potential customers that might be interested in automobiles. This content is often combined with other contest data and sold to numerous companies. Eventually, the provided information is attached to you through a marketing profile that may follow you forever.

In years past, I have always laughed at the idea of entering these contests. Today, I never pass up this opportunity. I always provide my real name, my false address from the address disinformation section mentioned earlier, and one of the "busy" telephone numbers listed previously. I like to use different numbers every time and watch for any online associations to me from these numbers. I then know which contest companies are selling my information.

Shopping Cards

Most grocery stores have a shopper's card program that provides discounts on merchandise. These are portrayed as opportunities to save money for being a loyal customer to the brand. In reality, these cards are closely monitored to learn about your shopping habits. This data is used to create custom advertising and offers. The only benefit of joining this program is the savings of the items that you purchase. The risk of joining is the guaranteed profile that will be created about you and sold to interested parties. You can enjoy the benefits without jeopardizing your privacy. This is a great opportunity for telephone number disinformation.

Practically all of the stores that utilize this type of savings program allow you to access your account by the telephone number that you provided during registration. You are not required to provide or scan your shopper's card. You can simply enter your telephone number to obtain the savings and attach your purchases to your profile. I have found the following telephone number to work at most stores.

867-5309

This number may not look familiar, but say the number out loud. This was the title of a song by Tommy Tutone in 1982 that gained a lot of popularity. This number is currently assigned to customers in most area codes. In fact, it is often sought after by businesses due to the familiarity. I never use this number with services that may try to contact me. Instead, I only use it when I register a shopping card at a grocery store.

If I am shopping in Chicago, I use an appropriate area code such as 847. If you ever find yourself at a Safeway store anywhere in the world, you can use 847-867-5309 as your shopper's card number and it will be accepted without hesitation. If you find that this number does not work at another chain, you should consider requesting a shopper's card and provide it as your number. Figure 15.12 displays my actual shopper's card application for the grocery chain Kroger.

I provided my real name, the disinformation address discussed earlier (which does not exist), a Chicago area code, the 867-5309 number, and a specific email address at my 33 Mail account. I will never use that email account again, and will know which company provided my information when I receive unwanted email at Kroger@nsa.33mail.com. I can now provide 847-867-5309 as my member number when I shop at Kroger. Most importantly, you can too.

As a community service, I create new accounts at every store that I can in the number of 847-867-5309. The more strangers that use this number during their shopping, the more anonymous we all are. The data collected by the store will not be about one individual. Instead, it will be a collective of numerous families. If you locate a store without a membership with this number, please consider activating your own card with address disinformation.

Within weeks, this information will be associated with your real name. It will add an additional layer of anonymity by making any present legitimate information difficult to find and harder to prove accurate.

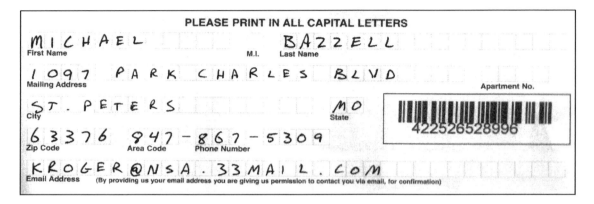

Figure 15.12: A Kroger Shopper's Card application.

Rewards Cards

Chapter Five discussed a method of using hotel reward programs to help convince a receptionist to accept your credit card in your alternate name. These programs can also be used to spread disinformation for your benefit. Many companies that offer reward programs share or sell the collected data to other interested businesses. If you have an account with a chain of luxury resorts, they are likely to sell your information to credit cards that cater to business travelers. If you are a rewards member of a fast food chain, they are likely to share your details with other food and retail companies. While some privacy advocates warn you to stay away from these traps, I encourage you to embrace them with disinformation.

Rental Vehicles

I travel often and find myself in a rented vehicle monthly. I joined various rewards programs in order to obtain substantial discounts and upgrades. I always provided my real name because a driver's license was always required to complete a transaction. However, the address and telephone number was never verified during the signup process. Every time that I would rent a vehicle, I was asked if I was a rewards member. I always advised yes, but stated that I did not know my membership number. The most common response was "What is your telephone number?".

Like many other programs, most car rental rewards clubs can access your account by telephone number. The telephone number is heavily associated with your name and a great opportunity to provide disinformation. The details that you provide will likely become visible either publicly or to data marketing companies. Providing your real name, disinformation address, and one of the telephone numbers discussed earlier will help create an inaccurate profile and may help eliminate your real telephone number that is currently on file with other companies.

You do not need to actually use any of the services that you register with. All of them allow you to join their rewards program before your make any reservations or purchases. The information below will take you directly to the online application process for some of the popular vehicle rental companies.

Enterprise: enterprise.com/car_rental/enterprisePlusCreateAccount.do
Hertz: hertz.com/rentacar/member/enrollment/contact-details
Thrifty: thrifty.com/BlueChip/Enrollment.aspx
National: nationalcar.com/index.do?action=emcIndex.do&type=uszl-withnav-header
E-Z Rentals: e-zrentacar.com/rewards/money_main

Phone Number Disinformation Results

A college student of mine once told me that her ex-boyfriend was constantly harassing her through telephone calls and text messages. She had changed her number once, but he was eventually able to find the new number through the internet. With her permission and assistance, we embarked on a telephone disinformation campaign before she changed her number again. Eventually, Spokeo and other services associated her name with three of the "busy" numbers, her email address with a 33 Mail account, and her home address with a non-existing building. Figure 15.13 displays a redacted view of one of these results. She was now ready to change her number for the last time, and keep it out of any public databases.

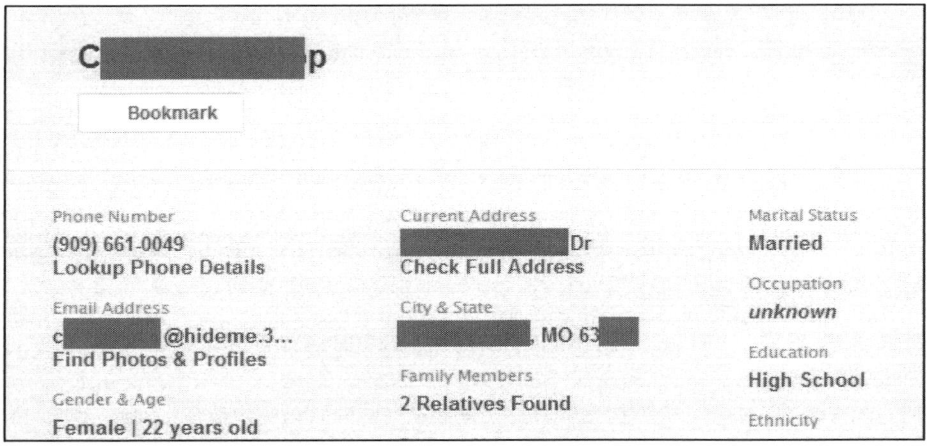

Figure 15.13: A redacted view of disinformation collected by Spokeo.

General Tips

✓ Consider always providing disinformation that will help you identify the leak of data when you find it. For example, if you request information from a reverse mortgage company with a goal of name disinformation, you should use a name that will remind you of this company, such as "Joe Reversi". When you receive unwanted mail at your residence attached to this name, you will know the original source.

✓ A benefit of disinformation involving companies that cater to a specific demographic is that your residence will now be associated with the same category. Requesting reverse mortgage information or a medical alert quote will likely indicate that older adults live at your residence. This can help mask your real interests.

✓ Never use your real name or alternative credit card name in association with your real address or telephone number. The goal here is to generate inaccurate details in order to help mask any real data that you cannot remove.

✓ Remember that it will be difficult to remove disinformation that you provide about yourself. If you have very little online information identifying your personal details, these techniques may not be appropriate for you. However, if there is an abundance of accurate details that you cannot remove, it is better to add bad information in order to hide the real content.

Chapter Sixteen

Future Habits

By now, you have learned how to hide from public searches on the internet. If you have applied the techniques, it will also be difficult for private investigators, attorneys, and marketing companies to find you. This success can be quickly ruined by repopulating your personal information into public view. Preventing new data from being collected about you is as important as removing your personal information. The way that you previously provided your personal details to others must change immediately.

In this chapter, I have provided the most common scenarios that will jeopardize your privacy. Reacting to these the wrong way will introduce your personal information back into the public. In each scenario, I have outlined the appropriate way of responding to the situation in order to protect your personal details. I hope that you use this chapter as a reference when you need some ideas on how to stop people and companies from intruding into your life.

From this point onward, you should never associate your home address with your name or the names of your family members. At first, this may sound difficult to do. To help with the transition, continue reading. There will be exceptions, which will be explained later. A three tiered system for providing personal information is helpful. Tier one is information that anyone can have, including companies that will share it on the internet. Tier two contains information that is somewhat private. You do not necessarily want the information to be leaked out, but it does not identify your home. Tier three is your real information which should be reserved for close friends and family and government requirements. The following table identifies the information for each tier. Items stricken should never be disclosed to the entities in that tier.

Tier One	Tier Two	Tier Three
Public Information	Private Information	Protected Information
~~Real Name~~	Real Name	Real Name
Misspelled Name	~~Misspelled Name~~	~~Misspelled Name~~
Alternate Name	~~Alternate Name~~	~~Alternate Name~~
~~Home Address~~	~~Home Address~~	Home Address
PO Box Address	PO Box Address	~~PO Box Address~~
~~Personal Email Address~~	Personal Email Address	Personal Email Address
~~Work Email Address~~	~~Work Email Address~~	Work Email Address
Anonymous Email Address	Anonymous Email Address	~~Anonymous Email Address~~
~~Home Telephone Number~~	~~Home Telephone Number~~	Home Telephone Number
~~Cellular Telephone Number~~	~~Cellular Telephone Number~~	Cellular Telephone Number
Anonymous Telephone Number	Anonymous Telephone Number	~~Anonymous Telephone Number~~
~~Date of Birth~~	Date of Birth	Date of Birth
~~Social Security Number~~	Social Security Number	Social Security Number
~~Primary Credit Card~~	Primary Credit Card	Primary Credit Card
Secondary Credit Card	~~Secondary Credit Card~~	~~Secondary Credit Card~~
Online Accounts	Utilities	Close Friends & Family
Online Purchases	Financial Accounts	Driver's License*
Magazines / Catalogs	Employer / W2 / IRS Returns	
Hotels	Vehicle Purchases	
Entertainment	Medical Records	
Vehicle Service	Airfare	
Shopping	Passport	
Clubs / Organizations	Licenses / Permits	

The following should explain any items that need further clarification.

Alternate Name: The name attached to your secondary credit card (Chapter Five)
Misspelled Name: A variation of your real name (Bazel vs. Bazzell)
PO Box Address: Either post office box or commercial mail receiving agency (Chapter Three)
Personal Email Address: Free email account such as Gmail (Chapter Three)
Work Email Address: Email account assigned to you by an employer
Anonymous Email Address: Forwarding email account (Chapter Three)
Anonymous Telephone Number: Forwarding number (Chapter Three)
Secondary Credit Card: Additional card in alternate name with your real number (Chapter Five)

* Many privacy advocates do not use their primary home address on their driver's license. Other options include a family member's address, your private office address, or a "ghost" address as explained in the book *How to Be Invisible*. Laws vary by state.

Age and Identity Verification

There will be times when you are "carded" in order to verify a minimum age. This may be at the grocery store when you purchase alcoholic beverages or to gain access to an "over 21" area at an event. For most situations, I do not mind displaying my driver's license. The employee is only looking at your birth date and no information is being collected into a system. This is not always the case. Recently, I attended an event at a local casino. Upon entry, everyone had to show identification for age verification. If you frequent the casino often, the player's card will escalate you through this process. Since I do not participate in these programs, I was stuck in line. I watched my friend ahead of me display his license which was scanned into a card reader by a gaming agent. The computer displayed my friend's driver's license photo and information. I had no doubt that his information had just been added to this chain of casino's database. He was allowed to pass. As my paranoia kicked in, I pretended to receive a cellular call and got out of line to retrieve a forgotten item from my car. When I returned, I walked through the line without showing my license and personal address. How did I do it? I displayed my passport.

Passports are accepted practically everywhere as proof of identity. They contain your name, date of birth, and a photograph. A passport contains a unique number assigned to you that can be used in place of a driver's license number. This number is much more difficult to trace by the private sector. A passport has never contained a home address.

I contacted my friend a few months later and inquired about the casino. I asked if he ever receives advertisements and offers from them. He replied that he gets coupons and announcements from them in the mail. After thinking for a moment, he said that he also gets mailings from other casinos owned by the same company. He verified that he had never signed up for anything through the casino. They must have used the data from his driver's license. I suspect that the data collected will eventually find its way to a company that will not keep it private.

Any time you need to provide proof of your name or age, consider showing your passport. While it can be scanned in the same manner as a license, very few establishments have the hardware devices to do this. Banks, hospitals, airports, and hotels are familiar with passports and should never offer resistance in their use.

Post Office Box Issues

There are occasions when companies will refuse a post office box as a mailing address. This has nothing to do with the deliverability of mail to the address. They just want your home address to add to your profile. Therefore, they have rules in place that will reject your box number in an online form submission. The only times that a physical house address must be verified are when you are establishing a new line of credit or completing official government paperwork. Any other company should only receive your post office box address. There is a way to usually force it.

Assume that your address is PO Box 9985, Chicago, IL 60601. There must only be one box with that number in that zip code. When your online form refuses to accept your address, enter it in reverse order. Enter it as 9985 Box, Chicago, IL 60601. The post office will know that any mailings to this address should be sent to your box. This format should meet any requirements in an online form. You may notice that some generic advertisements are addressed in this reverse format.

Outgoing Telephone Calls

When you make a telephone call, the receiver can identify you by your caller identification (caller ID). Since this is common knowledge, many people dial "*67" before the telephone number to hide their identity. This causes the caller ID display on the receiving end to display "Unknown Caller" or "Blocked Call". This does not work at large companies. If you attempt to block your caller ID when calling a toll free number, your call will not be blocked. Large companies have telephone systems that will still display your name and number regardless of masking attempts. Because of this, you should be careful when calling large businesses. If you call from your landline telephone, your information will automatically be populated into the company's database. You will now be more susceptible to receiving calls from the organization. If you call from your cellular number, your number will be collected, but not your name. When you discuss your account with the business, your number will be added to your customer profile. If this concerns you, consider these alternatives:

- ✓ Place the call from a pre-paid cellular telephone.

- ✓ Place the call through a VOIP service such as Google Voice (free).

- ✓ Contact customer service through internet services such as email or website chat.

- ✓ Request a call from the company to your anonymous number through an email message.

Vehicle Servicing

Having your vehicle serviced will usually result in your information entering advertising databases. Whether it is an oil change at a national chain or a repair at a local dealership, your information is being collected. This will eventually result in related advertisements at your home and direct marketing toward your preference in vehicles. An average visit makes the following information available:

- ✓ Full name, home address, and home telephone number

- ✓ Cellular telephone number for pickup notification

✓ Make, model, year, mileage, registration, VIN, and maintenance history of vehicle

✓ Services provided and services declined

✓ Estimated warranty expiration

This is the type of information that companies such as TowerData and Epsilon use to build custom profiles on you. This is why you receive mailings from auto dealers and warranty providers at specific times. Staying out of this system is difficult, but not impossible.

Your best option is to locate a trusted individual to service your vehicle either in a small shop or home. It is more affordable, service is usually superior, and you leave no trace. If you must visit a repair shop or dealer, never provide your real name and address. Use the information available about you in the first tier. Payment can be made with your secondary credit card in your alternate name. Is this overkill? Maybe. Use your best judgment.

Smart Phone Applications

If you have a smart phone, such as an Android or iPhone device, you probably have numerous "apps" on your phone that do amazing things. Every time that you install one of these applications, you are asked to agree to the amount of data that the application will have access to on your device. Most people agree to these terms without reading the details. This can expose you to great risk of divulging your personal information. There are many examples of these sneaky applications on the internet, but I will only document one here.

Mr. Number is an app on the Google Play store for Android telephones. It is marketed as an application to provide free texting over the internet and to screen incoming text messages and calls. You can set a list of people that you do not want to communicate with, and the software will forward these callers to voice mail without bothering you. Further, it will display the caller identification (caller ID) of many callers even if they are not in your contact list. Their website claims that the service will identify 80% of the incoming calls to the telephone. This includes both landlines and cellular numbers. This level of identification is impressive, which made me investigate how they collect cellular number information.

Mr. Number collects contact information from the telephones that it is installed on. When you install the application, it reports your entire contact list to a server. These entries are then added to a master database. If you had a friend's private number stored in your telephone as "Brad O'Neal", the number and name assigned to it are now in the database. If I install this application, and he calls me, the application will tell me that his name is "Brad O'Neal" without me already having his information stored. It will further identify personal details such as employer and a photograph if available from a public source such as LinkedIn. This is referred to as crowd sourcing. The hundreds of thousands of users that installed this application gave possession of their contacts list to Mr. Number to do whatever they want. How did they legally do this? The permissions required from the telephone should give the answer.

Every application on the Google Play store must document the permissions required from the device to function. These are the areas of information that the application can have access to. When you install the application, you will be asked to approve or reject these permissions. If you reject them, the software will not install. The following permissions were extracted directly from Mr. Number's Google website:

This application has access to the following:

- ✓ Allows the app to call phone numbers without your intervention.

- ✓ Allows the app to send SMS messages.

- ✓ Allows the app to receive and process SMS messages.

- ✓ Allows the app to modify the contact (address) data stored on your phone.

- ✓ Allows the app to read all of the contact (address) data stored on your phone.

The last two items on this list explain how this company can legally copy your contact list and add it to their database of numbers and names. You give them permission to do this when you agree to these terms. Now everyone in your contact list has lost the privacy of their cellular and landline numbers. Also, any of your friends that installed this application have now shared your contact information that is stored in their telephone. If this were not bad enough, the service will also let anyone type in a telephone number and display the caller ID information stored on the database. It eliminates the need for you to call someone for them to identify your number.

This is not the end; the following are additional permissions that you authorize:

- ✓ Allows the app to access the phone features of the device. An app with this permission can determine the phone number and serial number of this phone, whether a call is active, the number that call is connected to and the like.

- ✓ Allows the app to process outgoing calls and change the number to be dialed.

- ✓ Allows the app to write to the USB storage. Allows the app to write to the SD card.

- ✓ Allows the app to disable the keylock and any associated password security.

✓ Allows the app to prevent the phone from going to sleep.

✓ Allows the app to retrieve information about currently and recently running tasks.

I do not mean to pick on Mr. Number. There are thousands of applications that require you to grant similar permissions. I recommend that you read the permissions that you are granting to every application that you install. If something looks wrong, do not install the application. In my experience, the applications that offer any free service to interact with your telephone calls, text messaging, caller ID, or contact list are extracting all information from your telephone. It is not worth jeopardizing the privacy of you or your friends and family.

Monitoring

Now that your information is out of public view, you must continually monitor the entire internet for any new information that may surface. Recent studies have identified over 55 billion web pages in existence. The hard way to do this would be to scour Google every day looking for anything new identifying your information. Do not worry, this monitoring can be automated.

Google Alerts (google.com/alerts)

Google is a very powerful search engine. It can identify areas where your personal information, such as name and home address, are on display in a public website. Manually searching every week or month is a burden. Google Alerts can automate this search and send you an email when any new results appear. This free service will basically notify you when your information has appeared on a public site.

✓ Log into your new personal Gmail account. If you do not have a Gmail account, Navigate to **gmail.com** and create a new free account.

✓ Determine the exact searches of your personal information that would return appropriate results. This will vary depending on how common your name is. If your name is unique, such as Jeremiah Dressler, and you live at 4054 Brenner Street in Biloxi, MS, you should create the following alerts.

"Jeremiah Dressler"
"Jeremiah Dressler" "Brenner"
"4054 Brenner" "Biloxi"

The quotes should be included in the alert. If you have children named James and Chris, you should add the following alerts.

"James Dressler"
"James Dressler" "Brenner"

✓ However, if you have a common name, you will need to add more data. If you do not specify the exact search that you want, you will receive too many false positives for pages that are not about you. If your name is Brian Johnson, and you live at 1212 Main in Denver, CO, you should create alerts that are specific to you. These should include interests, a workplace, or associations. The goal is to search for the perfect amount of data to identify your public personal leaks without receiving irrelevant data. You will need to manipulate these searches until you achieve only the results that are about you.

"Brian Johnson" "1212 Main" "Denver"
"Brian Johnson" "volleyball" (a specific interest)
"Brian Johnson" "Denver" "Johnson Ford" (workplace)
"Brian Johnson" "Denver" "Colorado AARP" (association)

✓ If your landline telephone number is 314-555-1212 and your cellular number is 713-555-9999, you should add the following alerts.

"314-555-1212"
"314" "555-1212"
"713-555-9999"
"713" "555-9999"

These specific search terms will attempt to locate information placed within websites that match the terms inside quotes. For example, if a person search site created a new profile in the name of Jeremiah Dressler, Google would pick up on this and let you know. If a reverse telephone directory listed the term "Jeremiah Dressler" and the street of "Brenner" in the same page, this service would alert you. The quotes mandate that a result is only returned when those words are next to each other on the page. The telephone number examples would identify a website with your number even if the area code was separated from the rest of the number.

✓ Navigate to **google.com/alerts**. Supply the first alert that you want to create. The result type should be "Everything", frequency should be "As-it-happens", results should be "All results", and the delivery should be to your Gmail address. Figure 16.01 displays a sample of this entry. As you create the alert, you will see the current search results in the right column. Click "Create Alert" when complete and continue to add alerts.

✓ Click on the "Manage your alerts" button and review your alert settings. Here you can modify or delete an alert that you have created.

With a properly configured set of Google Alerts, you can be notified in real time as Google finds information about you and your family. You are not limited to these examples. In Figure 16.02, you can see that I have alerts in place for my website and book. If any website links to my website, or someone is discussing my other book, I can be notified and provided a link to the source. I also have alerts for "Michael Bazzell" and "Mike Bazzell" in case someone uses my shortened name.

Figure 16.03 displays an email from Google notifying me of a new alert. Google indexed a blog entry from my website and determined it to fit the criteria of my website alert. Notice that the alert is from my blog portion of my website and not my main website. This is because Google scans the entire website, not just the main pages.

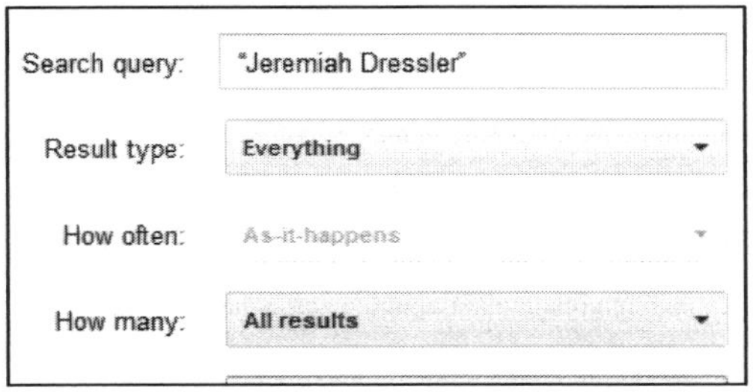

Search query:	"Jeremiah Dressler"
Result type:	Everything ▾
How often:	As-it-happens ▾
How many:	All results ▾

☐ "michael bazzell"	All results
☐ "mike bazzell"	All results
☐ "open source intelligence techniques"	All results
☐ computercrimeinfo.com	All results

Figure 16.01: A Google Alert entry page.

Figure 16.02: A Google Alerts management page.

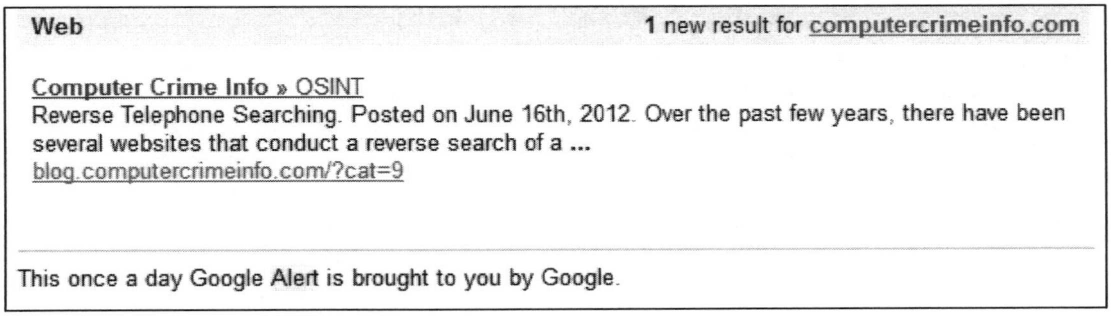

| **Web** | **1** new result for computercrimeinfo.com |

Computer Crime Info » OSINT
Reverse Telephone Searching. Posted on June 16th, 2012. Over the past few years, there have been several websites that conduct a reverse search of a ...
blog.computercrimeinfo.com/?cat=9

This once a day Google Alert is brought to you by Google.

Figure 16.03: A Google Alert.

Google Analytics (google.com/analytics)

This book has discussed how websites track you and collect information about your internet searches and history. You can use this same technology to track people that are looking for information about you. You can know when someone searches for you on Google, where they are located, and what they were researching in order to find you. This may sound expensive and difficult. The easiest way to apply this tracking technique is to create a free website and add Google Analytics. Not only is the service free, but the following instructions will eliminate the need for an analytics expert to set up your account:

✓ Navigate to **sites.google.com** and log in with your Gmail account information. Click the red "Create" button to start a new project.

✓ Provide the name of your site. This should be your real name. Contrary to the rest of this book, you want people to find this website. For the site location, supply your real name without spaces. If that name is taken, add generic information to the end of the name. If your name is Chris Johnson, "ChrisJohnson" will probably already be in use. Try "ChrisJohnsonHomeAddress". This will make more sense in a moment. Select the "Create" button to generate a new generic website.

✓ Click the small icon that looks like a pencil. This will allow you to edit your new website. For this site's purpose, change the title to "YOUR NAME's Home Address". Obviously, enter your real name. In the content box below it, type any names that you think people would search to find you. Since I have a fairly unique name, I have included different spellings of my last name with the full and shortened versions of my first name. I also included "telephone number" and "phone number". Notice that I did not actually place my number here, only a reference to it. Click "Save" when you are finished. Now, when someone conducts a Google search for "Mike Bazzell home address" or "Michael Bazel phone number", this new site will be in the results. If you have a common name, you may want to consider adding any term that is very public about you that would help with this bait, such as the name of your spouse or the high school you attended. It is important that you not include any information that would identify your home or children. You only want to make it easy for someone to find this page through a search. Figure 16.04 displays my new page.

✓ Navigate to **google.com/analytics**. Select "Create an account" and click the "Admin" tab in the upper right portion of the screen. This will present a page with a button labeled "+ New Account". Click this button. In the "Account Name" field, type your real name. In the "Website URL" fields, select http:// and then type the location of your new website. This will be the name you used earlier without spaces. In the example, I used "ChrisJohnsonHomeAddress". If this was your example, your website would be sites.google.com/site/ChrisJohnsonHomeAddress. If you have trouble with this, go back to the website that you created. When you can see the website, look at the address bar. It will display the exact URL of your site. Figure 16.05 displays the name and location of my new site. Agree to the terms and click "create account".

✓ On the next page, ignore everything and click "save". At the top of this page will be your new Google Tracking ID. It will look like UA-33333333-1. Select this entire ID and copy it.

✓ Return to your new Google website. Select the "more" button and click "Manage Site". In the "Statistics" portion of the page, check the box labeled "Enable Google Analytics for this site". Paste in the number you previously copied. Click the red "Save" button. It may take up to 24 hours for Google to add the analytics to your site.

✓ Navigate to **google.com/webmasters/tools/submit-url**. Enter the entire website address of your new site. In the previous example, it would be sites.google.com/site/ChrisJohnsonHome-Address. Click "Submit Request". This notifies Google and requests that they scan your website for keywords to be added to their search index. This will make the website appear in a search result when someone is trying to locate you. It may also take up to 24 hours to be activated.

In summary, this process created a free website with limited information about you in plain view. This will only be your name and possibly some other content that is not private to you. Since you added Google Analytics, you can track the visitors to this site and learn information about them. This will often identify why a person is trying to find you. You should now visit your analytics site and see what you find. There is an abundance of data available about the visitors to your website. Most likely, you will have very few visitors, if any at all. When you do receive visits, the Google Analytics portal will let you browse the data collected from the visit.

Figure 16.04: A Google Sites website with generic information.

Figure 16.05: The Google Analytics website entry page.

Analytics Reports

Now that you have Google Analytics installed and monitoring your website, you are ready to view reports about visitors.

✓ Navigate to **google.com/analytics**. Sign in to your Google account and select the name of your website. This will present an overview page of traffic to your site. If you see that there were no visitors, then you know that no one was at your site for the past 30 days. There is nothing else to see here. However, if you have visits, continue to the next step.

✓ In the left menu, click "Demographics" in the "Audience" section. Click "Location" and view the map to your right. This will identify the locations of people visiting your website. The dark green states have had the most visits and the white states have had no visits. Clicking on a state will open the state view and identify which cities have visited your site. This will never disclose the name of the person searching for you, but knowing the city and state the person is in could be helpful. Figure 16.06 displays a list of cities in Illinois that have visited my public site. The data also identifies the number of visits and the average time spent looking at the site.

✓ In the left menu, click "Traffic Sources" and then "Overview". This will present a summary of how people found your website. This will probably all be through search traffic. Scroll to the bottom of the page and view the data in the lower right portion. These are the exact searches that were typed into Google that led the person to your page. Figure 16.07 displays a portion of the analytics for my main website computercrimeinfo.com. These consist of people searching my name, the website name, and a combination of both. Figure 16.08 displays searches that I conducted that led to my new site.

This will be an important area to monitor on your website. If someone does visit your page, you can identify the terms that were typed to find you. A search of your name may not concern you. However, a search of "Mike Bazzell home address" from a location of a past stalker should raise your interest. The following true story may shed light on why this process is important.

In 2010, I was asked to assist with creating a Google Analytics site for a client receiving serious death threats. He suspected it was the family of a federal prisoner that he had testified against. A few months after the analytics were active, someone from Minneapolis, MN conducted a search on Google for my client's name and the term "address". A quick search of the suspect on the Federal Bureau of Prisons website verified that the suspect had just been released from federal custody. He had been housed in Minneapolis, MN. This was an early notification that this suspect had not forgot about my client.

If you have been the victim of harassment or stalking, you should execute your own bait website. I also believe that law enforcement should consider using analytics now instead of waiting until a problem arises. Analytic analysis, for example, could be created for businesses that want to monitor potential business or for an organization that wants to identify the best cities to advertise new services. If you are tech savvy, I encourage you to research Woopra (woopra.com). This free analytics service will also identify IP Addresses and employers of visitors. A live capture option will display notification of visitors in real time.

	City	Visits ↓	Pages / Visit	Avg. Visit Duration	% New Visits	Bounce Rate
1.	Chicago	115	1.74	00:02:23	57.39%	67.83%
2.	Peoria	67	2.64	00:03:10	61.19%	44.78%
3.	Danville	54	2.35	00:05:46	0.00%	59.26%
4.	Springfield	50	2.66	00:03:00	50.00%	54.00%
5.	Decatur	43	1.30	00:02:04	13.95%	76.74%
6.	Champaign	41	2.02	00:02:39	24.39%	56.10%

Figure 16.06: A Google Analytics demographics page.

☐	3.	computer crime info	28	2.75	00:02:38
☐	4.	computercrimeinfo	23	3.91	00:03:32
☐	5.	mike bazzell	15	3.33	00:01:29
☐	6.	mike bazzell computer crime	8	2.25	00:00:32

Figure 16.07: A Google Analytics search report.

☐	7.	where does mike bazzell work?	1	3.00	00:00:03
☐	8.	info on computer crime	1	1.00	00:00:00
☐	9.	mike bazzell home address	1	1.00	00:00:00
☐	10.	mike bazzell vehicle	1	1.00	00:00:00

Figure 16.08: A Google Analytics search report.

Conclusion

To keep up with the changes in various methods of personal information removal, read my blog at **computercrimeinfo.com** and visit the "**Hiding from the Internet**" links. There is a good chance that as you read this, new content has been posted about the very topic you are researching.

Hopefully, you have now eliminated all of the personal online information possible. You have changed your habits and no longer associate your real name with your home address. You have provided disinformation when appropriate and have a grasp on how companies extract and share all of your sensitive details. You should now conduct a post-assessment. You may choose to wait 30 days before completing this process. Many companies take some time to remove everything requested.

You should first re-visit Chapter One and repeat the techniques that were explained. This should give an immediate indication of your level of success. Next, visit the various people search websites in Chapter Two and conduct a manual search for your information. You will likely see great results with this category. After you have determined that your information is no longer present, I encourage you to continually monitor your personal details online.

The battle for privacy is never over. There will always be someone trying to obtain your personal information for profit. You may never be able to stop all of it. Staying on top of the information available to the public will create a strong layer of privacy. Many attempt to achieve privacy only when safety issues arise. It is often too late. You will never regret removing personal information, but you may have regrets if you do not. Nothing is more important than your safety and the safety of your family. We live in a chaotic and unpredictable world. Please consider reclaiming your privacy.

The amount of personal information collected about individuals will continue to escalate. This is a new form of currency for many businesses. We have never seen such an effort to individually target someone for the purpose of advertising. You do not have to accept this new standard. Use the techniques described to opt-out of this system.

I hope that this book will change the way that you interact with websites and businesses in the future. Every day, your privacy is jeopardized when you execute your normal routine. Whether through a website shopping experience or an in-person encounter with a sales person, there has never been a higher demand for your private details. Consider the lessons in this book and apply them to whatever situation you are in. Regardless of the scenario, you can be in control and ultimately decide who collects your private information.

Thank you for reading.

Index

24548238R00149

Made in the USA
Middletown, DE
29 September 2015